GENDERED NEWS

GENERED NEWS
MEDIA COVERAGE AND ELECTORAL POLITICS IN CANADA

Elizabeth Goodyear-Grant

UBCPress · Vancouver · Toronto

© UBC Press 2013

All rights reserved. No part of this publication may be reproduced, stored in a retrieval system, or transmitted, in any form or by any means, without prior written permission of the publisher, or, in Canada, in the case of photocopying or other reprographic copying, a licence from Access Copyright, www.accesscopyright.ca.

21 20 19 18 17 16 15 14 13   5 4 3 2 1

Printed in Canada on FSC-certified ancient-forest-free paper
(100% post-consumer recycled) that is processed chlorine- and acid-free.

Library and Archives Canada Cataloguing in Publication

Goodyear-Grant, Elizabeth, author
Gendered news : media coverage and electoral politics in Canada /
Elizabeth Goodyear-Grant.

Includes bibliographical references and index.
Issued in print and electronic formats.
ISBN 978-0-7748-2623-5 (bound). – ISBN 978-0-7748-2624-2 (pbk). –
ISBN 978-0-7748-2625-9 (pdf). – ISBN 978-0-7748-2626-6 (epub)

1. Women political candidates – Canada. 2. Women in mass media – Canada.
3. Sex role – Political aspects – Canada. 4. Mass media – Political aspects – Canada.
5. Journalism – Objectivity – Canada. 6. Elections – Canada. I. Title.

HQ1391.C3G66 2013   320.082'0971   C2013-902935-4
                                                  C2013-902936-2

Canadä

UBC Press gratefully acknowledges the financial support for our publishing program of the Government of Canada (through the Canada Book Fund), the Canada Council for the Arts, and the British Columbia Arts Council.

This book has been published with the help of a grant from the Canadian Federation for the Humanities and Social Sciences, through the Awards to Scholarly Publications Program, using funds provided by the Social Sciences and Humanities Research Council of Canada.

Printed and bound in Canada by Friesens
Set in Futura Condensed and Warnock by Artegraphica Design Co. Ltd.
Copy editor: Kate Baltais
Proofreader: Helen Godolphin
Indexer: Patricia Buchanan

UBC Press
The University of British Columbia
2029 West Mall
Vancouver, BC V6T 1Z2
www.ubcpress.ca

Contents

List of Tables and Figures / vii

Acknowledgments / xi

Introduction / 1

1 Visibility in the News / 24

2 Quality of News Coverage / 54

3 Who Is Responsible? Explaining Gendered News / 107

4 Backlash or Boost? The Effects of Attack-Style News / 139

5 Media Effects on Politicians' Experiences of Their Political Careers / 161

Conclusion / 185

Appendix 1   Issue Coding / 194

Appendix 2   Coding for CES and Media Reception Study / 199

Notes / 201

Works Cited / 211

Index / 232

Tables and Figures

Tables

1.1 Distribution of seats in Canada's House of Commons, by party, 2000 / 32
1.2 Distribution of news stories, by political party, four TV networks, 2000 election campaign / 34
1.3 Mean length of news stories, by political party, four TV networks, 2000 election campaign / 36
1.4 Length and number of party leaders' sound bites, CBC news, 2000 election campaign / 40
1.5 Party leaders' clips and ratio of sound bites to clips, CBC news, 2000 election campaign / 41
1.6 Length and number of candidates' sound bites, by sex, CBC news, 2000 election campaign / 43
1.7 Distribution of candidates' first mentions in print news, 2006 election campaign: challengers, incumbents, incumbent cabinet members / 46
1.8 Placement of candidates' first mentions in print news, by sex, 2006 election campaign / 48
1.9 Inclusion of photo of candidate mentioned first in article, by sex (print news), 2006 election campaign / 49

1.10 Attributions of speech of candidate mentioned first in article, by sex (print news), 2006 election campaign / 50

2.1 Party leader shown with family: sound bites and clips, CBC news, 2000 election campaign / 67

2.2 Length of party leaders' sound-bite speaking time, by attack-style behaviour (CBC news), 2000 election campaign / 74

2.3 Length of candidates' sound bites, by sex and tone (CBC news), 2000 election campaign / 75

2.4 Symbols of power shown with party leaders: sound bites and clips, CBC news, 2000 election campaign / 77

2.5 Mentions of campaign elements in news stories about party leaders (four TV networks), 2000 election campaign / 80

2.6 Focus of news stories about party leaders (four TV networks), 2000 election campaign / 81

2.7 Coverage of issues in news stories about party leaders (four TV networks), 2000 election campaign / 83

2.8 Nature of lead-ins in news stories about party leaders (four TV networks), 2000 election campaign / 87

2.9 Evidence offered in analytical voice-overs in news stories about party leaders (four TV networks), 2000 election campaign / 88

2.10 Mention of candidates' appearance, by sex (print news), 2005-06 election campaign / 91

2.11 Mention of candidates' personal romantic relationships, by sex (print news), 2005-06 election campaign / 91

2.12 Mention of candidates' parental status, by sex (print news), 2005-06 election campaign / 91

2.13 Horserace vs. issue coverage of candidates, by sex (print news), 2006 election campaign / 99

2.14 Tone of stories on candidates, by sex (print news), 2006 election campaign / 100

2.15 Issue coverage of candidates, by sex (print news), 2006 election campaign / 102

2.16 Issue coverage of male and female challengers (print news), 2006 election campaign / 103
3.1 Status of men and women in Canadian TV news, July 2011 / 114
3.2 Status of men and women in Canadian print news, July 2011 / 115
3.3 Issues addressed in political parties' press releases, 2000 election campaign / 131
3.4 Male and female challengers by political party, 2006 election campaign / 132
3.5 Male and female incumbents by political party, 2006 election campaign / 133
3.6 Attacks in parties' press releases, 2000 election campaign / 134
4.1 Ratings of news story, by party leader, 2006 election campaign / 151
4.2 Determinants of leaders' news story ratings (selected by party that was focus of story, binary logistic regressions), 2006 election campaign / 152
4.3 Determinants of leaders' news story ratings, testing interactive effects of sex and gender ideology (selected by party that was focus of story, binary logistic regressions), 2006 election campaign / 156

Figures

1.1 Vote intentions through the 2000 Canadian federal election campaign / 33
1.2 Distribution of news stories by TV network, 2000 election campaign / 35
1.3 Distribution of headline stories (four TV networks), party leaders, 2000 election campaign / 37
2.1 Attack-style coverage of leaders (CBC) / 70
2.2 Leaders' mean sound bite lengths, by attack-style behaviour (CBC) / 73
3.1 "Hard" versus "soft" issues, by sex (2000 election campaign) / 117

3.2 Evidence of horserace coverage, by reporter sex (CBC, 2000 federal election coverage) / 117

3.3 Percentage of female candidates and MPs, by election year and political party / 127

4.1 Predicted probabilities of positive news ratings, by McDonough aggressivity / 154

4.2 Predicted probabilities of positive news ratings, by Chrétien aggressivity / 154

Acknowledgments

This book is an intellectual product that benefited greatly from the guidance, support, and input of a fantastic collection of people. I am a lucky author, indeed, for the rich intellectual and emotional resources that have surrounded me and nourished my soul and creative energies. In no small measure, these people are responsible for helping me to produce my best work, while playing no hand whatsoever in this book's faults.

The genesis of *Gendered News: Media Coverage and Electoral Politics in Canada* in my early research at McGill University means that my first debts are to Elisabeth Gidengil, Stuart Soroka, and Jerome Black. Elisabeth's intellectual rigor is well-known in the discipline. She is and has been an important role model, even in the years since I flew the nest, so to speak. My peers at McGill were a smart and lively group, and the exchanges of ideas and experiences were great. I am grateful for their support and friendship. Cameron Anderson, Blake Andrew, Rachel Brickner, Allison Harell, Emmanuelle Hébert, and Jason Roy provided special insight, both related to the book and of a more social kind, during and since.

My colleagues at Queen's provided me with a new home, and I am grateful for their support and encouragement, particularly that of Scott Matthews, a dear friend who was my most frequent listener, sounding board, and practice audience as this book took shape. At the early stages, as well, the advice of Keith Banting, Janet Hiebert, Abbie Bakan, and others was indispensable.

Were every new academic to have such experienced, wise, and caring colleagues, a misstep among the junior ranks would become a rare thing indeed. The same must be said of Emily Andrew, the editor I have had the pleasure of working with at UBC Press, whose instincts seem infallible, and whose professionalism I admire greatly. Thank you for your attention and dedication to this project. The production team, particularly Anna Eberhard Friedlander, deserves a special thanks, as well.

Special recognition, of course, must be given to my husband and best friend, Andrew Grant. You understand when to offer advice and when silence is golden. You set a standard in your own academic endeavours that I am both proud of and aspire to. You allow me to make my own intellectual mistakes, and do not remind me of them later. You know the genuine meanings of patience, tolerance, and support.

Finally, I must go back much farther than my time at McGill or at Queen's, to my own beginning. Early on, my parents, Norman Goodyear and Siobhan Goodyear, impressed on me the value and joy of education. My inquisitiveness is in no small measure a product of the talents and attitudes they have passed to me. If I am at all equipped to forge a life and career of knowledge-seeking, it is because of them. My hope is that Andrew and I can do the same for our daughter, Audrey Kathleen, for whom gendered mediation, I hope, will mean very little. This book is dedicated to her.

GENDERED NEWS

Introduction

Women are numerically under-represented in politics by a large margin in Canada and across the globe. Despite important improvements on a variety of representational fronts since the early 1970s, the brief period of growth in women's candidacies and share of elected seats at the federal level over the 1980s and early 1990s has largely stalled, raising grave doubts about "the view that things are moving along nicely," a perspective that Bashevkin calls "flat-out wrong" (2009, 3). Why has women's political representation stalled? *Gendered News: Media Coverage and Electoral Politics in Canada* contributes to answering the puzzle of women's persistent political under-representation by focusing on the role of the news media. This book asks whether the news media contribute to the supply- and demand-side barriers to women's political representation. It argues that the news media often present gendered representations of female politicians and of the political world, which, in turn, can become formidable obstacles to women at all stages on the path to attaining elected office. Put differently, gendered news coverage can negatively impact both the supply of and the demand for women politicians.[1]

This empirical fact of women's political under-representation raises critical questions on both symbolic and substantive fronts, and it also means that legislatures operate with unnecessarily restricted talent pools. In Canada, from 1993 to 2011, there was a modest 7 percent increase in women's share of the seats in the House of Commons, from 18 percent in 1993 to

25 percent following the May 2011 federal election. Women's representation seems to have plateaued at around the 20 to 25 percent mark, a level that has been holding for the past fifteen years and that raises the possibility of a gendered "electoral glass ceiling" (Trimble and Arscott 2003, 51). When changes in women's proportions of House seats have occurred from election to election, the pattern has not always been one of growth. Women's share of seats fell slightly from 21.1 percent to 20.8 percent from the 2004 to the 2006 federal election. When we focus specifically on party leaders, the pattern is similar. Two female party leaders contested the 1993 federal election, then Prime Minister Kim Campbell and then NDP leader Audrey McLaughlin; yet, there has not been a woman heading a competitive political party in a federal election since 2000, when Alexa McDonough led the NDP. Gains are not irreversible.

Provincially, women candidates have not fared significantly better. Keeping sizeable provincial variations in mind, on average, women occupy just 22 percent of provincial legislative seats, although there has been a remarkable increase in the number of women premiers and provincial party leaders in recent years, including premiers Christy Clark (British Columbia), Kathleen Wynne (Ontario), Pauline Marois (Quebec), and Kathy Dunderdale (Newfoundland and Labrador). Women's representation at both these levels of Canadian government, however, remains stubbornly short of the so-called critical mass threshold – typically pegged at 30 percent of legislative seats – required for women to make a difference in politics. At the current rate of change – a 7 percent increase over eighteen years – Canada's House of Commons will not see a critical mass of female members of Parliament until 2029 or parity until 2075, well over half a century from now.

To attain elected office in politics, candidates must undergo three selection processes: they must select themselves to run; they must be selected by parties for nomination; and they must be selected by voters at the ballot box (Matland and Montgomery 2003). In many ways, the stubbornness of women's under-representation over these eighteen years is a puzzle, because many barriers at all three stages have been reduced, suggesting that women's shares of candidacies and legislative seats should be higher. Indeed, barriers erected by parties, fundraising, voter hesitation about women politicians, and women's positions in the candidate eligibility pool have all improved.

Political parties historically played formidable gatekeeping roles that tended to overtly scuttle women's prospects for elective office (e.g., Bashevkin 1993). Political parties certainly still have work to do to provide women the same opportunities for power and influence that men have enjoyed for our entire history; nonetheless, they have improved. Many parties have adopted formal and informal measures to enhance women's candidacies over the past few decades. Although Canada has not joined the roughly 110 countries in the world that have adopted some form of gender-based quotas, Canadian political parties have undertaken other steps to increase the number of women candidates and legislators. Several parties have informal "targets," some of which aim for gender parity in candidate nominations. Some parties have set up funds reserved for women candidates to assist them in their bids for office. Some have adopted formal recruitment policies aimed at identifying and recruiting women candidates, as well as candidates from other under-represented groups such as minorities and Aboriginals. The federal NDP falls within this last category. Parties no longer tend to run their female candidates overwhelmingly in so-called lost-cause ridings, although this still happens in rural ridings (e.g., Carbert 2009). To be sure, different political parties offer different levels of resources for, and obviously have different levels of commitment to, the recruitment of women candidates. More left-wing and centrist parties, predictably, tend to be more supportive than more right-wing parties. This partisan pattern is fairly consistent across countries of the developed West, and in Canada it became quite overt in the post-1993 shake-up that saw the emergence of the Reform Party, later the Canadian Alliance (e.g., Young 2002). In the main, however, political parties have become more hospitable to female office seekers over recent decades, as well as to female members more generally (Young and Cross 2003).

Political parties are key, but so is money, and there are important inequalities that must be taken into account. In Canada there is a persistent gender gap with respect to income. Women are paid roughly 84 cents for every dollar paid to men,[2] placing Canada's gender-income gap among the highest of countries in the OECD.[3] Earnings differentials can be important to self-selection into political careers and to success at the nomination stage, as well, because personal income can affect whether one can afford to run a political campaign and shoulder other costs associated with doing so, such as day care, transportation, and absence from paid work. Women do tend to earn less personally; however, we must also consider the abilities of candidates to fundraise if we are to glean a full picture of whether and how money hampers women in seeking office. Success at fundraising is a critical indicator of candidate quality and electability, and there is convincing evidence that women are not disadvantaged relative to men in raising campaign money (e.g., Young 2005). The recent overhaul of campaign and election finance laws in Canada, which has resulted in stricter restrictions on spending and contributing, has had the added advantage of practically levelling the playing field for all candidates, male and female, when it comes to raising and spending money on electoral campaigns.

In addition to the loosening of barriers to nomination and election, the supply pool of potential candidates has grown dramatically over recent decades. Women are better educated, more professionally qualified to run for office, and more connected to political networks than ever before, factors that actually should enhance their chances of selection at all three stages. Critically, women's presence in professional and managerial occupations has grown dramatically in the past few decades. In 2008, women occupied 50 percent of professional positions in business and finance in Canada, including 34 percent of senior management positions.[4] Law is becoming similarly feminized. Where women were just 5 percent of Ontario lawyers in 1971, over three decades later, in 2006, women accounted for nearly 60 percent of young lawyers and 38 percent of all lawyers in Ontario.[5] Women make up much smaller portions of senior lawyers, partners, and the like, but their entrance in large numbers into this critical pipeline profession should contribute to a larger number of female politicians as well. This has not happened, however, at least not yet.

Turning to the final stage of selection – being elected by voters – women fare well. In the aggregate, when other factors are equal, voters do not appear to be systematically biased against female candidates (e.g., Black and Erickson 2003). What this means is that voters have no baseline objection to voting for women. Sometimes, women actually enjoy an electoral advantage among voters. The problem, as always, is with the qualifier "when other factors are equal," which they often are not for many women candidates. When women have the same money, credentials, time, experience, networks, and other important resources as men, including media visibility and favourable coverage, they do not face disadvantage at the polls. As the following pages illustrate, the media play an important role in shaping voters' perceptions of female leaders and candidates and of the political world generally, thus influencing voters' support for female politicians.

What is the role of the news media in producing and reinforcing supply- and demand-side barriers to women's representation in formal politics? Broadly, this occurs mainly through a process of gendering in news coverage, whereby women politicians are systematically presented differently than their male counterparts. The term *gendered coverage* refers to all the ways that women politicians are presented differently than their male colleagues as a function of the fact that they are women, just as racialized coverage focuses on ethnic and/or racial markers of difference – such as foreign birth, country of origin, dress and appearance, religion, or language – and promotes a view of visible-minority news subjects as novel, atypical, or exotic (e.g., Abu-Laban and Trimble 2006; Fleras and Kunz 2001; Gershon 2012; Henry and Tator 2002; Saunders 1991; Terkildsen and Damore 1999; Tolley 2012; Zilber and Niven 2000a, 2000b). Gendering can occur in both the quantity and quality of the coverage received by female politicians. Quality is particularly important, for the quantity of coverage matters little if the news presents women politicians negatively. News coverage is gendered when it systematically presents women politicians as unique or different, or implies that women are alien to politics because they are women; focuses on them as women first, and politicians second; and devotes disproportionate and voyeuristic attention to their personal lives, including their appearance and family situation, often at the expense of coverage of their professional credentials and political experience. Gendered coverage can assume a variety of guises, many of which are examined in this book – in fact, even seemingly gender-neutral coverage can have deeply gendered implications when women are presented the same as men, using masculine frames. Yet, with all forms of gendered coverage, the underlying dynamic is stunningly singular: broadly, gendered coverage assumes a male model of politician as the norm and, therefore, depicts women as gendered beings, implicitly novel and foreign to, as opposed to natural and normalized in, the political sphere.

This book is rooted in and extends the gendered mediation thesis. The original articulation of this approach in Sreberny-Mohammadi and Ross's (1996) work on female MPs in Great Britain has been further refined by Canadian (Gidengil and Everitt 1999, 2000, 2003a, 2003b) and Australian scholars (Fountaine and McGregor 2002). Representing a second stage in the gender analysis of media coverage, the primary focus of the gendered mediation thesis is not explicit sex or gender bias in the news. Unlike in decades past, the news today very rarely contains explicitly sexist remarks or language; rather, the gendering is more insidious, and examples include covering politicians using ostensibly gender-neutral news frames that are, in fact, masculine in nature, as well as format techniques that present more filtered, mediated representations of women than men. More details are discussed further on in this introduction.

The gendered mediation thesis is rooted in two core premises, which explain why gendered coverage occurs. First, the news media reflect the culture in which they are situated, which is gendered. Second, the mechanics of the news media industry, which is dominated by men, reinforce the masculine character of the news. The idea that the news media reflect the culture in which they are situated is conventional wisdom among the bulk of communications scholars. For example, Gamson (1988) identifies several factors that shape media discourse about politics, and one of these is "cultural resonances," or what Benson calls "culturally available symbols and themes" (2004, 277). Indeed, journalism is a human endeavour that cannot occur outside the systems of shared meanings produced by a society. Gender as a system of meaning, therefore, affects both the selection and editing of news content, as well as citizens' reactions to news stories. The gendered mediation thesis and this book's content, more generally, rely implicitly on gender schema theory to help further explain exactly how gendered patterns of coverage are created by the news and by politicians themselves, as well as the effects of gendered coverage on citizens' perceptions of female candidates.

A schema is a mental framework, "a cognitive structure that contains a concept's attributes and links among those attributes" (Fiske 1984, 141). Gender stereotypes are "generalized preconceptions about the attributes of males and females," and "a gender schema represents a more generic knowledge structure about maleness and femaleness" (Bussey and Bandura 1999, 678); Halpern, in fact, conceptualizes them as equivalents (1988). Gender schema theory is more about process than content. Like other schema theories, gender schema theory provides an account of how individuals process information in light of existing, highly organized structures of knowledge and beliefs, such as gender stereotypes. As such, gender schema theory can help us to understand how individuals react to counter-stereotypical behaviour, for example, on the part of a female candidate, or why the news tends to cover the personal lives of women more often than those of men (e.g., Chang and Hitchon 1997). The primary points about schemas are that they are easily cued; when they are cued, they become accessible, and their application to the political world becomes more likely; they are used as filters through which to understand and process new information; they are used to make inferences in the face of information deficits; and individuals often confront challenges when presented with information that is discordant with the content of a schema. Gender is one kind of schema, but there has been ample work on how other schemas, too, affect the political world, including partisan schemas and race schemas, which provide individuals with generalized information and beliefs much in the same way that a gender schema does.

The second premise of the gendered mediation thesis is the notion that the news, in the broadest sense, is dominated by men – in terms of its personnel, structure and organizational culture, and economic imperatives (e.g., Chambers, Steiner, and Fleming 2004; Robinson 2005). This creates and reinforces gendered patterns of coverage in various ways. Chapter 3 presents evidence that the Canadian television and print news systems are both dominated by men and are distinctively masculine in their structure, their political economic imperatives, and their culture.

Gendered news can produce three main effects, and together, these make up a significant focus of this book in terms of linking patterns of coverage with outcomes related to women's political under-representation. First, gendered news media coverage of women politicians can have negative effects on evaluations of female candidates and office holders and, by extension, women's chances of winning and maintaining elected office. Second, gendered news coverage can have negative effects on women's willingness to run, an important supply-side consideration. Similarly, it may also implicitly discourage girls and young women from considering political careers when they mature, creating important socialization effects on future generations of political citizens. If girls and young women become alienated from seeking political office, the result will be a continuation of women's political under-representation for the foreseeable future. Finally, there is the impact on political women, who must navigate gendered news media throughout their careers, in addition to all the other challenges of office holding that they share in common with their male counterparts. Gendered news contributes to the idea that femaleness is different, alien to politics, or even *unwelcome* in politics. Knowledge of this constrains many women politicians, as later chapters demonstrate.

News Matters

Before turning to more specific discussion of the ways in which gendered coverage and its effects are analyzed in this book in the next section, it is instructive to first consider the specific question addressed by this book – the contribution of the news media to gender inequality in representation – within the larger context of the political communications as well as the political representation literatures. Doing so reveals the gaps in current knowledge, but also the potential power of the news media to affect electoral decision making on the parts of voters, parties, and would-be candidates. Various factors affect election to public office, some of which have been mentioned already, but there are multiple reasons for focusing, in particular, on the news media. First, we do have extensive evidence about political parties, electoral systems, and other influences on women's electoral prospects, but relatively little on the news media. Additionally, we know that the news media affect political life at all levels – a topic that will be treated in greater detail below and in the chapters that follow, including effects on candidates' individual political behaviours as well as effects on the overall tone of electoral campaigns. However, the issue is not just that the media affect how people think about and act in politics, which alone would suggest taking the media seriously. Media representations of reality tend often to be partial or distorted, and this fact makes it all the more important to ask questions about coverage and its effects. Professional news media have organized themselves according to norms of objectivity, impartiality, and truth seeking, prompting many citizens to regard the news as a trusted and authoritative source of information about politics and current events. Yet, the news presents a condensed, selective, and partial take on real-world people and events. Add to this the potential for the news to distort systematically or to present inaccurate or unfavourable depictions of groups, particularly marginalized groups such as racial minorities and women, and news coverage becomes a serious concern, indeed.

Another consideration that elevates concern about media is that, for many citizens, the media take the place of direct experience. Most communications between politicians and citizens are mediated in some manner or other. Few citizens will meet, much less become acquainted with, a prime minister, a party leader, or even a local candidate directly. At the same time, citizens do form opinions about political issues, events, and personalities of which they have no direct experience. As Zaller notes, "it is hard to imagine where many of these opinions come from if not from the mass media" (1996, 17). Depictions in the news of political personalities and issues actually take on the characteristic of reality for many citizens. As such, the tendency of the news to distort reality – sometimes in systematic and unfavourable ways – raises questions of utmost importance to political inquiry, such as how the media perform as conduits of information in democratic systems and why representational gaps persist in Canada and other countries.

At its core this book places considerable stock in the claim that news matters. The news media affect political life in all sorts of ways, and some of these are outlined below. The idea that the news media matter to electoral politics, indeed, politics generally, has not always been a popular claim. There have been remarkable swings in thinking about the mass impact of the news media. We are currently in a third era in the study of the effects of media, each characterized by a distinctive view of their impact. The first period saw its beginning around the First World War. Inspired by the apparent successes of wartime propaganda campaigns, the belief in the 1920s was that the media wield substantial powers of persuasion over public values and positions (e.g., Lippmann 1922). This "powerful effects" view saw the influence of the media as direct and immediate, like the effects of a hypodermic needle or a bullet, both popular analogies at the time. The 1940s ushered in a second period in the study of media. Until roughly the early 1970s, scholars rejected the powerful effects model in favour of a "minimal effects" paradigm. The core belief was that political preferences were extremely stable, mainly because of strong partisan loyalties acquired early in life through socialization, leaving little room for change during election campaigns (e.g., Campbell et al. 1960). The effect of political communication seemed to be reinforcement of existing partisan loyalties and political attitudes, not persuasion, especially given citizens' selective exposure to media messages in line with their pre-existing beliefs. As Blumler and Gurevitch aptly observe, the minimal effects paradigm was "part and parcel of an overall view that placed far more emphasis on the underlying stability of the world of politics than on its flux" (1988, 245), a tendency that was common in this era.

The third and current period of research on the effects of media has established that these effects are, indeed, not so minimal after all, although they tend to be largely indirect, cumulative, and cognitive, rather than direct, immediate, and persuasive. The shift in outlook among scholars is the result of changes in the political environment, as well as the evolution of the methodological tools available for media effects research. The political landscape has changed in important ways since the beginning of the minimal effects era in the 1940s, and some of these changes have created greater opportunities than before for political communications to affect the political attitudes and behaviours of citizens. For example, partisan loyalties have weakened, and electoral volatility has climbed across the globe (Dalton and Wattenberg 2000). That diminishing numbers of voters have standing commitments to particular parties means that greater numbers of voters do not filter political decision-making through partisanship. With looser or absent party ties, voters turn to alternate means of making sense of the political world, a process that includes deciding how to evaluate candidates and issues and, ultimately, how to cast ballots. Naturally, processes of partisan de-alignment translate into greater opportunities for political communications of all sorts to influence mass political behaviour.

This is not to say that the news media are currently thought to have uniform or widespread direct effects, and certainly, most scholars do not hold that the news media commonly have persuasive effects. Rather, current media effects research focuses largely on the indirect effects of media via processes of agenda setting, framing, and priming – prominent theories of media effects. Research on agenda setting, priming, and framing focuses on the multiple complex ways that seemingly routine choices made in the structure, format, and style of the news influence how citizens think about politics. These theories are at the core of current work on media coverage and its effects, including work that focuses on gender. Agenda setting occurs through decisions of the media about what to cover and how much time or space to accord each issue or story. Salience transfer often occurs as a result (e.g., McCombs and Shaw 1972; Cohen 1963; Iyengar and Kinder 1987), when citizens mimic the news media's decisions regarding the importance of events or issues.

Agenda setting is not limited to directing our attention to particular topics or events. Framing and priming are often thought of as second-level agenda-setting effects, for they shift our attention to the particular attributes of news topics (framing) and how these influence public opinion (priming). Framing is "to select some aspects of a perceived reality and make them more salient in a communicating text, in such a way as to promote a particular problem definition, causal interpretation, moral evaluation, and/or treatment recommendation for the item described" (Entman 1993, 52). In other words, framing is the process of attaching a "peg," storyline, or interpretive lens to a news item. Framing provides structure to the people, events, and ideas reported in the story by implicitly signalling to audiences which aspects of the story are most important as well as how to think about the facts, ideas, or events contained within it. One of the critical points about framing is that each story can be framed in a variety of ways. For example, a campaign story can be framed as a "horse race" between front-running candidates or as an example of public discourse about the future direction of the country (Mendelsohn 1996, 8). Coverage of terrorism routinely adopts a perpetrator-victim frame that simplifies the political, economic, and cultural complexities behind terrorist activity and also unambiguously assigns blame for terrorist attacks (e.g., Iyengar 1991). Even these few brief examples illustrate the power of framing to define issues, events, and political actors.

Priming is closely related, but turns our attention to how public opinion is *affected* by the selective processes of agenda setting and framing. By drawing attention through processes of agenda setting and framing to some issues, problems, or traits, the news can set the standards by which viewers judge candidates and office holders (e.g., Iyengar and Kinder 1987). The term *priming* refers to the fact that the news media can influence the criteria by which political evaluations are made. By prioritizing national security over health care during a campaign, for example, the media can indirectly influence the public to prefer candidates who are perceived to be capable handlers of policing, border control, and defence spending – in other words, candidates who are (or who are perceived to be) assertive, oriented towards law and order issues, or who possess tough stances on these issues. A key component of priming theory is the idea that citizens do not form evaluations or make decisions with all available information; rather, citizens use accessible information disproportionately, resulting in an accessibility bias. In politics, more accessible information is typically information that is emphasized more often or more extensively in the news (Iyengar 1990, 1991), which is to say that the news media is an agenda setter, as agenda-setting theory proposes and ample empirical work has demonstrated.

Analyzing the News for Gendered Patterns of Coverage

Getting into some of the specifics, gendered coverage manifests in election campaign news in a variety of ways, and the first step in identifying the different analytical categories involved is to separate considerations about quantity of coverage from those about quality of coverage. Visibility or the quantity of coverage was an important focus of early research, for women were often left out of the news. This certainly had something to do with the fact that women held very few seats in Canada's House of Commons prior to the 1980s, and even fewer prominent positions such as cabinet posts. From Ellen Fairclough's appointment as the first female federal cabinet minister in 1957 to the election of the first Mulroney government in 1984 there were only six women appointed to the federal cabinet in Canada. Visibility comes with prominence and importance, obviously, and as women have entered politics in greater numbers and have achieved prestigious positions within government, including as prime minister, the news media have paid attention. Even so, there has been ample evidence that for much of recent history female politicians' treatment by the news media amounts to "symbolic annihilation" (Tuchman 1978). Even when female politicians have occupied prominent political roles, marginalization of them and their credentials has occurred. The following is a telling example:

> After the 1990 invasion of Kuwait, [CBC's] *The Journal* aired a "special" on the condition of foreigners detained in Iraq during which the Tehran hostage crisis was recalled. Instead of drawing on Flora MacDonald's expert knowledge as Canada's external affairs minister during that period, *The Journal* assigned the commentary roles to former ambassadors Allan Gotlieb (Washington) and Ken Taylor (Tehran). (Robinson and Saint-Jean 1991, 135)

Although Gotlieb and Taylor were certainly appropriate sources for this story, MacDonald's exclusion as an expert commentator is curious given her political position at the time.

Turning to the content of coverage, which is in many ways the chief focus of this book, I use the gendered mediation thesis as a primary framework for structuring analyses of gendered news coverage. This said, the gendered mediation approach has much in common with lots of work that does not use it explicitly. Additionally, I also develop new theoretical insights as a result of the analyses that follow. Most notably, I propose the provision-presentation distinction in Chapter 3, which deals directly with how political women's own gendered behaviour affects their coverage in the news. It is impossible to ignore the empirical fact that women and men often behave differently in politics, as they do in other spheres, an issue that raises thorny questions about who is responsible for news coverage being gendered.

The gendered mediation thesis is not a departure from past approaches, but a refinement and progression of analytical focus, as noted previously. It has two chief benefits for the analyses that follow: first, its focus on seemingly gender-neutral coverage and, second, its focus on the format of the news. The gendered mediation thesis goes far beneath the surface – beyond the unequivocal use of stereotypes and sexist language in the news – to identify how and why ostensibly gender-neutral news can disadvantage female politicians. The gendered mediation approach certainly does not avoid or ignore coverage that is overtly sexist, blatantly stereotypical, or contains "women-specific narrative frames" (Gidengil and Everitt 2000, 106), for these are important focal points for all scholars of gender, media, and politics. However, the approach does direct particular attention to seemingly gender-neutral coverage, which on the surface appears to treat male and female politicians the same. The basic problem is that gender-neutral treatment often means framing both men and women using masculine language and imagery (e.g., Gidengil and Everitt 1999, 2003a, 2003b; Sampert and Trimble 2003; Trimble and Sampert 2004), a direct consequence of the fact that politics has been constructed as a masculine domain. The application of masculine frames to describe female politicians can appear unnatural to viewers, triggering a "basic schema incompatibility" (Butler and Geis 1990), in which new information conflicts with deeply embedded gender schema. To use Entman's words: "journalists may follow the rules for objective reporting and yet convey a dominant framing of the news that prevents most audience members from making a balanced assessment of a situation" (1993, 57). The idea of a woman landing a "knockout blow" or "keeping her stick on the ice," metaphors that are illustrative of how the news media tend to cover events like leaders' debates, is at odds with culturally defined norms of feminine behaviour. Historically, women have not been associated with war, sport, and games and, therefore, do not tend to be automatically credited with the traits needed to succeed in these domains, such as aggression, strength, autonomy, and competitiveness. If a job or a social role has been occupied predominantly by one type of person, it is natural that, over time, the role would become closely associated with that type of person. More concretely, men have enjoyed a near-monopoly on the domains of war, sport, games, and politics, so men and masculine traits are closely associated with these activities. Therefore, the use of masculine news frames that equate political debate with boxing matches and elections with horse races may convey the idea that women are alien to politics or that they do not possess the traits required to successfully compete.

As noted above, the second analytical advantage offered by the gendered mediation approach is that it pays attention to several important formatting issues. When thinking about the content of news coverage, a distinction always needs to be made between substance – *what* is said, represented, or depicted – and style or format – *how* things are said, represented, or depicted. Both the substance and format of the news can be gendered, and these are analyzed separately in this book. The following categories are used to organize discussion of patterns in the substance of news coverage of male and female politicians:

- *Representations of the personal* – personal lives, appearances, and personality or traits

- *Representations of the professional* – professional credentials; political experience; and attributions of success, the extent to which candidates' successes are ascribed to their own efforts and traits as opposed to the assistance of others (e.g., political and family connections)
- *Representations of viability* – opinion polls, electability, and the use of horserace frames
- *Representations of issues and positions* – the issues that candidates are associated with and, where possible, the positions they are said or implied to favour.

This categorization maps neatly onto the key criteria according to which individual candidates and politicians are typically evaluated: traits, credentials, competitiveness, and issues. As will be discussed in further detail in Chapter 2, the media tend to focus on women's appearances more than and in different ways than on men's. The media tend to frame women in stereotypical terms using culturally accessible feminine archetypes – seductress, mother, pet, and iron maiden (Kanter 1977a, 1977b) – that often pose dangers for their entrance into or advancement along political careers. Media coverage also tends to raise doubts, typically implicitly, about women's viability as candidates and office holders, often as a result of being framed according to the culturally accessible archetypes.

To analyze gendered patterns in the format of the news, this book draws from the insights of the gendered mediation approach. One of the primary objectives of the gendered mediation thesis is to examine the more oblique gender imbalances in political news. One way that it does this is by focusing on the format of the news. In particular, the gendered mediation thesis holds that the news presents a more mediated, filtered image of female politicians' words and actions compared with news coverage of male politicians. In line with the two core tenets of the approach – the news reflects societal gender codes and the news is dominated by men – female politicians' "behavior is subject to more evaluation and interpretation, because it opposes traditional feminine stereotypes" (Cantrell and Bachmann 2008, 430). Put simply, the news media must devote more time and space to interpreting, rather than simply reporting on, female politicians because women's presence in politics deserves explaining or decoding. This is not to say that audiences wonder, "What is that woman doing running for office?" but rather, "How should I think about this woman running for office?" This is where the disproportionate mediation comes in. As such, this book's discussion of the format of media coverage of female candidates is organized according to the following categories:

- *Speaking agentically* – to what extent are female candidates permitted to speak in their own words in the news media? Conversely, to what extent are candidates paraphrased or summarized by newsmakers for audiences?
- *Analytical and evaluative reportage* – to what extent is coverage of female candidates descriptive (the classic mode of hard news reporting) versus analytical and/or evaluative?

Data Sources, Electoral Context, and Book Summary

This is the first book-length and most in-depth investigation of gender, news, and electoral politics in the Canadian setting. The following chapters engage with questions about gendered coverage of candidates and politicians in Canadian news and the impact of that coverage on citizens' political perceptions of women, as well as on female politicians' own views of their political careers. If gendered news influences citizens' perceptions and decisions, by extension, gendered news will have an impact on elections. This causal chain is not difficult to conceptualize given recent evidence that news can matter. We know that the news can affect citizens' political judgments, both directly and indirectly, leading many scholars to view the news media as a significant political actor in its own right. This book's most important claims are (1) there are gendered patterns in news coverage of female politicians, and (2) these gendered patterns have negative effects on public discourse, collective attitudes, and political decisions, and on the under-representation of women in politics.

This book uses a rich combination of data, both quantitative and qualitative, to support its central arguments. Data from content analyses of news coverage of the 2000 and 2006 federal elections are presented. Specifically, this book uses data collected by the 2000 Canadian Election Study (CES) on television coverage of the 2000 campaign on four networks (CBC, CTV, SRC, and TVA)[6] and data collected by the McGill Media Observatory on print coverage of the 2006 campaign (*Globe and Mail*, *National Post*, *Vancouver Sun*, *Calgary Herald*, *Toronto Star*, *La Presse*, and *Le Devoir*).[7] At several points in Chapters 1 and 2, analyses are conducted on a randomly drawn subsample of the 2006 print news data set, rather than the full, original data set. The original data set produced by the McGill Media

Observatory coded 3,769 print stories on a range of variables. Naturally, when using secondary data, a need can arise to add to or amend the data set being used; in this case, to add variables necessary for the analysis of gendered news coverage. When it was necessary for me to construct and code additional variables in order to test the various aspects of the conceptual framework on quality of coverage, which forms the primary focus of Chapter 2, the decision was made to draw a much smaller sample of cases from the large number of stories in the original data set, because of resource considerations involved in adding seven new variables to a manually-coded content analysis that included more than 700 candidate stories. First, I excluded all the stories that focused on leaders, because there was no female leader in the 2006 race, and excluded all stories that did not focus on candidates. Some stories mentioned no actual people, and a very small number of stories mentioned non-candidates, such as provincial politicians and campaign organizers. Virtually all analyses of the 2006 data in this book – whether the full data set or the subsample – are on candidates. There are 713 candidate stories in the 2006 print news data set, and I drew a random sample of 20 percent of them for the subset on which new variables were content analyzed. This made for a subsample size of 143 stories. New variables coded in the subsample include those for direct quoting and paraphrasing of candidates, as well as indicators for media representation of candidates' personal and professional lives, described in greater detail in Chapter 2.

Both the television and print news data include major French-language news sources. The television news codes coverage from two public (CBC and SRC) and two private (CTV and TVA) broadcasters, and the print news codes coverage from seven major dailies that cover most of the regions. These data sets on television and print news are used to evaluate the coverage of male and female politicians in Canada, both their visibility in the news and the quality of their coverage, which are analyzed, in turn, in Chapter 1 and Chapter 2. The various media content data sources used in the chapters that follow enable multiple fruitful comparisons that permit the drawing of robust conclusions about the media coverage of male and female politicians: the female leader's (Alexa McDonough's) coverage versus that of her male counterparts in television news of the 2000 campaign; the female leader's versus female candidates' coverage in the 2000 campaign; female candidates' coverage in televised versus print news; and female candidates' coverage when there is no female leader in the race, as was the case in the 2006 federal election. Further detail on these data sources and electoral contexts will be supplied in relevant sections throughout this book.

Among the data sources used in this book, of particular interest is analysis of a mixed-method, three-part study of CBC news coverage and its effects in the 2000 federal election, which combines content analysis data of CBC televised news coverage of the entire campaign, individual-level attitudinal and vote choice data from the 2000 Canadian Election Study,[8] and the results of an innovative audience study on how real voters *actually responded* to CBC's news coverage of the 2000 campaign. This allows the powerful and compelling results that are presented in Chapter 4 about how the news affects voters' perceptions of male and female politicians.

Throughout this book, rich qualitative data are used to support the primary arguments including the results of a set of in-depth personal interviews that I conducted with federal politicians over 2004-2005, among them a number of party leaders (Alexa McDonough, Stockwell Day, Ed Broadbent, and Kim Campbell). This book also analyzes a variety of political autobiographies of Canadian female politicians, particularly their reflections on their news coverage and their relations with the media, as well as excerpts of television and print primary news sources in order to illustrate the overarching patterns identified.

In the chapters that follow, *Gendered News* tackles three questions: What are the patterns of gendered coverage? Why do such patterns occur? What are their effects? This entails examining, in Chapter 1 and Chapter 2, the quantity and quality of media coverage of politicians across the two federal election campaigns; in Chapter 3, why gendered coverage exists, including a compelling repudiation of the notion that more female journalists would fix the problem; in Chapter 4, the effects of gendered news on voters' perceptions of politicians; and finally, in Chapter 5, politicians' own media strategies and career trajectories. The remaining discussion in this introduction outlines each chapter in more detail.

Chapter 1: Visibility in the News

Analyses of news content can be divided into two categories: quantity of coverage or visibility and quality of coverage, as noted above. Chapter 1 focuses on the relative visibility of female candidates in election news. Using data from national televised and print election coverage of the 2000 and 2006 Canadian federal election campaigns, this chapter analyzes the volume and prominence of coverage received by female politicians compared with their male counterparts, and relative to women's share of candidacies overall. On the whole, according to common indicators of visibility and prominence, such as number of stories, number of sound bites (in TV news), and page number location (in print news), gender differences in candidates' visibility are becoming less common. Decades ago, female politicians were symbolically annihilated (Tuchman 1978) as a consequence of their invisibility in the news. Today, women seem to garner a roughly equitable share of coverage on most indicators. Female politicians are quite visible in the news, sometimes more than their numbers or positions warrant, in fact. The chapter analyzes explanations for this approximate equality in news coverage – which may be due to increasing normalization of women in political life or, alternatively, to the fact that news focuses disproportionately on that which is out of place, alien, or unexpected, suggesting that female politicians' visibility in the news, which sometimes outstrips that of their male counterparts, is a function of their seeming novelty in public life. This latter interpretation is that preferred by the gendered mediation approach.

This chapter sets the stage for an analysis of the complexion or quality of the coverage of female politicians in Chapter 2, and concludes with the critical point that visibility is always a secondary consideration to quality of coverage. High visibility in the news can even damage or, indeed, derail the political careers of female politicians if their coverage is negative in gendered ways.

Chapter 2: Quality of News Coverage
This chapter analyzes the complexion of female politicians' coverage in the news, focusing, this time, on the quality of coverage that women receive. News coverage can be gendered in a variety of ways, at times reflecting gender differences in the substance of coverage – *what* is said – at other times reflecting differences in the style or format of coverage – *how* things are said. This chapter systematically compares news coverage of male and female candidates in 2000 and 2006 according to both criteria. The chapter uses the following categories to organize discussion of gendered patterns in the substance of news coverage of politicians: representations of the personal, the professional, viability, and issues, as outlined earlier. Following this, the chapter focuses on the level of interpretive – highly filtered, as opposed to purely descriptive – reporting on female politicians compared with male politicians, and together with Chapter 1's discussion of the extent

to which female politicians are portrayed as speaking agentically, this provides a picture of gendered patterns in the format of news coverage of politicians.

Chapter 3: Who Is Responsible? Explaining Gendered News
Together, three factors account for gendered news coverage, two of which are identified by the gendered mediation approach: societal norms and the masculine news business. This chapter analyzes each and provides an account of how they fit together in the news system. First, the news is a reflection, in part, of our gendered society. The frames used to structure news stories about politics and elections are heavily reliant on masculine language, symbols, and metaphors that assign primacy to masculine traits. This is not done by journalists and news editors to intentionally harm female politicians personally or professionally or to provide an electoral edge to male candidates. Nothing so diabolical is at play. News is a largely masculine narrative partly because of *us*. News is a human endeavour and, thus, cannot avoid reflecting the widespread implicit assumptions that politics – indeed, power – is a masculine domain, and the ideal politician is cast in a male image. This is the simplest part of the explanation, and it is intuitively appealing to a wide variety of audiences.

Second, the structure and operation of the news system produce bias in favour of the status quo by implicitly discouraging news that challenges established gender norms. Much has been made in the literature about the potential for female reporters and editors to correct gender imbalances in political news; however, news bias does not occur at the individual level. Chapter 3 demonstrates this with data that illustrate the remarkable similarity in coverage by male and female reporters. Bias that can be attributed to the news media occurs largely at the systemic level, and it is a result of the political economy of the news system, as well as journalistic training, socialization, and work routines.

Third, this chapter presents the *provision-presentation distinction*, a theoretical innovation that links gendered news coverage to gendered behaviour by politicians in the real world. Put simply, female politicians themselves play a role in their own gendered mediation. This is not to say that female politicians want gendered coverage, and are to blame when it happens, but it is likewise inaccurate to portray female politicians simply as hapless victims of media complicity in the construction and perpetuation of gender stereotypes. Rather, media content is always a combination of provision and presentation – of real-world events *provided* for coverage and of how those real-world events are selected, interpreted, and *presented* by the news media. In some cases, female politicians receive gendered coverage because they behave in gendered ways. When former Prime Minister Kim Campbell publicly joked about her weight, is it surprising that the media reported it? Similarly, in a 2005 press conference, former Minister Anne McLellan said she was happy to welcome Belinda Stronach into the Liberal cabinet because of Stronach's "great shoes." In such cases, can we blame the media for trivializing women's policy expertise or focusing on what they wear? Can we blame the media for valuing women's appearances over their credentials just as McLellan seemed to value Stronach's shoe choices over her expertise and her business background? Would former Prime Minister Jean Chrétien have welcomed floor-crosser Scott Brison into his caucus with a public compliment on his silk ties and shiny cufflinks? Probably not, but the media likely would have reported the incident had it occurred. In a less charged example, many cases of gendered issue coverage can be attributed to *actual* differences in male and female politicians' issue priorities and positions. All political figures make choices that affect the mediation of their political personas, thorny terrain that few scholars have addressed seriously or systematically in the case of female politicians and coverage of them in the media.

Chapter 4: Backlash or Boost? The Effects of Attack-Style News
The first of two chapters on the effects of gendered news, Chapter 4 starts with the immediate, short-term effects of gendered news on public perceptions of female candidates and, by extension, their electoral prospects. Is the old saying right that there is "no such thing as bad publicity"? In the case of news coverage of female politicians, the answer in many cases must be disagreement. Concerns about gendered news stem, in large measure, from the knowledge that the news can have a measurable impact on collective political attitudes and decisions, as well as the evaluative criteria against which candidates are judged. The bulk of work on gender, media, and politics stops after demonstrating that the news is gendered, and then it assumes or infers that gendered news has negative effects on voters' perceptions of female politicians and, by extension, female candidates' chances at the ballot box. Very little of the literature analyzes the effects of gendered news, and my analyses of the effects of attack-style coverage of party leaders suggest that concern is warranted. This book provides evidence that attack-style coverage – which tends to exaggerate the aggressive behaviour of female candidates

– negatively affects women leaders. No similar harmful effect is found for male leaders.

Chapter 4 does not assume simplistically that gendered coverage is universally negative for female candidates' electoral prospects. There are scenarios in which women can benefit from gendered coverage, depending on the context of the election and prevailing political climate. This was a recurring theme in my interviews with federal MPs, presented in detail in Chapter 5, and it suggests the need for a more nuanced approach to the effects of gendered news. Gendered stereotypes contain a lot of content that reflects positively on female candidates, such as the association of femaleness with honesty, compassion, inclusivity, fairness, and ethical behaviour. Female candidates can and do use these stereotypical traits in attempts to shore up support among electorates. Hillary Clinton's emotional display during the 2008 New Hampshire primary, in the United States, whether genuine or put on, increased her appeal among voters, particularly female voters who favoured Clinton over Obama by a margin of 13 percent in the vote. The episode seems to have "softened" Clinton's image, not surprising given that the news so often describes Clinton as "overly ambitious, calculating, cold, scary, and intimidating" (Carlin and Winfrey 2009, 337).

Chapter 5: Media Effects on Politicians' Experiences of Their Political Careers

This second chapter on the consequences of gendered news, and gendered news practices, turns to the experiences of politicians themselves. Based on a series of personal interviews with Canadian politicians – from backbenchers to party leaders to Canada's first female prime minister – this chapter provides rich information on female politicians' own understandings of their mediation, as well as on how they formulate media strategies to deal with real or perceived disadvantages in media coverage, and to capitalize on those cases where femaleness and its associated gender norms can assist female office seekers. Interestingly, the patterns that male and female MPs identify in their media coverage often closely mimic those identified in the content analysis data presented in Chapter 1 and Chapter 2. This chapter focuses on comparative analyses of male and female politicians, keeping in mind that gender is one characteristic among others that affect media coverage.

Personal interviews and analyses of women's political memoirs demonstrate that media coverage and media relations shape and constrain political careers differently for female than for male politicians. Plainly stated, female MPs face an uneven media playing field, which, in turn, contributes to the continued under-representation of women in politics. The evidence presented in Chapter 5 suggests that female politicians engage in more personal censoring – of speech, behaviour, dress, and the like – in their self-presentations to media, largely out of a fear of negative gendered coverage, a finding that reflects considerable understanding, on their part, of the provision-presentation distinction. This self-censorship follows from the reality that women's speech, appearance, and behaviour are sometimes selectively presented, or misrepresented, in the news, a pattern found across the world. Female politicians often try to avoid certain types of media formats or situations, again, out of fear that the resulting coverage will be negative. In the end, the message is that female politicians face a variety of constraints, some of them self-imposed, that their male colleagues commonly avoid.

Conclusion

The findings of this study are synthesized in the Conclusion, and their implications are discussed for the representation of women at all levels of politics. The story that emerges from *Gendered News* is one that questions the contribution of the media to the political goal of equality, both in the treatment of candidates and their access to political office and in the creation of an equitable public discourse about politics that promotes fairness, respect, and inclusion. In that sense, this book is an analysis of the quality of political information that is provided for citizens. This story is focused on female politicians, but it can be readily applied to the experiences of political aspirants from other marginalized groups such as racial and ethnic minorities, immigrants, and Aboriginals, all of whom have been similarly "othered" by the media (e.g., Henry and Tator 2002; Zilber and Niven 2000). These linkages to other marginalized groups where relevant have been made in this book, and the Conclusion turns to this issue in some detail. As has been demonstrated, the relationship between politicians, newsmakers, and citizens is triangular and dynamic: all three sets of actors bear responsibility for the media's informational deficiencies, as well as for the remedial action necessary to correct current imbalances in coverage.

Moving beyond the immediate contents of this book, we must also consider the effects of gendered news on women in the candidate eligibility pool – educated, professional women who *could* be ideal candidates for office – and on young women. Demand-side barriers to women's representation in formal politics are being dismantled, as discussed above. As a result, supply-side problems have gained immense attention in recent years, resulting in evidence that women who possess the traits and credentials required for political careers do not choose this route nearly as often as men do. The news media have been implicated in turning women off from public office. If female members of the eligibility pool are conscious of the added (and negative and gendered) scrutiny that female politicians receive via political news coverage is it surprising that more of them do not consider a bid for office? That the typical readers of female politicians' autobiographies are women (McKenzie 2000), and likely the very same educated professional women who make up the candidate eligibility pool, suggests that if women do not draw their own conclusions about the difficulties that female politicians face in an increasingly mediated political world, then some of them are likely to read about these difficulties in the political memoirs of female politicians.

Remedial action is this book's closing theme, and it provides a pessimistic prognosis. Available options for tackling gendered mediation of female politicians – such as media regulation and increasing the number of female journalists – offer limited prospects for altering established modes of coverage, at least in the short to medium term. Gendered mediation is a function largely of collectively held stereotypes about the genders and about political leadership, as well as the structure and operation of the news system, both of which are resistant to change. Indeed, changing social norms about the role of women in politics means eliminating the widespread reaction to women in politics that Bashevkin describes as "women plus power equals discomfort" (2009, xi). Pragmatically speaking, women (and their male allies) must continue to embrace every opportunity to challenge prevailing norms and stereotypes, and political parties at both the national and constituency levels must continue to extend efforts to inform and prepare female (and male) candidates for dealing with an often fraught media environment. While doing this, female candidates and office holders will continue working to sidestep negative coverage in the media and exploit openings whereby gendered coverage may assist their electoral prospects and career trajectories, at least on an individual basis.

1
Visibility in the News

"There's no such thing as bad publicity" and the French "succès de scandale" (success from scandal) are statements about the desirability of attention. There are no shortages of politicians and campaign professionals who would disagree with the sentiments in the old sayings, for bad publicity and scandal have been the downfall of many candidates and politicians. Nevertheless, the old adages are telling illustrations of the often-presumed linkage between attention and political success. Of course, the relationship is not simply presumed. It can be very real. Modern campaigns are waged through the media, and an important focal point for candidates and party leaders is traditional news media outlets. It is among candidates' top priorities to be visible in media representations of campaigns, whether they be local, regional, or national media, and significant amounts of time and resources are devoted to attracting coverage. For party leaders, visibility in the news is essential.

Why is the quantity and prominence of candidates' and leaders' coverage in the news so important? Starting with the most immediate effects, in some contexts, visibility in the news can actually contribute directly to an election win (e.g., Gold 2005), often because media attention enhances a candidate's name recognition among voters (e.g., Bartels 1988; Lenart 1997; Mutz 1997). The volume of media coverage can also affect the duration of a candidate's stay in a nomination contest (e.g., Shen 2008). Visibility in the news suggests importance, seriousness, competitiveness, normalcy, and suitability to the competition and to politics generally. Perceptions of viability are commonly increased with media attention. When politicians are not covered, they can fall off the public radar, so to speak, and not just off voters' radars, but also off the radars of other politicians, party decision makers, and the like. If the national party executive, the riding association president, or the party leader gets the sense that a politician is not good at attracting coverage or is not assigned importance by newsmakers, promotion within the party or caucus may be negatively affected. To be sure, the media do not make visibility decisions singlehandedly, for they naturally tend to cover competitive leaders, parties, and candidates more extensively than less competitive or marginal ones, resulting in something of a cycle whereby competitive politicians are covered more, and the increased visibility, in turn, reinforces or even enhances their stock with the public and other politicians.

Visibility is closely connected with the concept of agenda setting. Citizens take salience cues from the media, and in this context, salience is attached to people rather than to issues or policies. Routine decisions about who to cover, for how long, in how much space, and in what sections of the broadcast or the newspaper implicitly assign importance or significance to those who are featured. Repeated absence from the news may, in contrast, imply triviality about those who are not covered, an outcome Tuchman wraps into her concept of "symbolic annihilation," a powerful descriptor for the consequences of media invisibility (1978). In other words, visibility determines who is most salient in media representations of politics, sending messages to citizens about who the central players are in an election. There is compelling evidence that citizens pick up on these cues, for they tend to equate media visibility with candidate quality (Bartels 1988; Jacobson 1992), a predictable process since many individuals are cognitive economizers (Tversky and Kahneman, 1974) who seek reliable shortcuts to political decision making that will minimize their expenditure of time and cognitive resources. When citizens lack adequate political information, as many do, or when an electoral environment is particularly complex – such as a campaign with multiple candidates who are relatively unknown – taking salience cues from the media may increase.

The level of attention from the news media clearly matters for candidates and politicians. This chapter focuses on structural content, which refers to the physical characteristics of the media and involves examinations of space (print news), time (broadcast news), and prominence (both). Following Manheim (1986), this book uses the concept of visibility to refer to the salience of politicians in the media, which is actually comprised of both quantity of coverage and prominence of coverage, two separate but related concepts. Quantity refers to the amount of coverage, and prominence is a measure of the placement, position, and other "framing mechanisms" (Ghanem 1997, 12), such as photos and pull quotes, that are used to highlight or mark a story out in relation to others. Visibility is important because, first, it increases the chance that the audience will become familiar with the politician; indeed, if a politician has high exposure in terms of the number of stories, as well as prominent placement and photos, she or he will be better positioned to claim a space on the public radar. Additionally, all of these indicators of quantity and prominence send signals about the importance of politicians.

The physical elements of the news media analyzed in this chapter are various, for this book analyzes both broadcast news and print news. Measurements across the two types of media are analogous, although typically not identical due to differences in format. For broadcast news of the 2000 federal election campaign, the chapter analyzes the number and length of stories covering male and female candidates; story order and headlined news stories, both of which indicate prominence; and the sound bites and clips included within each story. For print news of the 2006 federal election, the chapter analyzes indicators such as number of stories that male and female candidates received, page number and section, the use of photos, and so on. In contrast to structural content, substantive content refers to what has been said, written, or represented in a communication, a topic the next chapter takes up.

"Symbolic Annihilation"? Past and Present Findings Compared

Visibility was a major concern of early scholarship on media coverage of female politicians. A gender perspective on visibility involves assessing whether women receive an equitable share of coverage, both in terms of volume and placement. This does not necessarily mean coverage that is equal to that of men, especially considering that, in Canada, women's share of candidacies and party leadership positions has never been on par with that of men. Rather, equitable coverage means media visibility roughly commensurate with women's share of candidacies. In the Canadian context, earlier research demonstrated that women received much less coverage than men did (Robinson 1978; Robinson and Saint-Jean 1991, 1996). In part, this was because in the 1970s and into the 1980s there were very few female candidates and even fewer high-profile female candidates, such as cabinet members, party leaders, and powerful incumbents. Exacerbating the situation, women were infrequently assigned prestigious posts within parties, resulting in less media visibility for political women before they became candidates (Robinson and Saint-Jean 1996). Female political aspirants were unknown to journalists and the public prior to being elected, and media coverage of female office holders after their election did little to change this.

We can no longer assume that the news media will ignore political women; neither can we assume that where imbalances in quantity or prominence of coverage exist that such imbalances will be as large or as widespread as they were in the past. Automatic assumptions that female politicians face a visibility hurdle must be discarded, because who gets coverage is also affected greatly by the political context and the individual characteristics of the particular politician. With the passage of time and the accumulation of research, evidence has become increasingly mixed regarding women's visibility in political news. Cases of relative parity in the volume of coverage for male and female candidates have surfaced frequently, and in a variety of national contexts (e.g., Bystrom et al. 2004; Carroll and Schreiber 1997; Devitt 2002; Gidengil and Everitt 2000, 2003a; Kahn 1994; Kittilson and Fridkin 2008; Smith 1997). For example, Kittilson and Fridkin's (2008) cross-national comparison of coverage in the United States, Canada, and Australia found no significant gender differences in the amount and prominence of candidates' coverage, nor actually, in media attention to candidates' viability, family background, or the tone of coverage (see also Gidengil and Everitt 2003a).

There have even been cases where coverage of female office holders has outpaced that of their male counterparts (Bystrom, Robertson, and Banwart 2001; Carroll and Schreiber 1997; Trimble 2007; Trimble and Everitt 2010). For example, news visibility of female freshmen Congress members following the 1992 elections in the United States was greater than that of first-term male representatives (Carroll and Schreiber 1997). Granted, the 1992 "Year of the Woman" was an exceptional round of elections that witnessed a virtual doubling of the number of women in Congress. Press coverage of women elected in 1992 did not, however, fade as the term progressed; coverage of the twenty-four women elected in 1992 increased through 1993 and 1994, and most articles about these female representatives were featured in the front or national news sections of the papers (ibid.). As the novelty of the Year of the Woman class wore off, female office holders have continued to command considerable media attention in the United States. For example, controlling for incumbency and race competitiveness, this relative gender balance in news visibility was borne out in the 1994 senatorial and gubernatorial contests (Smith 1997). In the Canadian setting, there has likewise been evidence of disproportionate emphasis on female politicians in the news (e.g., Everitt and Camp 2009b; Trimble 2007; Trimble and Everitt 2010). Female contenders for conservative party leadership posts in the 1970s (Flora MacDonald), 1990s (Kim Campbell), and 2000s (Belinda Stronach), for example, were all more visible in the *Globe and Mail*'s print news than similarly situated male contestants (Trimble 2007).

In other contexts, however, gender disparities in news visibility have continued (e.g., Gingras 1995; Kahn and Goldenberg 1991; Lemish and Tidhar 1999; Monière and Fortier 2000; Norris 1997; Sampert and Trimble 2003; Serini et al. 1998). Considerable work remains to be done to explain why the volume of coverage of female politicians is proportional to their political presence in some contexts and not in others, but there are several factors that seem to be at work. Among them is the effect that gender-role stereotypes have on the amount of attention devoted to female politicians. Newsworthiness is defined by several criteria, and "the unexpected" is one of the stronger cues of newsworthiness (e.g., Bennett 2003; Ericson et al. 1987). The news "focuses upon what is out of place: the deviant, equivocal, and unpredictable" (Ericson et al. 1992, 233). Politicians are actually keenly aware of this fact; as one of my MP interviewees pointed out, "the news never reports the 600 planes that landed safely today, just the single one that didn't."

For female politicians, heightened news attention can result *because* they are women and, therefore, do not fit the typical (male) politician mould. There is something unexpected, surprising, or curious about women's presence in political life. The considerable news attention given to female candidates in the US 1992 "Year of the Woman" elections is a good example of this. Part of the reason for the attention to this cohort of female candidates was the novelty value of both their high numbers and the unprecedented rate of their electoral success. Similarly, Republican vice-presidential candidate Sarah Palin received more media coverage in the 2008 US presidential campaign than Democratic vice-presidential candidate Joe Biden (Bode and Hennings 2012).

Women may also attract increased media attention as a result of the presumed tension between their public and private roles and other violations of gendered double standards of behaviour. This has been exacerbated by the rise of "celebrity politics," whereby the boundaries between politicians' private and political lives are increasingly blurred (van Zoonen 2005, 2006). Gendered double standards in public life abound. Consider, for instance, how active dating, promiscuity, and even infidelity are celebrated, or at the very least tolerated, in male politicians. John F. Kennedy, Bill Clinton, and Pierre Trudeau are examples in this vein. The same behaviour in women not only attracts considerable media attention, but is often implicitly or explicitly criticized, a fact that political women like Belinda Stronach and Kim Campbell have faced. For example, during her political career, former Prime Minister Kim Campbell was dogged by references to her personal past, including a divorce, and even after she retired from politics, the media reported at length about her relationship with a younger man, a point Campbell herself notes in her autobiography (1996).

Increased media visibility may also come from less titillating contraventions of gender-role norms such as when women speak agentically and aggressively, when women demonstrate leadership ability and hard-nosed political styles, when female leaders take tough or uncompassionate stances on social issues. Society associates women and femininity with traits such as warmth, compassion, and gentleness, so a female politician acting even moderately aggressively can create a "basic schema incompatibility" in which actual behaviour contradicts deeply held cultural norms of appropriate female action and demeanour (Butler and Geis 1990; Hitchon and Chang 1995). Since surprising or unexpected behaviours are particularly newsworthy, instances of female aggression may be reported more widely or exaggerated in news stories, a pattern that characterized news coverage of Kim Campbell and former NDP leaders Audrey McLaughlin and Alexa McDonough (Gidengil and Everitt 1999, 2000, 2003a, 2003b). Subsequent chapters provide more comprehensive analysis of the quality of women's news coverage and the effects of gendered patterns of coverage on viewers' assessments of female politicians. For now, the point is that gender equity in visibility cannot always be taken at face value. Attention *must* be paid to the reasons for equity in visibility – whether it comes as a result of serious attention to female candidates or because of covering women as novelties or norm breakers.

The remainder of the chapter compares the visibility in the news of male and female politicians using data derived from content analyses of broadcast and print coverage of two Canadian federal election campaigns: 2000 and 2005-06. The media data for the 2000 federal election come from the Canadian Election Study's content analysis of election coverage on four major news broadcasts: CBC's *The National*, CTV's *National Edition*, SRC's *Le Téléjournal*, and TVA's *Le TVA Édition réseau*. These represent major

English- and French-language media outlets in the country. They also include two public (CBC and SRC) and two private (CTV and TVA) broadcasters; SRC, or Société Radio-Canada, is the French-language counterpart of the English-language CBC.

The CBC-SRC's coverage of the 2000 campaign is an interesting test of whether visibility in the news of candidates during election campaigns tends to be gender equitable. Both are public broadcasters, have taken steps to promote fairness and equity in broadcasting, and have developed explicit guidelines for sex-role portrayal in programming.[1] The CBC-SRC also promotes progressive employment equity policies that have resulted in rough gender parity in terms of the numbers of men and women in the organization, a fact that the organization discusses at length in recent annual reports and newsletters.[2] Finally, despite heightened reliance on advertising revenues, the CBC-SRC is a public broadcaster that reports annually to Parliament and receives a sizeable portion of its funding through an annual parliamentary appropriation. Consequently, of all mainstream broadcast media outlets in Canada, arguably the CBC-SRC should be least likely to deliver television coverage of election campaigns that is systematically gendered.

An important point to make before moving to results is that analyses of the news coverage of the 2000 federal election campaign are focused more on coverage of the party leaders than is the case for 2005-06, in both this chapter and the next, and there are two reasons for this. First, the media data for the 2000 federal election campaign come from television news, and the media data for the 2005-06 election campaign are derived from newspaper coverage. All news media are quite leader-focused during campaigns, but this tendency is more pronounced in television news, perhaps as a result of the smaller number and shorter length of stories on television news compared with print news. Hour-long televised news broadcasts, such as CBC's *The National*, have fewer precious resources of space and time to devote to coverage of personalities other than leaders. Second, there was a female leader of a major party – Alexa McDonough, then leader of the NDP – in 2000. In the campaign for the 2006 election, all the major party leaders were male, so there is more focus on candidates' than on leaders' coverage in analyses of print news of this race. The benefits of this particular combination of data sources are the multiple comparisons made possible: the coverage of the female leader versus that of her male colleagues in television news of the 2000 campaign; the coverage of the female leader versus female candidates' coverage in the 2000 campaign; female candidates' coverage in televised versus print news; and female candidates' coverage when there is no female leader in the race.

Visibility in Television News Coverage of the 2000 Federal Election

It is useful to begin by revisiting the broad features of the 2000 campaign in order to situate the following analyses of coverage. Making sense of news media coverage of men and women during any election campaign is contingent, to some extent, upon understanding the relative strengths, ideological positions, and electoral prospects of the parties and candidates in the race, as well as the notable events that occur throughout the campaign.

Five main parties contested the 2000 federal election in Canada: the incumbent Liberal Party under leader and Prime Minister Jean Chrétien; the Canadian Alliance (CA) under leader Stockwell Day; the Progressive Conservative (PC) Party under leader Joe Clark; the New Democratic Party (NDP) under leader Alexa McDonough; and the Bloc Québécois (Bloc or BQ) under leader Gilles Duceppe. In terms of location on the conventional left-right political spectrum, the parties' placements were the following: the Bloc and NDP on the left; the Liberal Party in the centre; the PC Party on the centre-right; and the Alliance on the right of the spectrum. The parties' platforms in the 2000 campaign attest to this characterization of their relative positions (e.g., Blais et al. 2002a; Dornan and Pammett 2001), as do party supporters' issue positions (Blais et al. 2002b). For example, the NDP and the Bloc both campaigned in favour of a nationally funded prescription drug plan, social programs, and environmental protection. The PCs and the Alliance – both on the right – paid attention to crime, and the Alliance put special emphasis on fiscal issues.

The parties' standings in the 36th Canadian Parliament (1997-2000) upon its dissolution were as follows: the Liberals had a majority with 161 seats; the Alliance was the Official Opposition with 58 seats; the Bloc had 44 seats; the NDP had 19 seats; and the PCs had 15 seats (Table 1.1). Upon its dissolution in 2000, there were four MPs sitting as Independents.

None of the party leaders in the 2000 federal campaign were newcomers to political life. This is an important point given that there is a "learning curve" for the acquisition of media savvy, and, moreover, it takes time to cultivate relationships with journalists. Jean Chrétien was first elected to Parliament in 1963, and he had served in the cabinets of prime ministers Pearson, Trudeau, and Turner. Chrétien was elected Liberal leader in 1990. In 1993, he became prime minister and was re-elected in 1997. In 2000, Chrétien was running for his third consecutive term as prime minister. He

TABLE 1.1

Distribution of seats in Canada's House of Commons, by party, 2000

Party	At dissolution	After election
Liberal	161	172
Alliance	58	66
PC	15	12
NDP	19	13
BQ	44	38
Independent	4	0
Total	301	301

had led the Liberals for a decade and had over thirty years of experience in the House of Commons.

Stockwell Day was a relative newcomer to federal politics in 2000, for he had only recently been elected Canadian Alliance leader that summer. However, Day had been a member of the Legislative Assembly (MLA) in the province of Alberta for fourteen years, from 1986 to 2000. Day spent a number of years holding prominent cabinet portfolios, including Labour, Social Services, and Finance, in the PC governments of Alberta Premier Ralph Klein, where he had also been the government house leader.

PC leader Joe Clark was a former leader of the Opposition and a former prime minister (June 1979 to March 1980). After losing the PC leadership to Brian Mulroney in 1983, Clark stayed in federal politics as a cabinet minister in Mulroney's governments until 1993. Clark retired from federal politics in 1993, but made a comeback as PC leader in 1998. Clark won a parliamentary seat in a Nova Scotia by-election in 2000.

Alexa McDonough's first runs at political office were for the federal NDP in Halifax ridings in the 1979 and 1980 federal elections. She was defeated in both. Her main political training ground was Nova Scotia provincial politics. McDonough was elected leader of the Nova Scotia NDP in 1980. The following year she won the provincial NDP's first seat for mainland Nova Scotia (as opposed to labour-friendly Cape Breton, where historically the NDP has had its most support in Nova Scotia). Until 1984, she was the sole New Democrat and the only woman MLA. She was re-elected in 1984, 1988, and 1993. McDonough retired from provincial politics in 1994 to pursue the leadership of the federal NDP, which she won in October 1995, replacing

Visibility in the News

FIGURE 1.1

Vote intentions through the 2000 Canadian federal election campaign

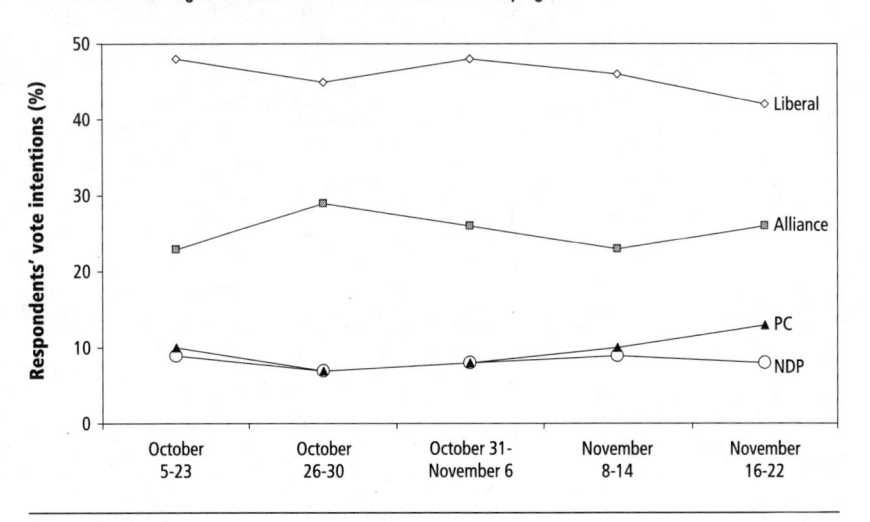

[Figure: Line graph showing respondents' vote intentions (%) from October 5-23 through November 16-22, with Liberal around 45-48%, Alliance around 23-29%, PC and NDP both around 7-10%. Source: Environics]

Audrey McLaughlin, the NDP's first national female leader. In 1997, Alexa McDonough achieved a number of federal-level "firsts" for the NDP. She became the first New Democrat elected to Parliament from the mainland of Nova Scotia; she was the first NDP leader to win federal seats in New Brunswick; and she was the first NDP leader to win a majority of Nova Scotia federal seats. In 1997, McDonough also returned the NDP to official party status – which the party had lost in the 1993 election – electing twenty-one MPs from across Canada.[3]

All leaders in the 2000 campaign had by then built impressive political careers. Nevertheless, it was clear from the start that the 2000 campaign was a contest between the incumbent Liberal Party under Jean Chrétien and the Canadian Alliance under Stockwell Day, and few seriously questioned whether the Liberals would win. Neither Clark and the Progressive Conservatives nor McDonough and the New Democrats were in a competitive position at any point through the 2000 campaign, at least not in terms of winning enough seats to form the government or the Official Opposition. The NDP and the PCs went into the 2000 campaign on roughly equal footing in the polls, as polling data collected by Environics illustrate (see Figure 1.1). The near tie between the NDP and the PCs persisted through at least half of the campaign period. Clark enjoyed a spike in his ratings in the third

TABLE 1.2

Distribution of news stories, by political party, four TV networks, 2000 election campaign

	News stories	
Party	n	(%)
Liberal	217	(26.3)
Alliance	167	(20.2)
PC	86	(10.4)
BQ	123	(14.9)
NDP	77	(9.3)
Other	12	(1.5)
None	143	(17.3)
Total	825	(99.9)

Note: Percentages do not total 100 because of rounding.

week of the campaign, owing primarily to a strong showing in the English-language televised leaders' debate (Blais et al. 2002a).

The 2000 federal election was held on 27 November, and the distribution of Parliament's 301 seats after the vote count was as follows (see Table 1.1): the Liberals won a third consecutive majority with 172 seats; the Alliance retained their Official Opposition status with 66 seats; the Bloc won 38 seats; the NDP won 13 seats; and the Progressive Conservatives won 12 seats.

What do the data tell us about the possibility of gendered patterns of leader and candidate visibility in televised news of the 2000 campaign? News coverage of Canadian politics centres squarely on the leaders, as noted above, especially during election campaigns, which are increasingly reported through horserace frames. In coverage of the 2000 campaign, stories about the Liberals were largely stories about Liberal leader and incumbent prime minister, Jean Chrétien, and the same was true of the other parties and leaders. Looking at a simple distribution of news coverage among the four parties that fielded a full slate of candidates in the 2000 campaign provides a cursory feel for the visibility of the parties and their leaders to the Canadian public. As Table 1.2 shows, Chrétien and Day received the most coverage in 2000, and together accounted for almost 47 percent of 825 stories featured on the four networks. The prominence of Chrétien and Day and their parties certainly makes sense considering that the 2000 campaign was a contest between the Liberals and the Alliance. The BQ and Gilles Duceppe followed with nearly 15 percent of the stories, then the PCs and Joe Clark

FIGURE 1.2

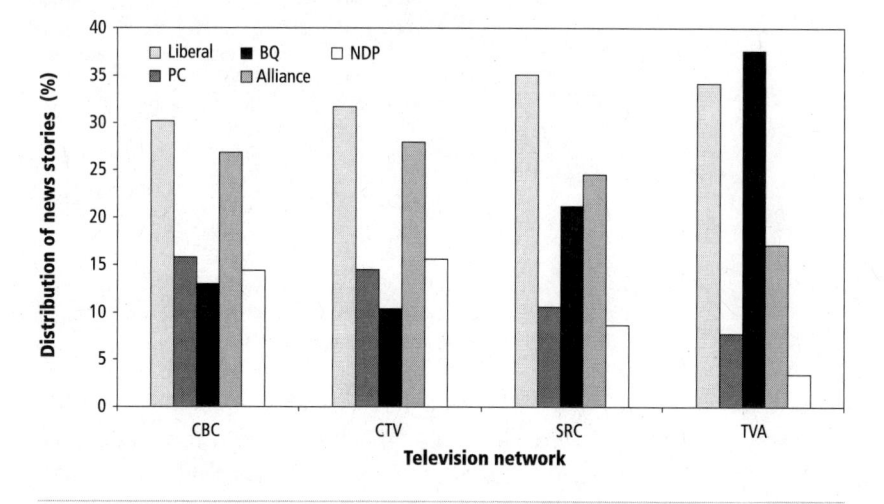

Distribution of news stories by TV network, 2000 election campaign

with 10 percent of the stories, and finally the NDP and its leader Alexa McDonough with 9 percent.

Coverage of the BQ is quite high considering that it does not run candidates outside Quebec, but this is accounted for, in part, by the fact that two French networks are included in the data set. If we look at coverage of the five major parties on the two English-language networks, the coverage of Duceppe and the BQ is much lower than on the two French networks, as Figure 1.2 shows. Looking at differences across networks, it is the French networks and the CBC that account for the small difference between Clark's and McDonough's percentages of stories. On CTV, the NDP and its leader's portion of stories is slightly higher than Clark's and the PCs' – of course, overall, the difference between McDonough's and Clark's visibility in terms of the number of stories is not large.

That McDonough received the fewest stories among the leaders of the full-slate parties in the French networks and the CBC does not mean a whole lot on its own, especially considering the small magnitude of difference between her coverage and that of Clark, her closest competitor throughout the campaign. It is necessary to examine other indicators in order to get a fuller picture. Story length also provides information about leaders' visibility in election news. Looking at the mean length of stories

TABLE 1.3

Mean length of news stories, by political party, four TV networks, 2000 election campaign

Party	Mean length sec.	(min.)
Liberal	126	(2.10)
Alliance	114	(1.90)
PC	73	(1.22)
BQ	82	(1.37)
NDP	53	(0.88)
Overall	89.6	(1.49)

about each of the parties and their leaders, Table 1.3 demonstrates that the female leader ranks last. Compared with an average of roughly two minutes for the two main contenders, and roughly one-and-a-half minutes for Clark and Duceppe, McDonough's average story length was less than a minute. What this means is that McDonough had not only somewhat fewer stories than the male leaders, but also far shorter stories, on average. The mean length of her stories was not even three-quarters that of Joe Clark's, the leader with the next lowest mean story length in the 2000 election campaign.

Moving from quantity to prominence indicators, the placement of stories in the newscasts of the four networks also contributes to the visibility of the party leaders. This prominence indicator can be related to section and page number in a newspaper. The closer a story appears to the front page in print news is a signal of its relative importance among all the news stories of the day; similarly, the most important, attention-grabbing stories on television news are typically placed closest to the top of the newscast (e.g., Eveland et al. 2002). Across the four networks, McDonough received no lead stories during coverage of the 2000 campaign (results not shown) – that is, the first story in the nightly newscast, as opposed to the second, third, fourth, and so on. Chrétien and Day had the bulk of lead stories, naturally, given their competitive positions in the campaign. Sixteen percent of Chrétien's and 8 percent of Day's stories were leads. Even for Clark and Duceppe, however, 4 percent of their stories were first up in the nightly newscast. All of Clark's lead stories were on the two English-language networks, and all of Duceppe's on the French networks. On the English networks, then, only Duceppe and McDonough were given no lead stories, even though McDonough's party ran a full slate of candidates from coast to coast to coast.

Visibility in the News 37

FIGURE 1.3

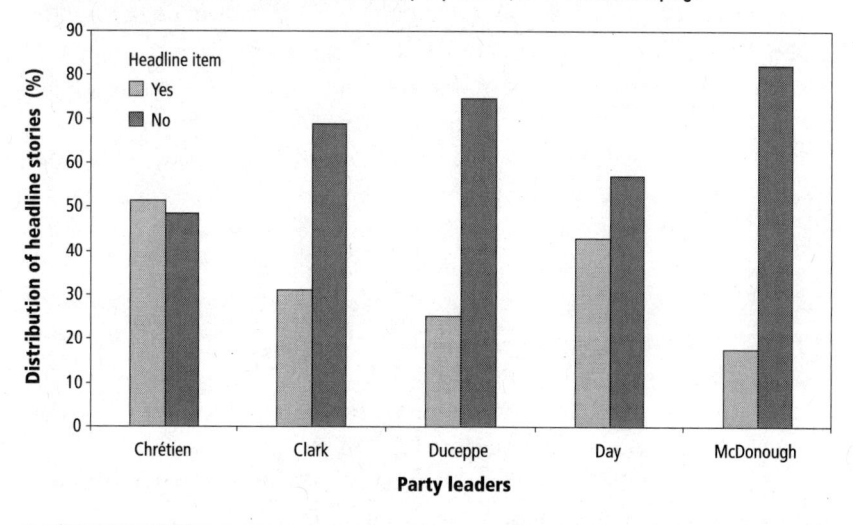

Distribution of headline stories (four TV networks), party leaders, 2000 election campaign

McDonough also received the lowest portion of headline stories (Figure 1.3). Immediately before and during the opening credits of a televised newscast, a voice-over narration of the stories coming up in the program is advertised to viewers, and the stories that correspond to these headlines are called "headline stories." Typically, the chief anchor narrates the headlines.[4] The headlines during the opening credits of the news program flag or introduce a selection of stories to come in the newscast – usually, the most important, interesting, or dramatic news items of the day. Therefore, headline stories can be considered an indicator of the importance attached to news stories, because they are advertisements of the best stories of the day and are designed to pique interest and prevent viewers from switching channels to another program. As Figure 1.3 shows, only 18 percent of McDonough's stories were headlined. In contrast, 51 percent of Chrétien's, 43 percent of Day's, 31 percent of Clark's, and 25 percent of Duceppe's stories were headline items. If we break it down by language of network (results not shown), even on the two English networks, Duceppe had a higher percentage of headlined items among his stories (21 percent) than did McDonough (19 percent).

On these initial indicators, McDonough and the New Democrats were the least visible among the major parties in the race in televised news of the 2000 campaign. McDonough and the NDP received the fewest stories, with by far the shortest mean story length, no lead stories, and the lowest percentage of headline stories. What should be made of these findings of consistent differences in visibility? On the one hand, McDonough's and the NDP's lesser visibility reflect the relative status of her and her party. McDonough and the NDP were never in a competitive position at any point during the 2000 campaign; yet, the same was true of Clark and the PCs as well as Duceppe and the Bloc. Clark was a former prime minister, which may account for his greater visibility in the media compared with McDonough, but McDonough was certainly no political newcomer, as the brief political biographies presented earlier in the chapter demonstrate. Certainly, for most of Canada's political history, the PC party was the other contender for power, although far less successful than the Liberals in terms of total years in office. The PCs' historical importance is likely a significant factor influencing the greater media attention paid to Clark and the PCs in the 2000 campaign compared with McDonough and the NDP.

Although the gulfs between McDonough's visibility and that of Chrétien and Day, the two main challengers in the 2000 election, are to be expected, there are reasons to question whether Clark and the PCs deserved greater media visibility than McDonough and the NDP. With the unprecedented defeat of the PCs in the 1993 federal election, the PC party became one of the minor players on the federal scene. Aside from the fact that the PCs had once been powerful, there were no immediately relevant reasons why McDonough should have received fewer stories, shorter stories, no lead stories, and a lower proportion of headline stories compared with Clark. McDonough and Clark went into the 2000 campaign with similar ratings in the polls (Figure 1.1), and this near-tie persisted through the first half of the campaign period until Clark's post-debate bump. In terms of House standings, the NDP went into the 2000 campaign with four more seats (19 seats) than the Conservatives (15 seats), and finished with one more seat (13 seats) than the Conservatives (12 seats) (Table 1.1).

Another CES data set that examines solely CBC's *The National* permits us to examine the components of televised news stories more closely, still considering its coverage of the 2000 campaign, but this time including stories that focus primarily on the four main leaders and parties that ran a full slate of candidates: the Liberals, Alliance, PCs, and NDP. This data set includes more detailed coding of the elements that constitute a news story: the lead-ins, sound bites, clips, and the wrap-ups. The chapter turns now to a finer level of analysis, from examining whole stories to looking at the constituent components of news stories, permitting closer investigation of the characteristics of coverage. At the substory level, three components of a news story are particularly significant: the lead-in or introductory segment of a news story, the wrap-up or concluding segment, and the sound bites and clips featured in between, each of which is explained in further detail below. Together, these constitute the "anatomy" of a televised news story.

A lead-in is the introductory segment of a story where an anchor presents the story or stories to come, usually from behind a desk in the news studio. Not all stories have lead-ins. Commonly, the first and second stories in a news program have lead-ins, and subsequent stories are generally less likely to have lead-ins. A lead-in can be thought of as an element of news production that cues audiences to the most important elements of the story to come, with the intention of preventing audiences from changing channels to a different program, news-oriented or otherwise. A lead-in is often used as a "hook" to maintain audiences' attention.

A wrap-up is the concluding segment of a news story, usually done by a reporter talking in front of a camera. Sometimes the wrap-up is a simple summary of the story; in other cases, the wrap-up is where "spin" is added to a story (e.g., Schokkenbroek 1999; Schultz 2005). "Spin" refers to the act of manipulating meanings, symbols, or images in order to influence political interpretations, so it is closely related to the idea of framing. Bennett identifies framing as one of the core components of spinning a story (2003, 134). Both spinning and framing involve applying an interpretive lens to a set of existing events or statements. Therefore, in cases where spin is added during the wrap-up of a story, journalists tell viewers not only what happened in the campaign that day, but also what the events mean or signify. As with lead-ins, not all stories have wrap-ups.

A sound bite is video footage of a person who is shown *and* heard talking in his or her own words. A sound bite is a form of direct, relatively unmediated communication from the speaker to viewers.[5] In coverage of a national election campaign, the figures in sound bites tend overwhelmingly to be the party leaders. To a lesser extent, sound bites are also shown of candidates, party officials, campaign workers, pollsters, and other experts, as well as citizens. When candidates are shown in national-level televised news coverage, they tend to be high-profile candidates, such as cabinet ministers or long-serving backbenchers.[6] Stories vary in terms of the number of sound bites they contain. Some stories have no sound bites, some have a single sound bite, and some have many.

TABLE 1.4
Length and number of party leaders' sound bites, CBC news, 2000 election campaign

Party leaders	Sound bites n	(%)	Mean length, sec.	Total length sec.	(min.)
Chrétien	156	(33)	8.16	1,274	(21.2)
Day	168	(36)	6.26	1,055	(17.6)
Clark	78	(17)	8.31	649	(10.8)
McDonough	67	(14)	8.57	578	(9.6)
All sound bites	469	(100)	7.83	3,556	(59.2)

Notes: $F = 10.15$; $p > F = 0.00$

Pairwise comparison of means tests reveals that Day's mean sound-bite length (6.26 sec.) is significantly different from all other leaders' sound bite lengths. The mean sound-bite lengths of the other three leaders are not significantly different from one another.

A clip is video footage of a leader, candidate, expert, citizen, or other person that is accompanied by a voice-over from a reporter or anchor. A clip is a more heavily mediated form of coverage that features narration by a journalist rather than the subject of the clip speaking in his or her own words (which is the case with sound bites). Lead-ins and wrap-ups will be analyzed in some detail in the next chapter. The remainder of this chapter's examination of televised news coverage of leaders and candidates will focus on sound bites and clips.

Looking more closely at the substory level, Table 1.4 presents several types of information about the sound bites each of the party leaders received in the 2000 election campaign: the mean length of the sound bites, the comparative number and percentage of sound bites, and the total amount of sound-bite speaking time that each leader had in the CBC broadcasts over the thirty-five-day campaign period. The first point to make about sound bites is that they are incredibly short, and have been getting much shorter over recent decades (e.g., Bennett 2003; Stephens 1996). The average length of a leader's sound bite in 2000 on the CBC news was 7.08 seconds. The typical news story has a number of sound bites, which is why the total number of sound bites is so large.

On average, as Table 1.4 shows, McDonough's average sound-bite length is basically on par with Chrétien's and Clark's, and is much longer than Day's. Pairwise comparisons of means testing show that the only significant differences were between Day's mean sound-bite length and the mean sound-bite length of each of the other three leaders. Nonetheless, McDonough had

TABLE 1.5

Party leaders' clips and ratio of sound bites to clips, CBC news, 2000 election campaign

Party leaders	Clips n	(%)	Ratio, sound bites to clips
Chrétien	186	(34)	156:186 = 0.84
Day	191	(35)	168:191 = 0.88
Clark	91	(17)	78:91 = 0.86
McDonough	77	(14)	67:77 = 0.87
Total	545	(100)	n/a

far fewer sound bites than either Chrétien or Day and somewhat fewer than Clark, resulting in less overall sound-bite speaking time for McDonough in the CBC news compared with the three male leaders of full-slate parties. McDonough received 71 seconds – over one minute – less total sound-bite time than Clark did (final column of Table 1.4). Of course, this was certainly related to the fact that McDonough and the NDP received the fewest stories compared with the other three leaders and their parties.

The distribution of clips was very similar to that of sound bites (Table 1.5). The first column of Table 1.5 shows the total number of clips of each leader contained in the 163 stories in the data set. In ascending order, McDonough received the fewest number of clips (77) followed by Clark (91), Chrétien (186), and then Day (191). Again, that McDonough received the fewest clips is a reflection of the fact that she received the lowest number of stories.

Another way to examine the prominence of leaders in news stories is to examine the ratio of sound bites to clips – in other words, the extent to which each leader was seen and heard talking in his or her own words versus the extent to which the leader was simply shown in a video clip while a journalist narrated. This is also an important indicator of the extent to which women are portrayed as agentic or autonomous speakers, as opposed to having their words and behaviours more heavily mediated by newsmakers, and as such, is one of the ways in which this book analyzes patterns in the format of men's and women's coverage. Past research has shown that the news tends to paraphrase women as opposed to letting women speak in their own words (in sound bites) or quoting women directly (in print stories) (e.g., Aday and Devitt 2001). The consequence may be that female candidates have less control over their campaign messages and their public personas (ibid., 68). In addition, perennial paraphrasing of female candidates may imply that women are less substantive, less "quotable," or less credible as speakers. In the context of televised news coverage, the difference between a candidate speaking for herself and a reporter paraphrasing a candidate is captured nicely in the distinction between a sound bite and a clip. A sound bite is akin to a direct quote; it lets a politician give her message directly to viewers. A clip is akin to being paraphrased, because the reporter may tell the viewers what the politician said or what her actions mean or signify.

As Table 1.5 demonstrates, all four of these leaders received more clips than sound bites in CBC's coverage. The second column of Table 1.5 shows the ratio of sound bites to clips for each leader. A score of 1 would indicate that a leader received the same number of clips as sound bites. The lower the ratio, the heavier a leader's coverage was on clips compared with sound bites. The key point here is that all four leaders received essentially the same ratio of sound bites to clips. Coverage of Alexa McDonough in the news of the 2000 federal election campaign had roughly the same balance of relatively unmediated sound bites to clips compared with the coverage received by her male counterparts.

Although local news channels may focus more on constituency-level electoral contests, national coverage tends to focus predominantly on leaders and to a much lesser extent on parties. Leaders are the most prominent political figures in televised news; but, there is some coverage of the other candidates, particularly high-profile incumbents and cabinet members. In 2000, this included coverage of candidates such as Allan Rock, minister of health; Anne McLellan, minister of justice; Elsie Wayne, prominent PC incumbent and former interim PC leader (April-November 1998); and Yvan Loubier, one of the BQ's co-founders.

Table 1.6 reports the same categories of information that were provided on leader sound bites earlier, only now focusing on candidates' sound bites. The combined total sound-bite speaking time provided to candidates was about 13 minutes, compared with an hour for the party leaders combined. Of these 13 minutes, male candidates received 10.6 minutes of sound-bite speaking time in news coverage in 2000 compared with 2.5 minutes for female candidates.[7] At first glance, this may appear unfair, but female candidates' proportion of sound-bite time was actually nearly equal to their proportion of candidacies. Of the 1,808 candidates who stood for election in

TABLE 1.6

Length and number of candidates' sound bites, by sex, CBC news, 2000 election campaign

Party leaders	Sound bites, n	Mean length, sec.	Total length sec.	(min.)
Men	97	6.57	635	(10.6)
Women	17	8.58	147	(2.5)

Note: $t = -2.72$; $p > t = 0.01$

the 2000 federal campaign, 373 or 21 percent were women. The 2.5 minutes of sound-bite speaking time allotted to female candidates represented 19 percent of the total sound-bite time allotted to all candidates. Thus, there was only a small difference between the proportion of female candidacies and the proportion of female candidates' sound-bite speaking time in the CBC news coverage of the 2000 election campaign. Although this is, nevertheless, a difference, with male candidates gaining a slightly larger share of the sound-bite time, this small gender difference is probably a function of the fact that male candidates were more likely to be incumbent and/or high profile, such as Liberal cabinet ministers. Indeed, all twenty-six members of Chrétien's cabinet at dissolution in 2000 sought re-election, and of these, nineteen were male.

Correspondence between women's candidacies and their news visibility was also found in analyses of print coverage of three provincial elections in Atlantic Canada in 1999 and 2000 (Everitt 2003). Thus, balance in the amount of time and space apportioned to candidates of both sexes may have increasingly become the norm in the Canadian setting. To foreshadow the next chapter, however, there seems to be an interesting linkage between women's visibility and their counter-stereotypical behaviour, particularly regarding high visibility of the female leader's and candidates' attack-style behaviour, reminding us that increased media attention is not always positive, nor is it necessarily the result of gender equitable treatment. As Chapter 2 demonstrates, for example, female politicians are accorded far more visibility and prominence in the news when they go negative or engage in attack-style behaviours, because both are counter to prevailing stereotypes about feminine behaviour. This was true of news coverage of both McDonough and other female candidates in 2000, and it indicates that considerations of quality and quantity of coverage are, in certain respects, highly intertwined.

Visibility in Print News Coverage of the 2006 Federal Elections

The campaign for the 2006 federal election is different in some ways from the election campaign in 2000. First, the 2006 race had fewer well-known leaders, since three of the four major national parties had relatively new ones. Paul Martin (Liberal), Stephen Harper (Conservative), and Jack Layton (NDP) were all "freshman" leaders in 2004, although by no means political newcomers, and 2006 was only their second election at the helm of their respective parties. Second, the campaign for the 2006 federal election, like the one in 2004, did not have a single female major party leader. In 1993, both major parties of the left and the right were led by women: Kim Campbell led the PCs and Audrey McLaughlin led the NDP. In the 1997 and 2000 federal elections, Alexa McDonough led the NDP. Accordingly, the analyses of print coverage of the 2005-06 campaign focus solely on comparisons of the coverage of male and female candidates.

Scandal was at the top of the election agenda in 2005-06. The Sponsorship Scandal[8] had been an issue for some time, but attention to the scandal increased dramatically during the campaign, and the Conservatives, NDP, and BQ certainly attempted to capitalize on the opportunity to criticize the Liberals and draw attention to governance issues more generally (Gidengil et al. 2006). Indeed, the Sponsorship Scandal was a centrepiece of the Conservatives' 2006 election platform. Additionally, during the 2005-06 campaign, allegations arose of insider trading within the Department of Finance, leading to an RCMP investigation. Female candidates may benefit in the media and at the ballot box when scandal, corruption, and governance become salient campaign issues. Since women are often stereotyped as altruistic, trustworthy, ethical, and other oriented (e.g., Eagly and Crowley 1986; Huddy and Terkildsen 1993b), female politicians are often perceived as less likely to engage in political corruption than are their male counterparts (e.g., Burrell 1994).

The campaign for the 2006 election was held over December 2005 and January 2006, with voting day occurring on 23 January 2006. The campaign was nearly eight weeks long, the longest Canada has had, in order to allow time off for the Christmas and New Year's holidays. The Conservatives had a "policy-per-day" strategy during this campaign, which saw them introduce a reduction in the GST (goods and services tax) from 7 percent to 5 percent over two years, a new child care allowance, and so on. The Liberal Party, in contrast, opted not to reveal anything major until after the Christmas/New Year's break, which meant that a lot of the news coverage went to Harper and the Conservatives in the first part of the campaign. In the end, Harper's

Conservatives won a minority government with 124 seats of the 308. The Liberals became the Official Opposition for the first time in a generation.

Looking at coverage of the candidates, which is more extensive in newspapers than on televised campaign news, analyses of the seven dailies' reporting of the 2005-06 campaign tell an interesting story about men's and women's campaign visibility. In the 2006 federal election, there were 1,634 candidates, 380 women and 1,254 men. Women represented 23 percent of candidates, as they did in the 2004 federal election. Looking at a few simple indicators of quantity of coverage, there is some evidence of equity, at least in the number of stories. For example, female candidates received 23 percent of first mentions in print news of the 2006 race (results not shown), a proportion identical to women's share of candidacies. A first mention refers to the person mentioned first in a news story. This is an important indicator of visibility, not only because it puts the mentioned person first in the article, but also because people tend to not read entire articles. One study suggested that only 12 percent of articles are read (as opposed to scanned or abandoned entirely) further than half their length (Garcia and Stark 1991). Consequently, what comes earlier in an article, such as a first mention, is what the article is about for many readers, regardless of what is written later.

Note that the gender breakdown of candidates' first mentions reported above excludes all stories where a party leader was mentioned first or where no particular person was mentioned in the story. As pointed out earlier, there was no female party leader in the 2006 election, so including the voluminous first mentions received by the four male party leaders inflates dramatically the number of first mentions received by male contestants in the campaign. There are 698 stories that mention a candidate first, compared with the 2,646 stories that mention a party leader first, so although gender equity in the number of candidates' first mentions may be positive, it is still the case that when there is no female leader in an election campaign, coverage is obviously overwhelmingly dominated by men. As a final note, Belinda Stronach received 33 first mentions in the 2005-06 campaign, far more than any other female candidate, and representing 20 percent of the 163 first mentions received by female candidates in 2006. If Stronach were not a candidate in 2006, visibility of female candidates in print news of the campaign would have been lower, raising some doubt about whether gender equity in the quantity of coverage would have been present. Without Stronach's 33 first mentions, female candidates would have had only 19 percent of all first mentions.

TABLE 1.7

Distribution of candidates' first mentions in print news, 2006 election campaign: challengers, incumbents, incumbent cabinet members

Type of candidates	Men n	(%)	Women n	(%)
Challengers	229	(43)	44	(27)
Incumbents	140	(26)	48	(29)
Incumbent cabinet members	166	(31)	71	(44)
Total	535	(100)	163	(100)

Note: Chi^2 = 14.26; df = 2; p = .001

How do the rates of first mentions vary with candidate type? There are different types of candidates in any race: incumbents – including both high-profile incumbents, often cabinet members or opposition critics, and rank-and-file backbencher incumbents – as well as challengers. Among male candidates, it is the challengers that attracted the most first mentions (43 percent) in 2006 (Table 1.7), in no small measure because of the large number of male challengers in any election. Indeed, 77 percent of the candidates in the race were men, and only a relatively small portion of the male candidates were incumbents. Among male candidates, challengers received the greatest proportion of first mentions, followed by incumbents, followed then by incumbent cabinet members. The pattern is reversed for female candidates. Among female candidates, challengers received the lowest proportion of first mentions, followed by incumbents, followed by female cabinet members at the top on this indicator of media visibility. As noted above, Belinda Stronach, then a Liberal cabinet member in her last re-election bid, led with 33 first mentions. She was followed next, though distantly, by Anne McLellan (21 first mentions), Olivia Chow (16), Liza Frulla (15), Hedy Fry (5), and then Maria Minna, Libby Davies, and Carolyn Bennett (4 each). A more general observation about this finding may be that women tend to attract attention mostly when they are quite high profile, perhaps because of having demonstrated their expertise in the political domain and their viability as candidates or because of fascination with their personal lives or personalities, as was the case with Belinda Stronach (e.g., Trimble 2007; Trimble and Everitt 2010). High-ranking political women may be deemed particularly newsworthy simply *because* of their position within the top political elite, an interpretation that fits well with the notion that the news focuses on that which is surprising, dramatic, or novel. In her analysis of three female candidates for conservative party leadership positions in Canada, Trimble demonstrates that women's visibility in the news often outstrips their actual "standing in the race" (2007, 972), which follows from the notion that "hegemonic masculinity in political life ensures that gender is interesting in and of itself" (974). In coverage of the 2005-06 campaign, Stronach received 33 first mentions, as noted, more than male Liberal cabinet members Ujjal Dosanjh (12), Jean Lapierre (20), and Pierre Pettigrew (26), for example. Upon closer inspection, one might easily make the case that some of these male candidates were, arguably, more "newsworthy" than Stronach, suggesting that she did receive more attention than her political standing actually warranted. Pettigrew, for example, was minister of foreign affairs during the campaign, one of the pre-eminent portfolios in the cabinet, and he had previously been minister of health, intergovernmental affairs, human resources development, and so on, not to mention one of the senior members of the government and Liberal caucus at the time. Ujjal Dosanjh was newer to the federal scene in 2005, when the election was called, but he had been the federal minister of health since 2004, and before that he had been a provincial party leader, BC's attorney general for five years (1995-2000), and the premier of British Columbia (2000-2001).

Prominence is just as important as quantity, for both contribute to visibility. Although there was overall gender equity in candidates' proportions of first mentions in 2005-06, where in the papers did readers see stories about female politicians compared with stories about their male counterparts? Placement provides salience cues to readers about the importance of different candidates. On a practical level, placement also greatly affects whether a story is actually read by voters. Focusing on section and page number, a story on the front page of a newspaper is much more likely to be read than one on page A17 or in later sections of a paper. One study suggests that the first six pages of the newspaper are the most engaging for readers, with interest in reading dropping off significantly afterwards (Garcia and Stark 1991). In coverage of the campaign for the 2006 election, there are no statistically significant gender differences in the placement of male and female candidates' stories across the different sections and page numbers of the seven dailies examined (Table 1.8). This is true even for the all-important front page, where the proportions of men's and women's first mentions were the same. Women were not buried in the back pages or in lifestyle sections, as had previously been the case with earlier generations of political women. This result holds, actually, regardless of the type of candidate, for there are

TABLE 1.8

Placement of candidates' first mentions in print news, by sex, 2006 election campaign

		Men		Women	
Section	Page	n	(%)	n	(%)
Section A	Front page	60	(11)	19	(12)
	A2-A5	144	(27)	48	(29)
	A6-A10	161	(30)	50	(31)
	A11-A20	77	(14)	19	(12)
	A21-A35	35	(7)	8	(5)
Sections B-C		39	(7)	12	(7)
Sections D-F		19	(4)	7	(4)
Total		535	(100)	163	(100)

Note: Chi^2 = 1.73; df = 6; p = .942

no gender differences in page and section placement among challengers, incumbents, or cabinet member incumbents (results not shown). At all levels of candidacy, stories about female candidates are placed similarly to those about male candidates.

In addition to placement, the use of framing mechanisms like photos and pull quotes provides a second common indicator of prominence. The chapter analyzes photos, but the data set does not code for pull quotes. Similar to placement, photos mark out a news story in relation to others, thus signalling salience about the subject of the story. Photos draw attention to a story (Mendelson 2003), increasing the likelihood that it will be scanned or read. As Table 1.9 shows, stories about female candidates are more visual than male candidates' stories. Fifty-six percent of stories that mention female candidates first include a photo, and for male candidates this proportion is 48 percent. Interestingly, if we look only at the front pages of the papers, male and female candidates have identical rates of photo inclusion in their stories – 47 percent of stories (results not shown). Even on the attention-grabbing front page, women are not disadvantaged in terms of this indicator of visibility. It is really on pages A2 to A5 where the female photo advantage emerges (results not shown). This is an important finding, because this is the front section of the newspaper. However, it is also quite necessary to ask why photos are more likely to be included for female candidates, and again, the answer may be *because* they are women. Results

TABLE 1.9

Inclusion of photo of candidate mentioned first in article, by sex (print news), 2006 election campaign

Photo included	Men n	(%)	Women n	(%)
No	276	(52)	71	(44)
Yes	250	(48)	92	(56)
Total	526	(100)	163	(100)

Note: Chi² = 2.95; df = 1; p = .047

presented in the next chapter show that print news is more likely to report on the appearance of female politicians than of male politicians, so the greater rate of photo inclusion in female candidates' coverage is likely linked to this disproportionate focus on their looks.

The final indicator of prominence or importance in print news – as well as being an important component in the quality of a politicians' news coverage overall – is the extent to which candidates are directly quoted in their stories. In television news, there was no gender imbalance in the proportion of sound bites attributed to the female leader and female candidates compared with their male counterparts in the 2000 federal election, or in the ratio of leaders' sound bites to clips. Similarly, female candidates are not disadvantaged relative to males in the rate of direct quoting in newspapers (Table 1.10). For both male and female candidates, about 60 percent of their news stories include a direct quote. Paraphrasing is relatively rare, and it appears to be imbalanced across male and female candidates in the 2005-06 print news subsample because of the large number of stories on then Finance Minister Ralph Goodale (13 in total), most of which focused on the income trusts probe that was launched midway through the campaign.[9] In five of these stories Goodale is paraphrased, presumably because the RCMP's investigation into the matter was ongoing and he sought to avoid public comment.

The final question to be addressed regarding print news is whether all newspapers behave similarly with regard to their treatment of male and female candidates, or are there differences across papers, which may suggest that one's experience of political news depends on one's preferred paper. In this analysis, close attention should be paid to *La Presse*, the *Globe and Mail*, the *National Post*, and the *Toronto Star*. The first two are Canada's

TABLE 1.10

Attributions of speech of candidate mentioned first in article, by sex (print news), 2006 election campaign

	Men		Women	
	n	(%)	n	(%)
Direct quotation	60	(58)	24	(60)
Paraphrase	11	(11)	1	(3)
Neither	32	(31)	15	(38)
Total	103	(100)	40	(101)

Notes: Chi^2 = 2.67; df = 2; p = .236
Percentages may not total 100 because of rounding.

newspapers of record – authoritative sources with large circulations – for the Quebec and English-language populations, respectively. The *Post* is the other major English-language national daily, and the *Star* has the largest readership of all of them, with its weekly circulation of 2.2 million in 2009 (overwhelmingly in the Greater Toronto Area) – this is a few hundred thousand more than the *Globe*, and more than double that of the *Post*.[10]

There do actually seem to be some differences across papers (results not shown). On first mentions, for example, female candidates garnered a low of 19.6 percent in the *Herald* (and the *Vancouver Sun* followed closely with 19.8 percent) and a high of 30.9 in Montreal's *Le Devoir*. Popular impressions tend to peg the *Calgary Herald* as a comparatively conservative paper, and *Le Devoir* is often seen as left-of-centre. Among the four papers that deserve special attention, women's proportions of first mentions in 2005-06 ranged from 20 percent in *La Presse* to 29 percent in the *National Post*. Here we see a different pattern – the paper typically viewed as more right-of-centre (at least in its editorial content), the *Post*, had a higher proportion of female first mentions than the paper often seen as left-leaning (at least on social issues), *La Presse*. Aside from *La Presse*, none of the "big four" had a visibility deficit whereby women had fewer first mentions in the press than their overall proportion as candidates would warrant. In the main, therefore, the quantity of coverage of female candidates compared with their male counterparts was quite good in the big four highlighted for special attention in this analysis.

There are some gender differences across papers regarding page placements, although these are fairly minor. In the *Calgary Herald, Globe and*

Mail, *La Presse*, and *National Post*, rough equality whereby men and women received similar proportions of first mentions on the front page and in various parts of the A section of the paper was the general trend. In two of the other papers – *Le Devoir* and the *Toronto Star* – women were *more* likely than men to see their first mentions in front-page stories. In the *Vancouver Sun*, front-page first mentions were at a lower rate for women than for men, but the reverse was true on pages A2-A5, still quite important pages of the paper. A mixed cross-paper report, to be sure, but one of the generalizations that may be drawn is perhaps that most papers have some equality in placement such that each gender group received similar proportions of first mentions across different sections of the papers, and a smaller number of papers gives women a visibility bonus on this indicator, again perhaps because of the news value of politically powerful women. Only the *Vancouver Sun* accorded a higher rate of front-page coverage to male than to female candidates. With this final point – and added to the fact that the *Sun* had the second lowest rate of female first mentions after the *Herald* – what might explain the *Sun*'s lag? Whatever the answer, it is not because Vancouver or British Columbia as a province had lower proportions of female candidates on which to report. British Columbia had 206 candidates in 2006, and 46 of these were women, which represents 22 percent of the provincial total, nearly identical to the national breakdown of 77 percent male and 23 percent female candidates. Additionally, Vancouver itself had some very high-profile women candidates, such as Hedy Fry and Libby Davies, so even if the *Sun* is Vancouver-centric, which is no doubt the case, there were prominent, high-quality female candidates in the city's ridings on which to report.

Looking at the final indicator, the inclusion of photographs in stories, there are few cross-paper differences (results not shown). In all the newspapers except *Le Devoir* and the *Vancouver Sun*, women's stories were more likely to include photographs. *Le Devoir* is the only one to present a lower rate of photo inclusion for women's stories than for men's, and the *Vancouver Sun* actually had an equal rate – 50 percent of men's stories and 50 percent of women's had photos. Among the papers that gave women photo bonuses, some of the differences in men's and women's rates of photo inclusion were quite striking. In *La Presse*, for example, photos were included in 70 percent of women's stories, versus 42 percent of men's. Among the big four, the *Globe and Mail*'s rates of photo inclusion were the closest to gender equal (52 percent and 48 percent of women's and men's stories, respectively).

Conclusion

In the main, there is lots of evidence pointing towards gender equity in visibility, especially in coverage of candidates, and the results are similar in print and televised news. As groups, male and female candidates often receive coverage that is proportional to their shares of candidacies. The news does not ignore female candidates, and in fact, on some indicators of prominence, such as inclusion of photos with print news stories, female candidates are more visible.

Comparing party leaders' coverage is more challenging, and not simply because the data on party leaders come from one election that includes only one female leader. It can often be difficult to tease out generalizations about leaders, because much of the coverage of them is idiosyncratic. This is part of the territory when doing comparative analysis of high-ranking political elites. However, with this in mind, it is clear that the female party leader in the 2000 federal election, Alexa McDonough, was less visible in televised news of the campaign. Although her lower visibility compared with top contenders Chrétien and Day is understandable, some of the differences between her visibility and that of Clark or Duceppe on certain indicators are puzzling, especially because there were differences on both quantity indicators (story length) and prominence indicators (lead stories and headlined stories). Even bearing in mind that the female leader's visibility lagged on a couple of indicators, there was also evidence of fairness and equity in leaders' visibility – for example, on their average sound-bite lengths and their ratios of clips to sound bites.

There are few gender-based visibility differences in televised and print news, and many of the visibility differences that were discovered – most of these in leaders' coverage – were not sizeable. Yet, before drawing firm conclusions about the visibility of women in political news, it is critical to ask *how* women are portrayed compared with men. This chapter started by noting the commonly held idea that "there is no such thing as bad press." This is not altogether true, however, as many public figures have discovered first-hand. Media coverage of Watergate conveyed that lesson to US President Nixon. Relentless clips of Howard Dean's scream during the 2004 Democratic primaries provide another example, as does media coverage of Kim Campbell during the 1993 federal election in Canada after her campaign aired the television ad mocking the appearance of Jean Chrétien's facial expression and movement, a result of Bell's palsy. All these cases illustrate that we have to ask questions about the characteristics of coverage before we decide that more of it is better than less. High visibility in the news can damage or even derail female politicians' political careers if that coverage is negative in gendered ways. It is to this topic that the next chapter turns, with a focus on how, rather than how much or how prominently, women are covered in the news.

2

Quality of News Coverage

Female political candidates are quite visible in the news, but what does news coverage convey about women as candidates for office, and how does the news coverage of women compare with that of men? In contrast to mounting evidence of gender equity in news media visibility, much of today's research points to no similar balance in *how* women and men are reported. Coverage of Canadian female politicians, like of those worldwide, tends disproportionately to highlight women's appearances and personal lives (e.g., Everitt 2003; Robinson and Saint-Jean 1991, 1995; Trimble and Everitt 2010); to rely on gender-based norms and stereotypes for framing women as candidates and office holders (e.g., Gidengil and Everitt 1999, 2002, 2003a, 2003b; Gingras 1997; Robinson and Saint-Jean 1991, 1995, 1996; Sampert and Trimble 2003; Trimble and Everitt 2010; Trimble and Sampert 2004); to draw attention to and often raise doubts about their electoral viability (e.g., Tremblay and Bélanger 1997); to overemphasize their concern for "soft issues," particularly so-called women's issues; and all the while offering less attention to women's professional credentials and political experience compared with what we see in the coverage of men.

Gendered coverage can assume different forms, as noted in the introduction to this book, and each form has its own characteristics and possible effects. The unifying commonalities are the differential treatment is *because* of gender and it has the effect of drawing attention to gender as an important marker of female politicians. Critically, drawing attention to gender is often unnecessary. As Lundell and Ekström note, "gendering refers to when a person's gender is emphasized without it being specifically context-relevant" (2008, 891). All forms of gendered coverage – even those that may benefit female politicians electorally – state or imply that women are atypical or unique political actors because of their gender; that the "normal" or prototypical political actor is male. It is against this male archetype that female politicians are described, considered, and evaluated, not only by the news, but often by political parties and voters, as well.

Sometimes, their portrayal as different may benefit female candidates electorally, depending on the context. Gendered coverage can have positive content and beneficial consequences, such as when women are portrayed according to feminine stereotypes as more honest or trustworthy than male politicians. Indeed, the literature on stereotypes notes again and again that group-based stereotypes typically have both positive and negative content, even if the two types are not in balance. Issue stereotypes that link women – and in the United States, African-American candidates (e.g., Niven and Zilber 2001a) – with "soft" issues, or with liberal positions on those issues, can benefit candidates when such issues dominate the political agenda, such as during the 1992 mid-term elections in the United States, dubbed the "Year of the Woman" for the number of freshman female Congress members elected (e.g., Dolan 2002). Often, however, gendered aspects of female candidates' coverage create conditions that may disadvantage women by drawing attention to the ways in which they do not fit the male politician archetype, in turn, raising questions about their suitability for the job, their ability to handle "hard" issues like the economy and national security, or their ability to balance their domestic and public roles.

Although there is debate about the effects of gendered coverage – on the supply of female candidates, on the election success rates of female candidates, and on the careers of female politicians – there is broad agreement that gendered coverage transcends national and cultural boundaries. Frames used to cover female politicians are remarkably similar from one place to the next, and also relatively enduring over time. There are also remarkable parallels between the patterns of gendered coverage that animate this book and those associated with coverage of other "non-traditional" politicians, as seen in the work on lesbian and gay politicians (e.g., Everitt and Camp 2009a, 2009b) and visible minority politicians (Fleras and Kunz 2001; Gershon 2012; Henry and Tator 2002; Saunders 1991; Tolley 2012; Zilber and Niven 2000a, 2000b), as well as on minority voters (Abu-Laban and Trimble 2006), all of whom are to varying extents homogenized as groups, evaluated according to criteria derived from stereotypes of their group, and portrayed as novel, atypical, or exotic "others." All this fits with the idea that politics has been historically constructed not only as a male domain, but more specifically as a white, Christian, heterosexual, male domain.

Substance and Format

There are different ways to organize analyses of the quality of coverage. In this book, quality of coverage is parcelled out into two separate elements, substance and format. With substance – what is said or represented about candidates and politicians – there are the following four dimensions of coverage:

- *Representations of the personal* – includes personal life, appearance, and traits and behaviours
- *Representations of the professional* – includes professional credentials and background, political experience and mettle, and attributions of success
- *Representations of viability* – includes opinion polls, electability, use of horserace frames
- *Representations of issues and positions* – attributions of policy concerns and policy positions

Critically, these categories match up fairly neatly with the primary criteria citizens use to evaluate candidates including traits, credentials, competitiveness, and issues. Candidates tend to be judged based on who they are, what makes them qualified, how likely they are to succeed, and their policy priorities and policy positions. Trait and credential information is communicated in media representations of the personal and the professional, competitiveness is communicated in representations of the professional and viability, and policy priorities and positions are communicated in representations of issues and positions. Discussed below, there tend to be a small handful of frames that are used to report on the personal, professional, viability, and issues of female politicians. As labels for these frames, I use Kanter's terminology (1977a, 1977b), derived from her research on women in the corporate sector, which suggests that professional women are understood or stereotyped as sex objects, mothers, pets, or iron maidens, regardless of their individuating behaviour. Conceptually, this typology figures prominently in this book's analysis of news coverage of the 2000 and

2005-06 election campaigns, similar to Carlin and Winfrey's examination of the coverage of Clinton and Palin in the 2008 US presidential election cycle (2009). Parts of Kanter's typology are comparable, both in labelling and content, to that developed by Robinson and Saint-Jean (1991) in their work on the Canadian system; their "woman of easy virtue" stereotype is virtually identical to Kanter's sex object stereotype, for example.

Format considerations are not about what is conveyed, but rather about the *way* things are said or represented in the news, which is another important component of the quality of coverage. With format, the following categories are examined in this book, the first of which was presented in the previous chapter:

- *Speaking agentically* – to what extent are female candidates permitted to speak in their own words in the news media (in sound bites on TV news, and in direct quotes in print news)? Conversely, to what extent are candidates paraphrased or summarized by newsmakers for audiences? In Chapter 1, analyses of the ratio of sound bites to clips in television news coverage of the party leaders and candidates found no gender differences, suggesting that according to this measure, McDonough and the female candidates covered in the CBC's news were not presented as less agentic than their male counterparts. Similarly, there was no statistically significant difference in the extent to which male and female candidates were quoted directly versus paraphrased in print coverage of the 2005-06 campaign.
- *Analytical and evaluative reportage* – to what extent is female candidates' coverage descriptive (the classic mode of hard-news reporting) versus analytical and/or evaluative?

These two aspects of news format speak to the level of mediation or filtering in the coverage of different candidates, a matter that receives considerable attention within the gendered mediation approach (e.g., Gidengil and Everitt 2000). The level of mediation matters for several reasons. First, when candidates receive more mediated coverage, voters may come to the conclusion that they are not adept at expressing their own thoughts or points of view, and therefore, it is necessary for news journalists to paraphrase or analyze their thoughts and actions. Second, mediation creates more opportunities for framing according to culturally available stereotypes. More mediation often means more gendered coverage.

Kanter's Typology

Kanter's (1977a; 1977b, 233-36) pivotal work on corporations identified four common stereotypes of professional women: sex object, mother, pet, and iron maiden. Kanter calls these "role traps" (1977b: 233). The gendered patterns of news coverage of female politicians, in Canada and worldwide, correspond with these categories quite well, so I use her typology to imbue greater meaning to analysis of precisely *how* political women's personal and professional lives, viability, and issue agendas are covered in television and print news.

Sex Object

The sex object role can be applied to both sexes. However, this role is applied more often to women, and the sex object frame is more fraught for female politicians, who are less able to capitalize electorally on being seen in these terms, unlike countless male politicians from Pierre Trudeau in Canada to John F. Kennedy and Bill Clinton in the United States. One of the hallmarks of this frame is a sexualized focus on representations of the personal, sometimes at the expense of adequately covering women's professional credentials and political experience. In the Canadian setting, a focus on appearances in the news coverage of women has been noted at all levels and in all sorts of campaigns, from party leadership campaigns to general election campaigns. In New Brunswick, for example, coverage of former NDP leader Elizabeth Weir focused more on her appearance than did the coverage of her male counterparts (Everitt 2003), and Allison Brewer's run for the NDP leadership in the province after Weir stepped down brought ample media analysis that framed Brewer according to her gender and sexuality as a lesbian woman (Everitt and Camp 2009a).

At the federal level, the focus on appearance and sexuality or romantic life often characterized coverage of former Liberal cabinet member Belinda Stronach (e.g., Trimble 2007; Trimble and Everitt 2010). Originally a Conservative Party of Canada (CPC) MP, and party leadership candidate, Stronach crossed the floor of the House of Commons to join the Liberal Party and Prime Minister Paul Martin's cabinet in May 2005. Reports of Stronach's run for the leadership of the Conservative Party in 2004 were littered with references to her clothes, her blonde hair, and her personal life (e.g., Trimble 2007). Stronach was called the "It-Girl of the Political Right" in the *Globe and Mail*, Canada's newspaper of record, and her leadership campaign was compared to "Paris Hilton Starring in The Simple Political Life."[1] When Stronach defected from the Conservative Party to the Liberal

Party, several male politicians publicly accused her of "whoring" or "prostituting" herself for a cabinet post. The media reported these statements widely, and published editorial pieces and political cartoons that played on the incident. One cartoon, for example, showed Stronach in bed with Liberal Prime Minister Paul Martin, with Stronach telling Martin, "I've always liked a Liberal man with a big caucus."[2] The play on words in this case surely requires no explanation. The cartoon sexualized Stronach and her relationship with the prime minister and made gender and her sexuality the primary focus. Stronach is not the first Canadian politician to change party affiliation; however, gender-specific story angles and sexual innuendos are not standard in coverage of male party switchers, such as Jean Lapierre, Scott Brison, and Keith Martin.[3] Reacting to the stir about Stronach's defection, CBC Newsworld ran a story about party-switching by male MPs. Looking for the most insulting news item from what was then the most recent case of male party switching (Brison), the worst their researchers uncovered was a headline reading, "Turncoat MP Damages Party."[4]

The above examples are illustrative of common patterns in Canada (e.g., Everitt 2003; Gingras 1995; Goodyear-Grant 2009; Trimble 2007), and also across the world. Preoccupation with appearance and personal life has been prominent in coverage of Hillary Clinton, particularly in her bid for the Democratic presidential nomination in 2008 (e.g., Carlin and Winfrey 2009; Carroll 2009; Lawrence and Rose 2009; Rossmann 2010); in coverage of 2008 Republican vice-presidential candidate Sarah Palin (e.g., Bode and Hennings 2012; Carlin and Winfrey 2009; Rossmann 2010); Elizabeth Dole's bid for the Republican nomination in 2000 (e.g., Aday and Devitt 2001; Heldman et al. 2005); and first female Speaker of the US House of Representatives Nancy Pelosi (e.g., Dabbousa and Ladleya 2010); as well as Condoleezza Rice's relationship with then President George W. Bush (Alexander-Floyd 2008). A preoccupation with appearances and private lives has also characterized news coverage of Australia's Pauline Hanson, founder of the right-wing, nationalist political party, One Nation (e.g., Deutchman and Ellison 2004).

Some may wonder where the harm lies in this type of coverage of female politicians. Moreover, journalists do comment on the appearances and romantic lives of men as well, as noted above. When Preston Manning, the former leader of the now-defunct Reform Party, had a hair and wardrobe makeover in the run-up to the 1997 Canadian federal election campaign, a burst of news coverage examining his new image ensued. Coverage focusing on dress and appearance was not uncommon for former Canadian prime ministers Pierre Trudeau and Brian Mulroney. Trudeau was often depicted as a dashing "man-of-style," and reporters and pundits regularly mentioned Mulroney's penchant for designer shoes. More recently, former Liberal Prime Minister Jean Chrétien's donning of a denim shirt at several points during the 1993 campaign earned him the nickname "Marlboro Man." The shirt was intended to make him appear more youthful and "hip" next to the younger Kim Campbell, PC prime minister and Chrétien's rival in the 1993 federal election. In the 2008 federal election campaign, Stephen Harper wore a light-blue sweater vest – the speculated purpose of which was to soften his image and make him appear more approachable – and this was a focus of some media coverage, especially after NDP leader Jack Layton made an issue of the vest in the English-language leaders' debate. The point here is that appearance *is* important in politics, regardless of sex and gender. Appearances send signals to voters about candidates' traits and behaviours. In addition to a politician's issue positions, character, and past record, the right image is a vital ingredient in making a successful appeal to the electorate.

Although personal image is important for male and female politicians alike, intense or protracted coverage of exterior appearance is not and never has been the norm for male politicians. More importantly, commentary on the clothes, appearance, or personal lives of men does not automatically tie in to their gender. Coverage of personal appearance has different and potentially more damaging implications for women than it does for men. It is often simply more problematic for women. Naomi Wolf makes the point forcefully in her well-known book, *The Beauty Myth*:

> Aren't men, too, expected to maintain a professional appearance? Certainly: They must conform to a standard that is well groomed, often uniformly clothed, and appropriate to their context. But to pretend that since men have appearance standards it means that the genders are treated equally is to ignore the fact that ... men's and women's appearances are judged differently; and that the beauty myth reaches far beyond dress codes into a different realm (1997, 48).

The principal argument of Wolf's book is simple: although women have breached societal power structures with increasing boldness and success since the 1950s, "the ideology of beauty is the last one remaining of the old feminine ideologies that still has the power to control those women whom second wave feminism would have otherwise made relatively uncontrollable" (10-11).

Culturally speaking, women have long been seen as objects of beauty intended for the male gaze, and discussion of women's physical appearance in political news necessarily directs attention to their gender, detracting from their other qualities, qualities that may be more germane to politics and elections. Kanter (1977a; 1977b: 235) concluded that being perceived through the seductress or sex object stereotype "blotted out all other characteristics" of the corporate women she studied. Emphasis on female politicians' looks not only draws attention to their gendered sexual identities, but it implicitly raises questions about their political competence. Culturally constructed gender identities have paired men and masculinity with the public sphere, the mind, objectivity, and rationality. Women and femininity, on the other hand, have been associated with the private sphere, the body, subjectivity, and emotion. Therefore, news coverage that calls attention to the physical appearances of female politicians can buttress deeply rooted unconscious beliefs that women's principal value is in their aesthetic, as opposed to their cerebral, attributes (e.g., van Zoonen 1994, 2005).

Mother
The mother role can be seen in various different patterns of gendered news coverage of female politicians. This can arise most explicitly with coverage that focuses on a female politician's marital status, children, or domestic circumstances generally (e.g., Bode and Hennings 2012; Devitt 2002; Everitt 2003; Jamieson 1995; Muir 2005; Robinson and Saint-Jean 1991, 1995; Ross 2002; van Zoonen 1998, 2000a, 2005, 2006). In contrast, reportage of male politicians is more likely to place emphasis on the candidate's occupation, political service, and accomplishments (Davis 1982; Jamieson 1995). These differences in coverage are particularly striking considering women in Canadian federal politics tend to be better qualified for office than their male counterparts (Black and Erickson 2003).

When the spouses and children of female politicians become news, female office seekers may be viewed as "selfish" or undutiful for pursuing their own professional satisfaction. Perhaps equally damaging, they may be identified as "wives" and "mothers" first and as "politicians" second. The former are caring, nurturing, and selfless (in other words, "feminine"), while the latter are independent, powerful, and assertive (in other words, "masculine"), so there is a tension. The traits associated with "wife" and "mother" are at odds with the masculine construction of the social role "politician." Ultimately, "the language used in the coverage of female politicians emphasizes their 'otherness' and implicitly critiques them for deviating not only from the orthodox boundaries of their true gender, but also from the traditional expectations of masculine politicians" (Everitt 2005, 389). Not simply a Canadian or American phenomenon, media scrutiny of female politicians' "conflicting" roles occurs across the globe from the Netherlands (e.g., van Zoonen 1998, 2000a, 2005) to Germany (e.g., van Zoonen 2006) to Finland (e.g., van Zoonen 2006) to the United Kingdom (e.g., Ross 2002; Ross and Sreberny 2000) to New Zealand (e.g., Fountaine and McGregor 2002) to Australia (e.g., Muir 2005) to India (e.g., Bathla 1998, 2000). Indeed, as headlines lamenting neglected husbands and children reveal (e.g., van Zoonen 1998, 2005), female politicians often confront difficulties projecting a political persona whose private and public lives are integrated in a convincing and balanced whole.

Interestingly, married fathers do not appear to face the same challenges as their female counterparts (e.g., van Zoonen 1998, 2000a, 2005). Wives and children are seen as supporting characters that enable men to pursue political careers. Thus, as Everitt (2005, 389) points out, the widespread assumption among citizens and media is that "men's public and private worlds can be integrated while women's public and private worlds are in conflict." Male politicians regularly appear at campaign events with their wives and children in tow. In 2000, Joe Clark's daughter, Catherine Clark, accompanied him throughout much of his campaign. The fact that she is young, attractive, articulate, and photogenic was likely seen as a benefit by his campaign team. Men are able to use the "family man" image as political capital suggestive of their loyalty, dependability, and integrity, while women find it difficult to successfully portray themselves as "great family women" (van Zoonen 2000a, 117; see also van Zoonen 2005; Muir 2005). Not only can men generally use their family lives to their advantage, even when male politicians are (or are alleged to be) unfaithful – or promiscuous, in the case of single men – their political careers are not necessarily damaged. Former President Bill Clinton's affair with former White House intern Monica Lewinsky is a fitting example, for his popularity increased after the affair (e.g., Newman 2002; Zaller 1998). Similarly, the purportedly unstable marriage and infidelity of former Dutch politician Ruud Lubbers "was treated as exotic rather than deviant" (van Zoonen 1998, 52). In the Canadian context, Pierre Trudeau's singlehood did not hamper him prior to his marriage to Margaret Trudeau, and neither did their marital difficulties and his alleged involvements with other women afterwards.

In sum, most scholars see this type of reportage as potentially damaging to the credibility of female politicians. Yet, some have suggested that this type of coverage simply reflects the fact that women are more likely to be newcomers to political life who need "introductions" as both candidates and as individuals. The electorate does not yet know the female candidates – as opposed to their more entrenched male colleagues – so personal coverage is a necessary learning tool for voters. There are reasons to be skeptical about this argument. For example, Devitt's (2002) analysis of US gubernatorial races finds that incumbent women are just as prone to personal coverage as newcomer women, so the focus on women's personal lives does not cease after they become known to the electorate. Moreover, newcomer male candidates, who presumably also need personal "introductions" to voters, do not receive any more personal coverage than do incumbent males. Newcomer status has no bearing on the extent to which journalists report on personal aspects of a male candidate's life.

The mother stereotype is also often reflected in how female politicians' traits and issue priorities are covered in the news. Evidence of gender-based trait and issue stereotyping are among the most consistent and robust findings in the gender, media, and politics literature (e.g., Kittilson and Fridkin 2008). Female politicians' coverage tends to draw attention to, and often exaggerates, stereotypically feminine traits, often those associated strongly with mothering and nurturance, such as warmth, passivity, expressivity, cautiousness, and orientation towards communal rather than agentic goals (e.g., Bystrom et al. 2004; Devitt 2002; Heldman, Carroll, and Olson 2005; Huddy and Terkildsen 1993a; Kahn 1996; Kittilson and Fridkin 2008). Issue coverage tends to follow similar patterns. Issues are frequently divided into two broad categories: "hard" issues and "soft" issues, and past research suggests that news coverage tends to associate female politicians with "soft" issues such as health, education, child care, and lifestyle – those where maternal qualities such as care, nurturance, and other-orientedness are primary. Men are more likely to be associated with "hard" issues such as defence, finance, foreign affairs, and trade (e.g., Carlson 2001; Carroll and Schreiber 1997; Kahn 1996; Kahn and Goldenberg 1991; Kittilson and Fridkin 2008; Norris 1997), which means that issue coverage tends to reflect traditional gender stereotypes.

It is difficult to assess which causal factors are responsible for trait and issue stereotyping of female politicians in the news, a topic tackled at greater length further on in this book. For now, it is enough to point out that newsmakers are not solely, or perhaps even mostly, responsible. Both female and male politicians sometimes present themselves on the campaign trail in gendered ways. Female candidates sometimes campaign on stereotypically feminine traits and issue priorities (e.g., Bystrom et al. 2004; Herrnson et al. 2003; Iyengar et al. 1997; Kahn 1996; Niven and Zilber 2001a; Shames 2003), although recent work suggests this particular pattern of gender differences may be changing, as more female candidates focus on traits associated with toughness (e.g., Bystrom 2006; Dolan 2005). Female politicians also tend to hold more liberal welfare policy preferences than do their male counterparts (e.g., Poggione 2004; Thomas and Welch 1991), findings that echo patterns of public opinion in the electorate.

Pet

The third stereotype in Kanter's typology is the "pet" role, which sets out a dependent and passive role for women, whose political position or power is attributed to some, more powerful, male figure. Sometimes, the linkage between political women and their more powerful male mentors or supporters is very explicit in the news. For example, an Australian backbencher, Jackie Kelly, was actually called Prime Minister John Howard's "pet" in a 2004 story in the *Sydney Morning Herald* (Kittilson and Fridkin 2008, 384). Although usage of the term *pet* is rare, coverage that unduly attributes female politicians' success to male mentors or predecessors, or even to male relatives, is within the pet frame.

Iron Maiden

Finally, the iron maiden frame is a common one for female politicians, and for powerful women generally, for they are seen to violate established gender-role norms that prize passivity and gentleness in women. The original iron maiden was a torture device, an iron cage or vaultlike container, fitted internally with sharp metal spikes that would skewer the victim trapped inside. In the news media, the iron maiden frame is often applied to women who are deemed too masculine or who seem to possess too many masculine traits such as strength, assertiveness, decisiveness, and ambition. Although it may work for some women by allowing them to demonstrate that they have the right traits for political leadership – the best-known example is Margaret Thatcher, the "Iron Lady" – this frame can be quite negative. It can lead to unkind and inappropriate portrayals of political women as "shrews," "bitches," and "ball busters," terms that have been applied to women such as Hillary Clinton (e.g., Carlin and Winfrey 2009; Carroll 2009; Lawrence and Rose 2009) and Sheila Copps (e.g., Copps 1986, 2004). More importantly, "projecting competence through demonstration of masculine traits such as toughness ... is ... the primary cause of the double bind" (Carlin and Winfrey

2009, 337). Women can get caught in a losing scenario in which they are critiqued for violating expectations about feminine behaviour and taking on masculine traits or behaviours. The fact that women's counter-stereotypical behaviours are often unduly exaggerated by the news media (e.g., Gidengil and Everitt 1999, 2000, 2003a, 2003b) can aggravate the problem, an issue examined in detail in Chapter 4. At the same time, when they do conform to feminine stereotypes, female politicians are often portrayed as too soft, passive, or lacking leadership qualities and authority. This is the double bind: feminine is too soft, and masculine is too hard; either way, women often have trouble fitting the model, which can create barriers to political success, even to women's decisions to enter the political arena in the first place.

How Are Women Covered? The 2000 Federal Election in TV News

This section (on television news) and the next (on print news) examine how male and female politicians are covered. Analyses are organized according to the framework outlined at the start of this chapter for dividing different qualitative categories of news content. Substance of coverage is subdivided into representations of the personal, professional, viability, and issues. Throughout, examinations of the substance of men's and women's coverage are interpreted in large measure through the lens of Kanter's typology, the chief benefit of which is to illustrate the narrow confines that gender-role stereotypes impose on political women. Format of coverage focuses on two categories that examine the extent to which female candidates are presented as autonomous speakers – examined in Chapter 1, for it is also an indicator of prominence – and whether their news coverage is more mediated than that of male counterparts. Emphasis in this section is on the CBC-specific data set, for it has far more variables with close attention to particular aspects of the news than the data set that includes the four television networks (CBC, SRC, CTV, and TVA). When the four-network data set is used, this is clearly indicated.

Representations of the Personal

Focusing first on coverage of party leaders, for they are the most prominent political figures in national news of the campaign, several patterns emerge. The sex object and mother frames predict that coverage of political women will be more preoccupied than that of men with their romantic lives (for single and divorced women) and family roles (for married/common-law women, and women with children). Indeed, the rise of celebrity politics, as van Zoonen (2005) calls it, puts the personal lives of politicians on public display. Other scholars have used terms like the *personalization* of politics to refer to the same process. Celebritization can offer important benefits to male politicians, who can derive electoral advantages from the use of the private sphere as a "stage for the performance of integrity" (91). For women, celebritization or personalization of politics can be challenging. Attention to women's private lives is difficult to turn to their advantage, for it tends to draw attention to role conflict between their public and private lives. Moreover, "neither does celebrity culture offer an alternative frame for women to draw political capital from: apart from family life, female celebrity is predicated on appearance, sexuality, and ... femininity" (95). Trimble and Everitt's (2010) analysis, which uses the political career of Belinda Stronach as an illustrative case, demonstrates the limitations of the politics of celebrity for women. Stronach was hyper-sexualized in media coverage, which focused relentlessly on her clothes, hair, sex life, and overall appearance, with comparatively little attention to her issue priorities, political positions, or performance in Parliament. As a result, she was often portrayed as a one-dimensional "bimbo heiress."

Such coverage does not appear to be inevitable, however. Women's appearances and personal lives are not always exaggerated in coverage, even in this era of celebrity politics. In the 1976 contest for the leadership of the Progressive Conservative Party (Trimble 2007), news coverage of Flora MacDonald was nearly the same as for her male counterparts in terms of attention to appearance and marital status. Trimble and various other colleagues also report little attention by the news media to the appearances and personal lives of New Zealand's Helen Clark and Jenny Shipley (Trimble, Treiberg, and Girard 2010) and former Canadian Prime Minister Kim Campbell (Trimble and Treiberg 2010), although other work draws contrary conclusions. For example, Fountaine and McGregor (2002) suggest that motherhood themes played heavily in the coverage of both Clark and Shipley. Shipley herself used her status as a mother in an attempt to soften her image and become more relatable to voters, as well as to make Clark, who does not have children, appear "remote" (5).

On important fronts, CBC's coverage of the 2000 campaign does not follow the patterns anticipated by the celebritization account. As Table 2.1 shows, each of the three male leaders was far more likely to be shown in clips and sound bites with his family members than was Alexa McDonough. For the male leaders, about 10 percent of their sound bites and clips show them with a family member – typically their wives and/or children – while only

TABLE 2.1

Party leader shown with family: sound bites and clips, CBC news, 2000 election campaign

Shown with family	Chrétien n	(%)	Day n	(%)	Clark n	(%)	McDonough n	(%)
Yes	39	(11)	33	(9)	18	(11)	1	(1)
No	303	(89)	326	(91)	151	(89)	143	(99)
Total	342	(100)	359	(100)	169	(100)	144	(100)

Note: Chi^2 = 15.20; df = 3; p = .00; Cramer's V = 0.12

one of McDonough's clips and none of her sound bites show her with a family member. The sole story to feature McDonough with a family member was broadcast on 19 November, close to the end of the 2000 campaign. Narrated by CBC anchor Allison Smith, the story is primarily about McDonough's criticisms of Chrétien and a call for more New Democrats in Parliament. Smith ends the story with the two observations that "McDonough, who visited a craft show today, has been joined by her two sons for the final week of the campaign."[5] Previous findings suggest that the media tend to stress women's familial and romantic attachments more than those of male politicians; nevertheless, this is not the case in the CBC's coverage of party leaders in the 2000 campaign. The men in the race are the ones shown with spouses and children, for the most part.

Explaining the differences in Table 2.1, of course, must start from the fact that McDonough is divorced, while Chrétien, Day, and Clark are not. At this point, it is important to remember the fundamental distinction between provision and presentation, which is discussed in much greater detail in the next chapter. The patterns we see in Table 2.1 are, I argue, a function of the party leaders' own behaviour, not the selective processes of news production. Likely, it was McDonough's own choice to mostly avoid mixing her personal and professional lives in her campaign appearances. Indeed, in a personal interview, McDonough mentioned that she had made efforts to minimize her family's exposure to the public eye throughout her entire political career.[6] These issues will be revisited in Chapter 5 – a full-length discussion of interviews with male and female politicians about their political careers – but McDonough made two important points on the issue of family. First, McDonough's status as a divorced woman is one reason she kept her personal life out of the public eye. Put simply, she suspected her divorce would be used to discredit her. Second, McDonough has deliberately shielded her children from media scrutiny. There is every reason to believe, therefore, that the near absence of family members in McDonough's clips and sound bites is a function of her own self-censoring, which, in turn, is based on her expectations of how the media would present her as a divorced woman. McDonough's strategy demonstrates the cyclical and dynamic nature of the relationship between politicians and the media. McDonough has deliberately kept her personal life separate from her professional life, resulting in virtually no media coverage of her family or romantic attachments; however, her strategy is based on expectations about how the media would cover personal aspects of her life, as well as how the coverage would influence both her political image and her family members.

Why would McDonough be hesitant to present herself to the media as a divorced woman, either with or without romantic attachments? This is a common dilemma confronted by many female politicians, a large number of whom are divorced or separated. In Canada, female politicians routinely face unfavourable media coverage of their personal lives. Trimble's (2007) analysis of Belinda Stronach's bid for the CPC leadership in 2004 is demonstrative, for Stronach's marital status was mentioned four times as often as Stephen Harper's in newspaper articles, and, more importantly, Stronach was described by the media as "a 'single mom millionaire' ... and, less flatteringly, a woman with two failed marriages" (Trimble 2005, 13).

Seemingly, media scrutiny tends to intensify when divorced female politicians have active dating lives. Media focus on Belinda Stronach's relationship with Conservative MP Peter MacKay was intense, particularly when they split up following her decision to cross the House floor to join the Liberals, in May 2005. News coverage depicted MacKay as a braveA-faced jilted lover, and Stronach as an opportunist who exploited and then discarded him. However, divorced women who avoid romantic attachments do not escape scrutiny. When divorced female politicians are single, suspicions are raised about their sexuality, which is related to the "spinster" stereotype that permeated coverage of early women politicians (Robinson and Saint-Jean 1991), such as Agnes McPhail, Nellie McClung, and, later, Flora MacDonald and Pauline Jewett. As former NDP leader Audrey McLaughlin wryly put it, "Thank God I've got grandchildren or I'd be called a lesbian."[7] This is a potential problem for single female politicians generally, for singlehood is implicitly viewed as unnatural for women and, therefore, as evidence of homosexuality, in certain cases. Media speculation about sexual orientation in the coverage of both former US Attorney General Janet Reno (e.g., Jamieson 1995) and New Zealand Prime Minister Helen

Clark (e.g., Fountaine and McGregor 2002) are telling examples. In the end, dilemmas about how to present their relationships to the media and citizens is another manifestation of the "double bind" (Mandel 1981) faced by female politicians: "If she is a widow, she is suspected of having killed her husband. If she is divorced, she is unstable. If married, she neglects her husband, and if single, she is abnormal" (Allard 1987, 106, quoted in Robinson and Saint-Jean 1991, 137).

Personal traits and behaviour patterns are also focal points for representations of the personal in news media. One of the key themes in research on election coverage is the extent to which candidates engage in attacks on their opponents as well as the tendency of news coverage to emphasize this aspect of campaigning. Indeed, news focus on conflictive behaviour is expected given that conflict and drama are among the conventional criteria of newsworthiness (Bennet 2003; Ericson, Baranek, and Chan 1987, 1992).

A rich literature has developed debating the effects on candidates' personas and electoral results when they go on the offensive. Chapter 4 grapples with these debates at length. For the following analyses, it is sufficient to simply point out that there is evidence that attack-style politics, in general, *can* rankle audiences (e.g., Mutz and Reeves 2005), demobilize voters (e.g., Ansolabehere and Iyengar 1995; Kahn and Kenney 1999), increase political cynicism (Ansolabehere et al. 1994), and encourage negative feelings about the attacker rather than about the intended target (Basil, Schooler, and Reeves 1991). For female politicians, there can be particular dangers, especially a "backlash effect" against women who contravene stereotypes prescribing passive and cooperative feminine behaviour (Rudman 1998; Rudman and Glick 1999, 2001; Rudman and Fairchild 2004; Rudman and Goodwin 2004).

This section focuses on news coverage that shows party leaders "on the attack" – acting and speaking in a conflictive manner.[8] According to the two types of aggressivity, verbal attack[9] and aggressive body language,[10] stories about Alexa McDonough presented her as more confrontational or conflictive than the three male party leaders (Figure 2.1). Seventy percent of McDonough's twenty-seven stories showed her attacking another party or leader. Clark was the next most confrontational leader (53 percent of his stories depicted him on the attack). The two front-running leaders, Chrétien and Day, had the lowest proportions of attack-style stories. Chrétien's relatively smaller proportion may be explained by the fact that as incumbent prime minister, he spent more time on the defensive than on the offensive.

FIGURE 2.1

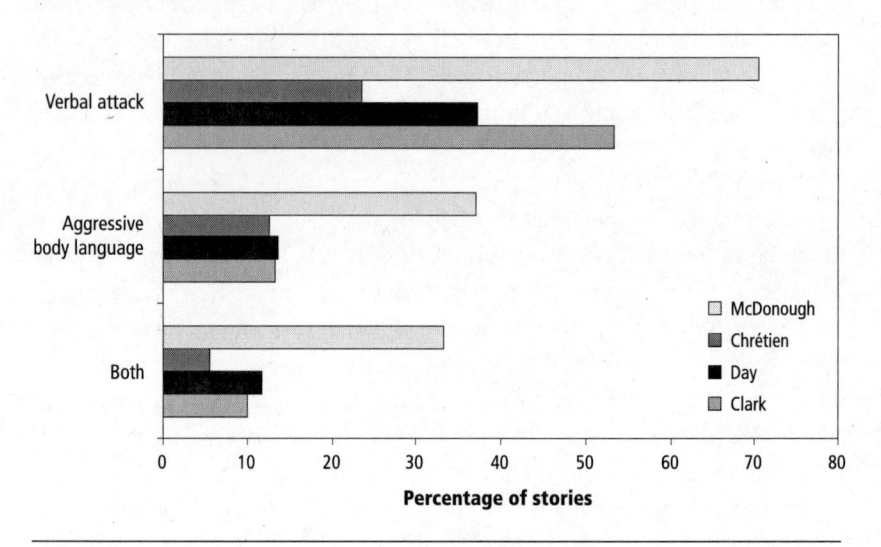

Attack-style coverage of leaders (CBC)

[Bar chart showing percentage of stories for Verbal attack, Aggressive body language, and Both, comparing McDonough, Chrétien, Day, and Clark]

Regarding Day, he and his campaign team devised a strategy early on of avoiding "mud slinging" in the campaign, resulting, presumably, in fewer attacks on his rivals, which is reflected in the news coverage.

For body language, McDonough's stories were more than twice as likely than the male leaders' to show her finger pointing, fist clenching, or hand chopping, and 33 percent of McDonough's stories showed her both speaking and gesturing in a confrontational way. The stories that depicted verbal and non-verbal attacks simultaneously are of particular interest. Each form of aggressive behaviour likely reinforces the other, giving citizens a stronger perception of candidate "incivility," to use Mutz and Reeves' (2005) terminology. Compared with 33 percent of McDonough's stories, only 6 percent of Chrétien's, 12 percent of Day's, and 10 percent of Clark's stories show them attacking another party or leader while also using aggressive body language.

Part of the explanation for differences between McDonough and the male leaders in terms of whether they were shown combining verbal and non-verbal aggressivity is differences in shot lengths. The male leaders were more likely to be shown in close-up (i.e., head and shoulders). Thus, their arms and hands, both key communicators of body language, often were not visible. McDonough was more likely to be shown from the waist up or from about the mid-calf up. Due to different shot lengths, McDonough's hands and arms were visible more frequently in her sound bites, and, consequently, she was seen gesturing more often than the male leaders.

To emphasize, depictions of combative behaviour were seen in a much larger portion of the relatively smaller amount of coverage McDonough received compared with her male colleagues. The proportion of McDonough's stories that showed her on the attack *and* using aggressive gestures was three times greater than the proportions for the male leaders. McDonough had the lowest number of stories among all the leaders in 2000, but the highest relative and absolute number of stories that combined verbal attacking with aggressive gestures. A response may be that she was simply more aggressive than her male rivals, which was then simply reflected in the news. How politicians are covered is a product of their own behaviour plus news production, as noted previously. It is difficult to judge the extent to which results presented in Figure 2.1 accurately reflect the leaders' actual behaviour, but available evidence suggests that McDonough *was not* more conflictual or aggressive in reality than were her male colleagues (e.g., Blais et al. 2002a; Gidengil and Everitt 2003a). Indeed, Gidengil and Everitt's (2003a) analysis of the 1997 and 2000 English-language leaders' debates reveal that McDonough was less aggressive in the debates, but that the news portrayed her as more aggressive in televised, post-debate coverage, evidence consistent with that presented here. For the 1997 debate, "there was not a single indicator of confrontational behaviour on which McDonough ranked first or even second," and the authors contend that McDonough switched to an even more "low-key style of debating" in 2000 (566). In other words, McDonough's level of aggressive debate behaviour, which was relatively low to begin with, was even lower in the 2000 leaders' debate compared with earlier campaigns. There are no obvious reasons why McDonough would be more confrontational on the campaign trail than in the debates. Arguably, televised leaders' debates are the most adversarial events of a campaign, the events in which all leaders – particularly those of opposition parties – go on the offensive with well-rehearsed talking points and statements. Therefore, one might predict that leaders, including McDonough, would be less aggressive outside the debate arena. By extension, therefore, the data presented here are consistent with evidence for the gendered mediation approach, for female politicians do appear to be presented as unduly aggressive in television coverage of election campaigns.

Additional reasons to be skeptical that coverage of McDonough simply reflects a more aggressive political style are provided in the next chapter, by comparing the proportion of attacks in parties' press releases in 2000 with the proportion of attack-style coverage received by the leaders (see Table 3.6), as well as by research on women's self-presentations to the media, a topic examined in greater detail in Chapter 5. The way that female politicians talk about their self-presentations to the media in personal interviews, as well as in their autobiographies, does not fit with the notion that women's political style is more combative than that of men. My discussions with Canadian women MPs suggest that they endeavour to *minimize* the appearance of conflictive behaviour because of fears of being depicted as "shrill" or overly aggressive – in other words, to avoid the iron maiden frame that tends to be applied to assertive, powerful female professionals. Others have reached similar conclusions. Shames (2003) demonstrates that female politicians' self-presentations in political advertisements tend to emphasize "femininity" and social issues as opposed to "masculinity" and "hard politics." Her study of American political commercials covering the past three decades suggests that women successfully play down masculine traits associated with aggressiveness and "politics as usual." A focus on "femininity" symbolizes an outsider status that can work to women's benefit. Black and Erickson (2003) ponder a similar question, for they raise the possibility that Canadian female candidates benefit from their outsider status, from their different political styles, and from public perceptions that female politicians are more honest and ethical than their male counterparts (e.g., Alexander and Anderson 1993; McDermott 1997, 1998).

Weight is added to the claim that female politicians' aggressive behaviour is unduly emphasized in media coverage when we analyze verbal attacks in a more dissected form. Indeed, a leader can only verbally attack another political party or leader in a sound bite, which is the only portion of the news that shows leaders speaking in their own words. Figure 2.2 shows the mean length of each leader's sound bites, but separates the sound bites according to whether or not they show the leader attacking another leader or party. All leaders had longer average sound-bites when they attacked another party or leader – not surprising given that conflict is a key criterion of newsworthiness (Bennett 2003; Ericson, Baranek, and Chan 1987, 1992). It is plain that McDonough was given much more unmediated speaking time when she behaved confrontationally towards another leader or party. Her average sound-bite length more than doubled when she was on the offensive, from a mean of 5.9 seconds to a mean of 11.5 seconds when she attacked another leader or party. The long sound bites McDonough received when she attacked certainly help to account for the finding in Table 1.4

FIGURE 2.2

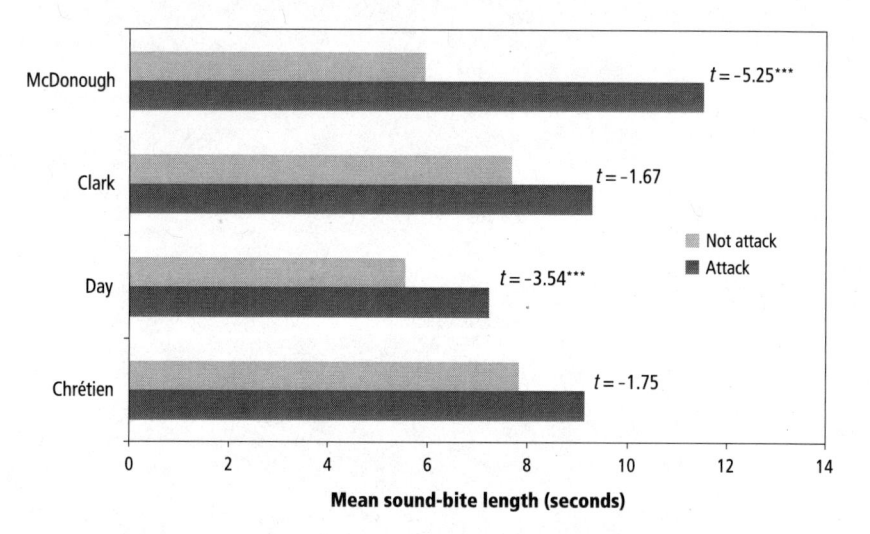

Leaders' mean sound bite lengths, by attack-style behaviour (CBC)

Leader	Not attack	Attack	t-value
McDonough	~6	~11.5	$t = -5.25^{***}$
Clark	~7.5	~9	$t = -1.67$
Day	~5.5	~9	$t = -3.54^{***}$
Chrétien	~7.5	~9	$t = -1.75$

Mean sound-bite length (seconds)

Notes: T-tests were conducted to assess whether the means of the two groups are statistically different from each other, in this case testing whether the mean sound bite length differed significantly when a leader went on the attack. Statistically significant results are marked:
* = $p < .05$; ** = $p < .01$; *** = $p < .001$

(Chapter 1) that McDonough had the longest average sound bites generally. For the male leaders, the average difference in the mean length of sound bites of attack- versus non-attack–style was 1.4 seconds.

Tabulating all of the sound bites provides a total for the amount of time each leader was seen in CBC's 2000 campaign coverage speaking to audiences in his or her own words. Figure 2.2 establishes that McDonough's sound bites were much longer when she went on the attack. As Table 2.2 shows, if we look at the leaders' total sound-bite speaking time, the majority of McDonough's sound-bite time in 2000 showed her on the attack. McDonough received 6 minutes of attacking sound-bite coverage versus 3.5 minutes of non-confrontational sound-bite time. The reverse is true for Chrétien, Day, and Clark. The majority of the male leaders' sound-bite speaking time did not show them on the attack.

The significance of Figure 2.2 and Table 2.2 is highlighted when we remember that politicians have no control over which sound bites are chosen for inclusion in news stories or how long individual sound bites will be. This is the task of newsmakers – of the producers, videographers, and editors

TABLE 2.2

Length of party leaders' sound-bite speaking time, by attack-style behaviour (CBC news), 2000 election campaign

		Total sec.	(min.)
Chrétien	Attack	352	(5.9)
	Not attack	916	(15.3)
Day	Attack	513	(8.6)
	Not attack	542	(9)
Clark	Attack	283	(4.7)
	Not attack	366	(6.1)
McDonough	Attack	363	(6.1)
	Not attack	211	(3.5)

who make news programs. As the gendered mediation thesis predicts, the news accords more prominence to a confrontational McDonough than to a subdued McDonough. The fact that the average length of McDonough's sound bites increased so dramatically when she was on the offensive in the absence of similarly large increases for the male leaders suggests that her confrontational coverage cannot be explained entirely by her own behaviour. Rather, newsmakers chose to include a large number of confrontational sound bites in McDonough's news stories, and they chose to make them lengthier than non-confrontational McDonough sound bites. Indeed, whether it is the camera people shooting the sound bites on location, the reporters covering the stories, or the producers and editors who select and format sound-bite segments, the evidence suggests that a sound bite of a female leader on the attack is worthy of valuable extra seconds in the nightly newscast.

The gendered mediation thesis predicts that the news exaggerates female aggressivity. The news is a predominantly masculine discourse created and maintained by (1) culturally constructed gender-role norms that link certain qualities (competence, assertiveness, and independence, for example) with maleness and other qualities (warmth, compassion, and dependence, for example) with femaleness and (2) the masculine nature of the journalistic profession itself. In determining newsworthiness, events and people that are unexpected, "deviant," dramatic, and counter-intuitive have high news value, particularly as "infotainment"[11] news formats have become

TABLE 2.3

Length of candidates' sound bites, by sex and tone (CBC news), 2000 election campaign

		Mean length, sec.	Total length sec.	(min.)
Men	Negative	7.78	195	(3.3)
	Not negative	7.39	273	(4.6)
Women	Negative	11.38	91	(1.5)
	Not negative	6.50	9	(0.2)

Notes: t-test for male candidates: $t = 0.58$; $p > t = 0.56$
t-test for female candidates: not performed because the "not negative" category is, in fact, a single sound bite

increasingly popular (e.g., Bennett 2003; Blumler and Kavanagh 1999). Because conventional gender-role stereotypes do not associate aggressivity and conflict with femaleness, a female politician acting even moderately aggressively can create a "basic schema incompatibility" in which actual behaviour contradicts deeply held cultural norms of typical/appropriate female action and demeanour (Butler and Geis 1990; Hitchon and Chang 1995). When women attack, therefore, it is all the more newsworthy, because it is surprising and atypical.

Although not overly visible in national television news, candidates' sound bites present similar patterns regarding the exaggeration of women's counter-stereotypical behaviour. Table 2.3 reports the mean length of sound bites and total sound-bite speaking times for male and female candidates, breaking the information down according to whether a candidate's tone towards a party or leader was markedly negative as opposed to neutral or positive. The measure used to code candidate negativity is different from the measure that asked whether a leader was on the attack, and thus the information presented in Table 2.3 should not be interpreted in precisely the same way as the information presented on leaders' attacks, strictly speaking. The negativity measure for candidates is probably not as powerful an indicator of conflictive behaviour, because coders were not asked specifically if the candidate was on the attack. However, it still offers some insight that can add to the preceding analyses of party leaders.

In sound bites where candidates did mention a party or leader, women are presented as more negative speakers than their male counterparts are. On average, the length of female candidates' sound bites practically doubled if either their tone or words towards a party or leader were negative. Male candidates' sound bites were only slightly longer, on average, if the men were negative. In total, women's sound-bite time when talking about a party or leader was overwhelmingly negative (1.5 minutes negative compared with 0.2 minutes not negative), and the opposite was true for men. The majority of men's sound-bite statements about a party or leader were not negative (4.6 minutes not negative compared with 3.3 minutes negative). Female candidates, like the sole female leader in 2000, were depicted in sound bites as more conflictual or negative than were their male counterparts.

Representations of the Professional
All four party leaders in 2000 were quite experienced, as discussed in the previous chapter. Chrétien and Clark had been prime ministers; McDonough had been federal NDP leader for five years, as well as former Nova Scotia NDP leader; and Day had been in cabinet in Alberta. The group had professional qualifications and experience in abundance, although McDonough was the only one who had never served in a government in some capacity. The content analysis scheme included coding of objects that appeared in the leaders' sound bites and clips. Several of these objects can be categorized as unambiguous symbols of institutionalized governmental power,[12] suggesting to the viewer that the politician in the frame is well suited to the role of party leader, prime minister, or Opposition leader. Such objects are the Canadian flag; the exterior of the Parliament Buildings in Ottawa; the interior of the House of Commons, Senate, and Supreme Court; and Parliament Hill more generally.

According to the gendered mediation thesis and more general work on women and leadership, female politicians are less likely than are their male colleagues to be linked with overt visual symbols of power that characterize politics as a profession. Table 2.4 shows the percentage of each leader's clips and sound bites (combined) that showed him or her with one of the identified symbols of political power. Clearly, there are partisan differences here. The two front-running leaders, Chrétien and Day, were linked with symbols of power much more than the other two were. This is unsurprising for two reasons. First, Chrétien and Day knew they were the only real competitors for the prime ministership, and, therefore, they likely exploited every opportunity to stand in front of the Parliament Buildings or display a Canadian flag at their press conferences. The stakes were high for both the contending leaders, and each probably consciously used symbols of power as a backdrop in his photo opportunities to enhance the perception

TABLE 2.4

Symbols of power shown with party leaders: sound bites and clips, CBC news, 2000 election campaign

Symbols of power	Chrétien n	(%)	Day n	(%)	Clark n	(%)	McDonough n	(%)
Yes	73	(21)	107	(30)	7	(4)	1	(1)
No	269	(79)	252	(70)	162	(96)	143	(99)
Total	342	(100)	359	(100)	169	(100)	144	(100)

Notes: Chi^2 = 85.51; df = 3; *p* = .00; Cramer's V = 0.29

among voters that he was the "right man for the job." Second, because the media also knew that the Chrétien-Day rivalry was the big story of the 2000 campaign, they may have been more likely to show clips of these leaders that linked them with symbols of power.

Beyond the obvious partisan difference in linkages with symbols of power, Table 2.4 also shows that McDonough was the least likely to be linked with a symbol of power in the CBC's coverage of the 2000 campaign. Of her 144 clips and sound bites, only one showed her with one of these important symbols. Clark did not receive a lot of power-symbol coverage, but he did receive more than McDonough, perhaps because Clark is a former prime minister. Overall, it would be difficult to draw firm conclusions from Table 2.4, although it is yet another case where McDonough is at the bottom in terms of an indicator of positive news coverage.

In terms of explicit mentions of professional qualifications and political experience, there is relatively little in the CBC's national news coverage generally, which is understandable given the constraints, but even taking this into account, there is virtually no mention of women's professional and political qualifications for office. Of the four leaders, three were well known to the electorate, so Day tended to receive more focus on his background and political experiences. For example, early in the campaign, *The National* reported that "Stockwell Day was a member of the Alberta legislature for fourteen years, and during much of that time he was whip, deputy house leader, house leader and deputy Premier."[13] This is an impressive collection of experiences, indeed. In the same newscast that night, a story also mentioned Chrétien's long record of success in that he had been elected ten times in the riding of Shawinigan,[14] and this was not the only edition in which Chrétien's number of election wins or thirty-seven years of service were mentioned.[15] For other male candidates, professional credentials were mentioned in addition to their years in office or their status as incumbents. For example, Allan Rock's background as a lawyer was mentioned in one edition, and he has a sound bite in which he provides a summary that leaves little doubt as to his fitness for office and his accomplishments as justice minister:

> I learned when I was practicing law and acting for people with the government on the other side that when you have sometimes a faceless bureaucracy with what seems like limitless resources, cases can go on for years and make it very difficult for the average citizen to respond. When I became Minister of Justice and Attorney General in 1993, I introduced mediation and fact finding and third party resolution outside the courtroom of disputes between people and the government because there's a real imbalance between the two of them.

Peter Mancini's background as a lawyer was also mentioned on the same night, although again, it was the candidate himself who drew attention to his professional qualifications, not the journalist or anchor.

In contrast to all the mentions of professional and political qualifications for male politicians, women's news stories tended to contain fewer mentions, and less material about their professions. Aside from a single clip that mentioned the length of McDonough's political career, there was nothing else about her background or experience. Like Day, she was also in provincial politics prior to her tenure as federal NDP leader, but this was not mentioned. Her background as a social worker was never mentioned in *The National*'s broadcasts. Other women were sometimes referred to as incumbents or by some cabinet or critic position they held at the time, but none of the female lawyers (such as Anne McLellan) had their professions mentioned. There was only a single mention of a female candidate's professional background throughout *The National*'s entire coverage of the campaign – Bev Braaten, the PC candidate for Langley-Abbotsford, mentioned her previous career in the banking industry. This was a self-mention that appeared in a sound bite of Braaten, like the mentions of Rock's and Mancini's law careers. These three examples, which are from a very small group of mentions of professional qualifications through the course of the campaign news, may suggest that it is in candidates' sound bites where professional background mentions occur. If this is true – if men's and women's stories mention their professional qualifications at different rates – perhaps it is because there are differences in the extent to which men and women talk about their own qualifications and accomplishments, a notion that would fit with past work on women's tendency to undervalue their own credentials for candidacy (e.g., Lawless and Fox 2005, 2010). That said, it is important to keep in mind that news media choose the sound bites and clips that allow such representations to occur, and as such, it bears reminding that these are not unmediated political communications.

Representations of Viability

Overlap exists between representations of the professional and representations of viability. The extent to which candidates or leaders are presented as possessing the right credentials and experiences to succeed in political life is a function of both their qualifications and viability, and the former is an important influence on the latter. A candidate with poor qualifications or little political experience may suffer reduced viability as a result, depending on the electoral context at hand, which is then reflected in media coverage. The main difference between representations of the professional and of viability is that viability is less general. It is more focused on the ability to win the election at hand. I use several indicators to give a general sense of the level of viability focus in leaders' stories: coverage that focused on the campaign over issues, on leaders over parties, and coverage that included mentions of polls, debates, ads, and other important campaign elements. I also include more detailed analysis of *what* was said or implied about the viability of the male leaders and female leader in their coverage.

The literature generally hypothesizes that female candidates tend to receive more viability coverage (e.g., Aday and Devitt 2001), which is thought to raise questions about their quality as candidates and their ability to win. Kahn (1994, 1996) found that female Senate candidates receive more horserace coverage, less issue coverage, and lower viability ratings than men. The first question, then, is whether McDonough received more viability coverage than her male competitors. The most obvious indicator of viability is polls. Looking at coverage of political leaders across the four networks, McDonough was tied with Duceppe for the lowest proportion of poll mentions (Table 2.5). For both McDonough and Duceppe, 3 percent of stories mentioned polls, compared with 10 percent of each of Day's and Chrétien's, and 7.5 percent of Clark's. Also, none of McDonough's stories was *mainly* about polls, although a small percentage for each of the male leaders was (Table 2.6). McDonough received a much lower proportion of mentions of electoral battles – another important indicator of viability coverage – in her stories compared with those of the four male leaders (22 percent compared

TABLE 2.5

Mentions of campaign elements in news stories about party leaders (four TV networks), 2000 election campaign

Mentions of	Chrétien n	(%)	Day n	(%)	Clark n	(%)	McDonough n	(%)	Duceppe n	(%)
Polls*	24	(10)	17	(10)	7	(7.5)	2	(3)	3	(3)
Debates	35	(14)	22	(13)	11	(12)	5	(7)	8	(8)
Party strategies***	146	(58)	107	(63)	46	(49)	32	(44)	54	(52)
Electoral battles***	78	(31)	56	(33)	30	(32)	16	(22)	48	(47)

Notes: * = $p \leq .05$; ** = $p \leq .01$; *** = $p \leq .001$

with 31 to 47 percent of the male leaders' stories), and a lower proportion of mentions of party strategy (44 percent of her stories compared with 49 to 63 percent of the male leaders' stories). Viability indicators for which there were no significant differences are mentions of leaders' debates, as well as gaffes and problems, so the inevitable missteps made on the campaign trail do not seem to be mentioned at a higher rate in the female leader's coverage.

Many of the important aspects of campaigns as contests were mentioned at a lower rate in McDonough's stories than in stories about male leaders. The differences are often modest, but they do seem consistent regarding polls, electoral battles, and party strategies. As such, the important question is what were the main focal points of McDonough's stories? If they mentioned polls, electoral battles, and party strategy less, what content filled the available space? Looking at the main focus of leaders' stories in the four networks (Table 2.6), it's clear that McDonough had a much higher proportion of stories that focused on leaders' activities or mixed campaign trail reporting – 62 percent of McDonough's stories compared with 20 to 45 percent of male leaders' stories. This is the kind of reporting that shows leaders attending community events, meeting people, and so on. McDonough had no stories that focused *primarily* on polls, ads, or debates – events with which campaigns are strongly associated – which may have given viewers the sense that she was not an important player in the election. Granted, her obvious comparator, Joe Clark, did not fare much better on these indicators, but he was not invisible. McDonough did well in terms of other story topics. She had the second highest proportion of stories that focused primarily on party strategies; she had no stories that were primarily about gaffes; and

TABLE 2.6
Focus of news stories about party leaders (four TV networks), 2000 election campaign

	Chrétien		Day		Clark		McDonough		Duceppe	
Focus	n	(%)	n	(%)	n	(%)	n	(%)	n	(%)
Polls	13	(5)	2	(1)	3	(3)	0		3	(3)
Ads	6	(2)	7	(4)	1	(1)	0		3	(3)
Debates	17	(7)	6	(4)	2	(2)	0		1	(1)
Leader's activities/ campaign trail	49	(20)	36	(21)	38	(41)	45	(62)	46	(45)
Party strategies	52	(21)	47	(28)	19	(20)	18	(25)	20	(19)
Electoral battles	26	(10)	19	(11)	16	(17)	4	(5)	11	(11)
Campaign problems	25	(10)	26	(15)	4	(4)	2	(3)	9	(9)
Campaign gaffes	11	(4)	8	(5)	0		0		3	(3)
Other	45	(18)	18	(11)	8	(9)	4	(5)	7	(7)
None	7	(3)	1	(1)	2	(2)	0		0	
Total	251	(100)	170	(100)	93	(100)	73	(100)	103	(100)

Notes: Chi^2 = 265.57; df = 54; p = .00; Cramer's V = 0.23

only two that were about problems, the lowest proportion among all five leaders' stories.

Flowing naturally from these findings, it's no surprise that McDonough's stories focused predominantly on her as leader, rather than on her party, for nearly two-thirds of NDP stories were primarily about the leader's activities on the campaign trail, as mentioned above (Table 2.6). Canadian electoral politics and media coverage of it both tend to be leader-centric, to be sure. The majority of all parties' stories are about the leader. However, fully 90 percent of the NDP stories in the data set focused on McDonough, rather than on the party (results not shown). The other parties had a greater balance of leader and party focus: 71 percent of Liberal stories, 77 percent of PC stories, 75 percent of Alliance stories, and 69 percent of Bloc stories focused on the leader.

In terms of representations of viability across the four television networks, the picture that emerges of coverage of McDonough in the 2000 federal election campaign is this: she was front and centre in coverage of the NDP, personifying the party on television news of the campaign. However, her stories mentioned polls, party strategy, and electoral battles less often than the male leaders' stories did (Table 2.5), and she had no stories that were predominantly about polls, ads, or debates (Table 2.6). Her coverage was focused predominantly on her day-to-day activities, often social or interactive events in communities – which may be a function of the NDP's campaign emphasis – and linked her less often with the competitive aspects of a national election.

Looking at what was said of McDonough and her leadership of the NDP in terms of viability, much of it was fairly critical or negative, focusing, for example, on the fact that the NDP had not won an Ontario seat – in the country's "industrial heartland," as the 22 October 2000 broadcast of CBC's *The National* pointed out – in two elections and that it had struggled throughout the campaign in an effort to retain its four Saskatchewan seats.[16] In a story aired during the first half of the campaign, also on *The National*, the NDP's struggle for seats in Ontario is highlighted with reportage of a campaign event in Windsor. The story starts with the observation that "the New Democrats don't have any seats in the province right now. So today, McDonough went to a place the party used to be able to count on. But ... she ran into problems of image and identity." Mansbridge continues by noting that "a warm greeting from a small friendly crowd, even if some aren't so sure of Alexa McDonough's name," after which the on-site coverage starts with an unidentified man saying, "Everybody, let's give Alexis a good welcome to the city of Windsor." As noted previously, McDonough had led the NDP for five years, and had led the party in the previous federal election. She was not a newcomer. The gentleman who introduced her to the crowd in Windsor that day likely made an honest enough mistake, but the question is why this became newsworthy for the CBC? Presumably, it was meant to illustrate for the purposes of the story just how far the NDP was from regaining ground in the industrial parts of Ontario; however, the fact that it had been shut out for two elections, that its polling numbers were down so far, and the like were probably sufficient. Moreover, the fact that the observation about the name mistake led the story, rather than the increasing mismatch between the NDP's and unionized workers' policy priorities may suggest that leadership, rather than ideological or policy issues, is what has pushed workers away from the party. Speaking about the NDP's campaign in its final day, one CBC reporter summarized it this way, "Other than the media, [McDonough] had trouble getting anyone's attention. A problem that trailed her for most of the campaign. She usually attracted only small crowds and was often preaching to the converted."[17] Joe Clark's campaign was never

TABLE 2.7
Coverage of issues in news stories about party leaders (four TV networks), 2000 election campaign

Type of issues	Chrétien n (%)	Day n (%)	Clark n (%)	McDonough n (%)	Duceppe n (%)
Soft	111 (45)	81 (48)	28 (30)	43 (59)	20 (19)
Hard	65 (26)	41 (24)	19 (20)	7 (10)	35 (34)
No main/ uncodeable	75 (30)	48 (28)	46 (50)	23 (32)	48 (47)
Total	251 (100)	170 (100)	93 (100)	73 (100)	103 (100)

Notes: $Chi^2 = 71.65$; $df = 8$; $p = .00$; Cramer's $V = 0.21$

characterized this way, despite having faced similar problems. As discussed in the previous chapter, McDonough's party went into the 2000 campaign with more seats than the PCs, and the two were tied in the polls for much of the four weeks leading up to election day. The PCs pulled ahead following a particularly good debate performance from Clark (Blais et al. 2002a), but the primary point here is that the competitive position of the two parties was similar before and during the campaign.

Representations of Issues and Positions

Compared with the male leaders, stories about McDonough and the NDP in CBC's coverage of the 2000 campaign were more likely to emphasize soft issues (Table 2.7).[18] Nearly 60 percent of McDonough's stories had a soft issue as their main focus. In contrast, 48 percent of Day's, 45 percent of Chrétien's, 30 percent of Clark's, and only 19 percent of Duceppe's stories focused on soft issues. Interestingly, it is the primary left and right parties that have the highest levels of soft-issue coverage in this campaign, a pattern we can understand given the importance of social policy for the NDP and moral and lifestyle issues for the Canadian Alliance.

Moving to hard issues, all of the leaders' stories were less focused on hard issues – the economy, security, and trade, for example – than on soft issues. This reflects the issue agenda on which the 2000 campaign was fought. Health care was the dominant issue in the news, in party platforms, and in party press releases. As Blais and his colleagues explain in detail (2002a: 40), health care was the most prominent issue in English-language news, followed by public finances, ethics, and social programs. In addition, health was also prominent in the parties' own platforms. References to health topped all issue mentions in the Liberal platform, and mentions of health were second only to public finances in the Alliance platform (20). In press releases, the most dominant issue mentioned by the Liberals was health, and the same was true of NDP releases (27). Public finances were the dominant issue in Alliance and Conservative press releases, and the second most dominant issue in Liberal and NDP releases (27). In short, social issues, health care, and other soft politics issues were very important in the 2000 campaign, and the two leading parties in the campaign discussed these issues frequently.

Despite the predominant focus on soft issues in the 2000 campaign generally, hard issues were important. As Table 2.7 illustrates, only 10 percent of McDonough's stories focused on a hard issue. The male party leaders all received much more coverage of hard issues than did McDonough (from 20 percent of Clark's stories to 34 percent of Duceppe's). Although some of the seeming gender differences may be legitimately a function of gender-based issue stereotyping, other factors are important to the division of soft- and hard-issue coverage among the leaders. The relative dearth of hard-issue coverage for McDonough is likely because she was the leader furthest to the ideological left of the five, and parties of the left are commonly perceived as weaker on or less interested in hard issues, particularly economic issues, than leaders of centre or right parties (Ansolabehere and Iyengar 1994; Bélanger 2003; Holian 2004; Kaufmann 2004; Nadeau and Blais 1990; Petrocik 1996; Petrocik, Benoit, and Hansen 2003; Scarrow 1965). In other words, McDonough's relative lack of hard-issue coverage is partly attributable to her partisanship or ideology. Moreover, the focus on soft issues in stories about McDonough and the NDP was predictable given the party's campaign platform in 2000. Blais and his colleagues' (2002a) analyses of party press releases in the 2000 campaign provide evidence that the news simply picked up on the NDP's focus on health and social issues. Over 35 percent of the NDP's press releases focused on health, compared with roughly 20 percent of the Liberal and Conservative releases and less than 10 percent of Alliance releases (27, Figure 1.2). In addition, the NDP was second only to the Bloc Québécois in terms of the proportion of press releases about social issues (ibid.).

Level of Mediation: Descriptive versus Interpretive Coverage
This section analyzes the nature of commentary made during news stories by reporters and anchors in order to gain an understanding of the extent to which female candidates and politicians are more filtered or mediated in

news coverage than are their male counterparts, a principal hypothesis of the gendered mediation approach. Scholars working within the gendered mediation paradigm have typically relied on Rakow and Kranich's (1991) theory of "woman as sign" in the news to understand why women's actions and speech would be more filtered than those of their male colleagues. According to Rakow and Kranich, women function in the news as "signs" or conveyors of meaning, rather than as authors or creators of meaning. They start from the premise that the news is a masculine discourse that reflects our culturally constituted norms and expectations, which means that men "do not ordinarily carry meaning as 'man' because the culture assumes maleness as given" (13). Rakow and Kranich are quite clear that the sign "woman" does not necessarily reflect reality. Indeed, "'woman' has meaning not because it refers to some real, predetermined entity that the word tags, but because it is different from another sign 'man'" (10). The difference for women, however, is that they do not define what "woman" means. The category "woman" has already been rigidly defined, and women's role in the news, therefore, is to passively reflect this culturally bound "other" juxtaposed against the male subject.

The consequences of women's function as sign in the news are various. Primary among these is that women's authority as creators of meaning is undermined, and this happens through a variety of news practices. First, past work has suggested that female politicians will be seen less often as speaking news subjects (e.g., in sound bites) compared with their male colleagues. This may mean that women disproportionately receive fewer sound bites in news stories compared with men or that women receive shorter sound bites. The result is the same: disproportionately less air time for direct communication with viewers/voters in their own words and voices. Chapter 1's analyses of the party leaders' and candidates' sound bites in television coverage of the 2000 federal election campaign and the inclusion of direct quotes in print coverage of the 2005-06 campaign do not support this claim, however.

Second, female politicians' speech will be paraphrased, interpreted, and/or analyzed more often than the speech of their male colleagues. This is another way that the news is thought to undermine women's abilities to create their own meanings and represent their own views – in other words, to speak for themselves. Past research demonstrates that this particular mode of filtering female politicians is common practice in news coverage of women. For instance, during the 1993 Canadian federal election campaign, 43 percent of statements made about Jean Chrétien in coverage of the

English-language leaders' debate were classified as descriptive; yet only 31 percent of the statements made about Kim Campbell's debate performance were descriptive (Gidengil and Everitt 2000). Coverage of Campbell was mainly interpretive, telling voters not only what she did and said but, more importantly, what her actions and words meant or signified, which creates openings for gender-stereotypical framing and priming to creep into news stories. Similar practices occur in American media. Print coverage of Elizabeth Dole's bid for nomination as her party's candidate for the US presidency included fewer direct quotes and more paraphrasing of her speech compared with coverage of her male opponents (Aday and Devitt 2001; see also Devitt 2002).

Finally, when female politicians' speech is analyzed or interpreted, news stories will be less likely to include evidence linking the analysis to reality. In other words, newsmakers will be less likely to explicitly tie their analyses of female politicians to the women's actions, speech, or political beliefs. To be clear, this is not meant to contend that newsmakers produce these sex differences in coverage knowingly or maliciously. Rather, like Rakow and Kranich (1991), my analyses of news content and production reflect the belief that "news media personnel work within a taken-for-granted meaning system in which it simply makes sense to do these things" (12).

This section analyzes the second and third types of coverage (interpretation and evidence-giving), focusing on the segments of television news stories where journalists report – in the lead-ins, the voice-overs for clips, and the wrap-ups – to ask whether one gender group receives more interpretive coverage (analytical or evaluative), as opposed to straightforward descriptive coverage, than the other. In the main, results are mixed in terms of differences in the distribution of party leaders' descriptive, analytical, and evaluative coverage in lead-ins, voice-overs, or wrap-ups.[19] In terms of the relative distributions of descriptive versus analytical and evaluative (together called interpretive coverage in the remainder of this section), there are no statistically significant gender differences for the four leaders in the voice-over or wrap-up segments (results not shown). The lead-ins to stories do show differences, but the primary difference does not seem to be gender based (Table 2.8). Keeping in mind that the bulk of lead-ins are descriptive, regardless of party leader, the two front-running candidates, Chrétien and Day, received much more interpretive coverage than did the other two, McDonough and Clark, suggesting that competitiveness is the critical variable predicting whether interpretation is offered in news stories of party leaders. McDonough does have a significantly higher portion of interpretive

TABLE 2.8
Nature of lead-ins in news stories about party leaders (four TV networks), 2000 election campaign

	Chrétien		Day		Clark		McDonough	
Lead-in	n	(%)	n	(%)	n	(%)	n	(%)
Descriptive	25	(50)	27	(58)	19	(81)	13	(70)
Interpretive	25	(50)	20	(42)	4	(19)	5	(30)
Total	50	(100)	47	(100)	23	(100)	18	(100)

Notes: $Chi^2 = 14.07$; $df = 4$; $p = .01$; Cramer's V = 0.23

coverage than her closest competitor, Clark, however, which may be due to gender, as predicted by the gendered mediation approach.

The 1 November 2000 broadcast of *The National* provides an illustration of the McDonough-Clark lead-in difference. CBC Chief Anchor Peter Mansbridge gave the following lead-in to the story about Clark: "Conservative leader Joe Clark zeroed in on both the Alliance and the Liberals while campaigning in Borden, Prince Edward Island, today." This descriptive lead-in told viewers simply that Clark focused on Chrétien and Day in his campaign activities that day, which was an accurate description.[20] Mansbridge did not tell audiences how to think about Clark's actions or speculate on the motives behind them.

In the same newscast, Mansbridge introduced a McDonough story with the following statement: "Alexa McDonough spent the day trying to colour parts of Ontario NDP orange. The New Democrats don't have any seats in the province right now. So today, McDonough went to a place the party used to be able to count on. But, as Raj Ahluwalia reports, she ran into problems of image and identity."[21] In this lead-in, Mansbridge applied an interpretive lens to McDonough's actions. The story was about a rally she attended in Windsor, Ontario. McDonough's speech at the event focused on health care, although Mansbridge's lead-in suggested that she was campaigning in heavily unionized Windsor in order to mobilize what used to be a strong base of working-class support for the NDP. Mansbridge's statement that McDonough "ran into problems of image and identity" attributes reasons to the party's struggles in Ontario that are not explicit in the content on which the news report is based.

The content analysis also coded whether analytical commentary included reference to any form of evidence that would substantiate the interpretations offered to viewers. The omission of supporting evidence to validate

TABLE 2.9

Evidence offered in analytical voice-overs in news stories about party leaders (four TV networks), 2000 election campaign

	Chrétien		Day		Clark		McDonough	
Evidence	n	(%)	n	(%)	n	(%)	n	(%)
No	33	(46)	20	(28)	17	(54)	16	(67)
Yes	39	(54)	52	(72)	14	(46)	8	(33)
Total	72	(100)	72	(100)	31	(100)	24	(100)

Notes: Chi^2 = 25.877; df = 3; p = .00; Cramer's V = 0.25

interpretations of female candidates' electoral viability, issue positions, or past records may lend greater weight to journalists' opinions about or analyses of female candidates. According to past research, print news is less likely to make reference to supporting "evidence or reasoning" in relation to quotations of female candidates compared with those of male ones (Aday and Devitt 2001, 56). Indeed, this was precisely Devitt's (2002) finding in his analysis of gubernatorial candidates in the United States, a result with considerable weight considering that a governorship is a common stepping stone to the White House (446). For television news of the 2000 campaign in Canada, findings are not mixed at all on this indicator. For analytical lead-ins, voice-overs, and wrap-ups, the rate at which evidence is offered for newsmakers' interpretations of leaders' speech and behaviours is significantly lower for McDonough than for the male leaders on all counts.[22] Every one of McDonough's analytical lead-ins and wrap-ups fails to offer evidence or reasoning to substantiate the interpretive content. For the male leaders, the situation is different; many analytical lead-ins and wrap-ups present evidence (results not shown). For voice-overs, the distribution is more balanced, but offering evidence is still much lower when McDonough is interpreted (Table 2.9). Two-thirds of her analytical voice-overs offer no evidence to support the analysis offered, a proportion that is higher than Clark's and substantially higher than Day's and Chretien's level of unsubstantiated voice-overs.

Concrete examples illustrate nicely the differences between substantiated versus unsubstantiated analysis in clip voice-overs. A story about Day and the Alliance discussed Day's efforts to emphasize the Grand-Mère affair, a scandal highlighted regularly throughout the 2000 campaign whereby Chrétien had allegedly called the Business Development Bank of Canada to help a financially troubled hotel (L'Auberge Grand-Mère) in his riding. Reporter Eric Sorensen had this to say about Day's activities that day: "Day hopes [Grand-Mère] has an effect on the campaign. Almost four weeks into the race, the Alliance has stalled in the polls. On Edmonton television this morning, Day bemoaned what he called unfair attacks by the Liberals on him, though he admitted those attacks are working."[23] Sorensen provided a piece of analysis, for he gave the impression to voters that Day hoped Grand-Mère would improve his own chances in the campaign by diminishing Chrétien's popularity. The reasoning Sorensen offered for this interpretation of Day's thinking was the Alliance's stalling in the polls, which was a well-documented fact at that point.

A few days before this, Laurie Graham reported a story about McDonough and the NDP. McDonough had spent the day campaigning in Nova Scotia. Speaking during a clip of McDonough shaking hands with people in the crowd, Graham had this to say about McDonough's "strategy": "So Alexa McDonough continues campaigning, not so much to win new seats as to protect the ones the NDP has."[24] Graham did not mention in the voice-over – or in the story at all, for that matter – whether McDonough was visiting a riding currently held by the NDP, which would have provided supporting evidence (however tenuous) for the claim that McDonough's strategy was to focus on NDP strongholds. Graham simply tells viewers this was McDonough's strategy.

How Are Women Covered? The 2005-06 Federal Election Campaign in Print News

In this section, I focus on candidates, not party leaders, since there was no female leader in the 2005-06 race. Some of the same patterns discovered above in televised news coverage are repeated in candidates' coverage in newspapers, although there are important differences. In some cases, these differences are likely a function of the fact that print news has much more content than television news (e.g., Druckman 2005), creating greater opportunities for mediation.

Representations of the Personal

Coverage of personal romantic relationships, appearances, and parental status is more common in coverage of female candidates than in that of male candidates. I use three indicators of personal coverage: whether a news story explicitly mentions a candidate's appearance,[25] whether it explicitly mentions a candidate's personal romantic relationship status,[26] and whether it explicitly mentions a candidate's parental status.[27] On all three indicators of personalized coverage, female candidates are more likely to receive such mentions in print news. Starting with appearances (Table 2.10), 18 percent of stories about female candidates made some reference to their external appearance, versus only 3 percent of male candidates' stories. Women's relationship status was reported in 25 percent of their campaign stories, versus in only 6 percent of men's (Table 2.11). The candidate covered most reliably in this way was Olivia Chow, whose stories rarely failed to mention that she was NDP leader Jack Layton's wife. All four of the Chow articles in the 2006 print news subsample explicitly mentioned her marriage to Layton. There is one article about Nina Grewal, a Conservative MP from British Columbia whose husband Gurmant Grewal was also a Conservative MP, in the subsample, and it referred to her as "the missus."[28] Parental status was explicitly mentioned in 13 percent of women's stories and in only 4 percent of men's (Table 2.12). Women received more personal coverage than men on all three indicators, and the consistency of the finding across different indicators is telling. However, it is also the case that in most of the articles covering women there was no mention of any of these aspects of their private lives.

What do newspapers print in cases of personalized coverage? What does such coverage look like? Belinda Stronach was certainly the primary female recipient of highly personalized, highly gendered election coverage in 2005-06, a finding that is not surprising given past work on the treatment of her in the news (e.g., Trimble 2007; Trimble and Everitt 2010). Coverage of Stronach regularly mentioned her appearance, her love life, and her family, and she was framed consistently in accordance with the sex object stereotype. An article that appeared in the news section of the *Toronto Star* about her win in the 2006 race summarizes Stronach like this:

> Slim, blond and striking, she was scolded for her lack of loyalty to Tory leader Stephen Harper and for the resulting breakup with her boyfriend, Conservative Deputy Leader Peter MacKay. She became the Liberal minister for human resources and skills development – an instant political icon – praised by many for standing up for what she believed in and for putting principles before love.[29]

The article does not have a negative tone overall. In places, it offers quite complimentary descriptions of Stronach's hard-fought win in what was "one of the most bitter and intensely personal races in the country." That said, the article makes reference to her blondness, her slim build, and her

TABLE 2.10

Mention of candidates' appearance, by sex (print news), 2005-06 election campaign

Mention of appearance	Men n	(%)	Women n	(%)
Yes	3	(3)	7	(18)
No	99	(97)	33	(82)
Total	102	(100)	40	(100)

Notes: Chi^2 = 9.3; df = 1; p = .00

TABLE 2.11

Mention of candidates' personal romantic relationships, by sex (print news), 2005-06 election campaign

Mention of relationships	Men n	(%)	Women n	(%)
Yes	6	(6)	10	(25)
No	96	(94)	30	(75)
Total	102	(100)	40	(100)

Notes: Chi^2 = 10.5; df = 1; p = .00

TABLE 2.12

Mention of candidates' parental status, by sex (print news), 2005-06 election campaign

Mention of parental status	Men n	(%)	Women n	(%)
Yes	4	(4)	5	(13)
No	97	(96)	35	(87)
Total	101	(100)	40	(100)

Notes: Chi^2 = 3.5; df = 1; p = .06

beauty, as well as her "lack of loyalty" to both Harper and her "boyfriend," MacKay. It reminds readers that Stronach was attacked by her colleagues in the House of Commons, and by the media and the public, for exercising an independent mind (if the defection was primarily the result of principle, as she has always maintained) or for being ambitious (if it was primarily for political career gain). Either way, independence and ambition are not qualities that tend to be critiqued in male politicians. The article also says that she was "scolded" for the defection, suggesting that she was reprimanded for her transgression like an insolent child, infantilizing her as a result.

Another news article begins by noting, "It is like being on the set of *Friends*. Belinda Stronach is sitting in an upscale coffee shop in her riding of Newmarket-Aurora, looking for all the world like Jennifer Aniston in her calf-length boots and tan leather jacket, as fans bask in her fame."[30] The article compares Stronach to an actress – someone who is always playing a role, and who is stereotyped as flighty and superficial – and draws attention to her clothes. Over and over, coverage of Stronach contains examples like these, for articles regularly describe her clothes, hair, face, and/or body; her past relationships with Peter MacKay, her ex-husband, and even rumoured linkages with Bill Clinton and others. Coverage of Stronach treats these pieces of information as though they are relevant to her political career and her policy positions.

Stronach is not the only one, however. Even though Stronach has received the most gendered of political news coverage in the country in recent years – which raises questions about why she should be covered this way so consistently – the patterns described above are not unique to her. An article titled, "TV Star Brings Glamour Factor to Churchill: Tina Keeper," says that the Liberal candidate, who used to have a role on *North of 60*, "looks every bit a northerner in a grey parka with a newly sewn collar of badger fur courtesy of her mother ... she is wearing a stylish black suit under the parka and silver jewellery that would not be out of place in the fashion-conscious haunts of Toronto, Ottawa or Vancouver."[31] Perhaps the article is suggesting that an Aboriginal female candidate in Churchill who wears clothes or accessories that would be considered fashionable in urban centres is noteworthy or somehow unexpected. The article calls Keeper a star several times, and suggests that many are "caught off-guard by her focus on gritty issues."

Rona Ambrose, Conservative MP for the Alberta riding of Edmonton-Spruce Grove, is also regularly portrayed using a sex object frame. An article published early in the fifty-five-day campaign for the January 2006 federal election noted, "Rona Ambrose is the type of politician parties love – young, ambitious, smart, articulate. As a bonus for the Conservatives, she is a policy wonk who also happens to be attractive and stylish. She was voted sexiest female MP in a Hill Times survey this year."[32] The article does mention traits commonly associated with successful politicians generally – ambition, intelligence, articulateness – but then goes on to add stylishness and sexiness to the list of her positive attributes. The central focus of the article is Ambrose's role as the party's chief spokesperson for its child care policy, but then it incorporates her personal life into analysis of her suitability for the role, noting,

> It cannot have been an easy issue for her to tackle. Ms. Ambrose does not have her own children, the reasons for which she describes as personal and complicated. She has decided to not talk publicly about the specifics – she and her husband, Bruce, guard their privacy – but suffice to say it is noble of her to have championed the issue.

The implication here is that there is something awful or perhaps painful in her childlessness; a secret to guard, making it a noble choice for her to then "champion" the child care issue. Implicit in this discussion is the idea that her own parental status is related to her role in child care policy, or more generally, that her personal experience is related to her role in formulating and speaking for public policy on the issue. Moreover, even though Ambrose has obviously tried to shield this aspect of her personal life from media intrusion, the journalist makes an issue of her childlessness, which may have negative consequences given that voters tend to rank childless women lower than mothers, fathers, and childless men (Stalsburg 2010). Furthermore, drawing attention to Ambrose's childlessness in the context of her role in child care policy may undercut her expertise on the issue, since childless women may "lose the traditional 'female advantage' on child-care and children's issues" (373).

For many older, often more experienced female politicians, personal coverage that focuses on appearances and personal lives seems less common, perhaps because many of the older candidates are also incumbents or otherwise well known for their political experience – such as Liza Frulla's experience as a deputy in the Quebec National Assembly before taking on a federal seat in the House of Commons, and Hedy Fry's long occupation of the Vancouver Centre seat and experience as a cabinet minister. Incumbents have records in office to analyze, and they may have more in the way of political or professional credentials to discuss, so candidates such as Hedy Fry and Anne McLellan receive little focus on their appearances and personal lives in print news of the 2006 election campaign. This proposition is difficult to test with the 2005-06 subsample, because the numbers in subcategories become too small for reliable analysis. However, looking at explicit reference to men's and women's looks, relationships, and parental status by whether a candidate is a challenger or incumbent suggests the speculation is accurate (results not shown). Women with experience in office tend to receive less personalized coverage, a finding consistent with the idea that once women "prove" themselves as politicians, their coverage tends to be more like that of male politicians (e.g., Fowler and Lawless 2009).

Of course, this is a generalization, and it is not applicable to all candidates. Young women or women relatively new to politics are not always covered in the sex object frame, and older or more experienced political women do not always avoid it. One difference that is fairly notable is that in various cases, older women are portrayed in the mother frame. For Carolyn Bennett – who was an incumbent Liberal cabinet minister in the Toronto riding of St. Paul's in 2005-06 – this frame was applied multiple times in print coverage. "This doctor who wears power-politics pinstriped suits but has this total earth-mother side"[33] is how one article describes her, and it goes on to note that "she doesn't burn incense in the constituency office or canvas in Birkenstocks. The [earth mother] vibe comes from all the years Bennett immersed herself in the mysteries of childbirth."[34] This does not constitute an explicit reference to her parental status, but is in line with the mother frame. Going on to explain Bennett's popularity with her expectant patients – Bennett is a family physician – the article wonders "maybe it was her distinctive voice that coaxed the babies out of the womb – a Demi Moore rasp combined with Sean Connery's way of turning an 's' into a 'sh.'" Or perhaps she is a very skilled and experienced obstetrician who is adept at handling births.

In terms of personal traits and behaviours, print news, like television news, frequently focuses on, and perhaps even exaggerates, female politicians' aggressive behaviours, sometimes using explicitly gendered frames. One illustrative example from 2005-06 is coverage of the contest in the constituency of Vancouver Centre, where long-time Liberal incumbent and cabinet minister Hedy Fry and rival NDP candidate Svend Robinson, both high-profile politicians, competed for the seat. In an article titled, "Fur Likely to Fly as Robinson, Fry Square Off," the journalist claimed that the rivalry had been dubbed "The Battle of the Divas."[35] Use of the term *diva* to describe Robinson feminizes him and also potentially activates stereotypes about gay males which depict them as flamboyant. Stereotypical coverage of gay men is fairly common; in one survey of gay candidates in the United States, for example, 71 percent of respondents said that the use of gay stereotypes had occurred in their media coverage (Golebiowska 2002). As Everitt and Camp note, "like women, they too are frequently presented in a distinct manner, accentuating their otherness, limiting the perception of their abilities and interests and pushing them to the corners of political discourse" (2009b, 27). The article continued with the claim that the race between the two candidates "could develop into one nasty little cat fight," that it will be "one of the most closely watched contests in the country for its entertainment value," that the Conservative candidate is hoping that "Svend and Hedy claw each other's eyes out and can't find their way to the finish line," and at one point the article says "Rarrrrrrr," "that is the sound of one cat angrily pawing the air at another. Get used to it." Granted, this is a column, not a hard news story. Nonetheless, the focus on the "cat fight" occupied so much space in the article that it said little about the two candidates' records in politics – and both were experienced veterans – and little about what they promised to do in the constituency if elected.

Personalized coverage is rarer for male politicians, and when it does occur, there seem to be important differences in what was said or represented. First, descriptions of male politician's appearances were often much briefer than those described above for female politicians. An article about the possibility of Lorne Nystrom's return to politics compared the young Nystrom with the older version: "the curly head of hair is still there, but the lines in the face hint at the reality that he will soon be 60."[36] Another article described Scott Brison at a campaign stop as "wearing a confident smile and a bright red sweater that matches the Liberal posters on the white walls." There was no protracted analysis of male candidates' clothes, hair, or overall "look." Moreover, coverage of men seemed qualitatively different from that described above of Ambrose, Stronach, Keeper, and others, for example, which tended to play directly into feminine tropes that sexualize and often trivialize. Explicit reference to marital status or romantic relationships in men's coverage was very infrequent in the 2005-06 subsample as well, and when such mentions were made, they tended to be descriptive and brief, rather than laden with inference or innuendo and in-depth. For example, one article in the subsample noted that Mississauga-Brampton South Liberal incumbent Navdeep Singh Bains "lives in Mississauga with his wife, Brahamjot."[37] An article about former Governor General Ed Schreyer's return to electoral politics as a federal candidate in 2006 noted that "some, including his wife, Lily, are not as sure Schreyer should be taking on the life of a busy parliamentarian. His wife, he admits, 'wasn't talking to me for a few days, but she is now.'"[38] Obviously, this is an issue that Schreyer brought up himself in the interview with the reporter, for there is a quote included about the effect of his wife's reservations.

Representations of the Professional
Women undoubtedly received more personalized coverage that focuses on their looks, relationships, and children (or seemingly inexplicable childlessness); indicators of the professional, however, reveal more balanced coverage. For the 2005-06 print news subsample, three aspects of coverage were coded: explicit mention of candidates' educational background or attainment,[39] explicit mention of their professions or occupational history,[40] and explicit mention of their experience in politics.[41] On all three indicators, there were no statistically significant differences between coverage of male and female candidates (results not shown). Thus, although there was gendering in the personalized, appearance-focused coverage of female politicians in the 2006 campaign, it is difficult to claim that this systematically came at the expense of coverage of their credentials, both professional and political, at least in terms of the extent to which stories explicitly referenced their professional and political credentials at least once.

Looking in more detail at the substance of print news stories, many women covered in print news of the 2005-06 campaign garnered lots of press attention to the professional and political factors that made them good nominees for their parties. Indeed, in various cases, the same women who received highly personalized coverage, described above, also received ample attention to their credentials. Rona Ambrose was touted in the campaign as a shoo-in for the cabinet, as a "quick and enthusiastic study, with a punishing work ethic," and as someone who speaks several languages.[42] She was always mentioned as an incumbent. In another article, the journalist described her win in the 2004 election as a "landslide," noted that she "worked on fiscal, social and constitutional issues for the Alberta government," and it also stated that she does not come from a political family.[43] In other words, she was portrayed as a winner who took her seat handily last time around, as someone with experience in government, and as someone who rose to political prominence on her own, not as the result of family connections.

Other women received similarly positive coverage of their credentials. Josée Verner, the Conservatives' Quebec regional chair at the time and candidate for the riding of Louis-Saint-Laurent, was presented as a "communications consultant and former aide to Quebec Premier Robert Bourassa."[44] Diane Ablonczy, long-sitting MP for Calgary-Nose Hill, was described in the same article as "an articulate lawyer," and Ambrose's MA in political science and background as a senior intergovernmental affairs officer in the Alberta public service were also mentioned. Bev Oda, who won her Durham riding in that election, was a senior television executive and commissioner for the Canadian Radio-Television and Telecommunications Commission before entering politics, and these experiences were mentioned in the article. Liza Frulla is someone whose credentials also received a lot of coverage. Calling Frulla a "star candidate," one article notes that she had been a cabinet minister in the Quebec provincial government, that she is a graduate of the University of Montreal, and that she was the first female sports reporter in Quebec electronic media.[45] It also notes that Frulla was the vice-chairperson of the No Committee in the 1995 Quebec sovereignty-association referendum, and that she claims credit for bringing almost $100 million in investment to her riding. Paddy Torsney, who was an incumbent Liberal candidate in the riding of Ancaster, was called a "twelve-year parliamentary veteran" and "a popular, likeable local MP ... who has seen off challengers in four successive elections."[46] This article continued by noting that Torsney was "relying on her reputation for 'delivering for Burlington' to see her through, pointing to $12 million in new infrastructure money for the city, as well as national initiatives such as the 'do not call' telemarketing legislation." This coverage of Torsney explicitly said that she is a repeat winner at the ballot box, and can serve up a fairly sure win to her party on election night. Two final examples that deserve mention for the consistent coverage of their professional and political credentials are Hedy Fry and Carolyn Bennett, both incumbent Liberal candidates in 2005-06, both cabinet ministers at the time, and both doctors. Use of the title "Dr." was common in coverage of both, and discussion of their profession and career highlights was more common in their news articles than not. For Hedy Fry, the fact that she defeated a prime minister – Kim Campbell, in 1993, in Fry's first run for office – is mentioned often in her coverage, and is typically used to signal her political skill and ability to win.

Even coverage of Stronach, who received the most consistently and blatantly personalized coverage in the race, regularly mentioned her professional and political credentials including that she was the CEO of Magna International, an auto parts company; that she had been ranked the second-most powerful businesswoman in the world outside the United States by *Fortune* magazine; that she was a Liberal cabinet minister; that she was on the Dean's Council at the JFK School of Business at Harvard University; that she had received an honorary doctorate of law from McMaster University;

and so on.[47] That said, coverage of Stronach's professional and political credentials also regularly contained reference to her father and sometimes to her political mentors. Sometimes explicit and at other times implicit, Stronach's success was frequently attributed to powerful men. Reference to her position as CEO of Magna was often quickly followed by statements like "the auto-parts company started by her father, Frank,"[48] or she is simply referred to as an "auto parts heiress."[49] Both suggested that her success in the industry came as the result of her father's hard work and initiative, not her own. Her 2005 floor-crossing is sometimes referred to as something orchestrated by powerful men to help Martin win a non-confidence vote on the budget – one article describes the defection as having been "masterminded by former Liberal Premier David Peterson,"[50] raising questions about Stronach's political autonomy and independence.

Reference to powerful men was uncommon in coverage of female candidates who were politically established (Stronach was one of the exceptions), but it did occur. For example, Susan Whalen, who was the Liberal candidate in Essex and had been a Liberal MP for three terms until losing in 2004, was described as being part of the "Whalen dynasty" – "her father, Eugene, a senator who was an agriculture minister in Trudeau's cabinet, was the MP from 1935 to 1968."[51] Although uncommon for experienced or well-known female candidates, coverage of female newcomer candidates seems more likely to contain linkages with powerful male relatives. The young NDP candidate for Churchill, Niki Ashton, for example, was regularly linked to her father, Steve Ashton, who was the water stewardship minister in the Manitoba government at the time.[52] This article referred to her as a "political blueblood," suggesting that her success in politics was inherited rather than earned, much as a royal title would be. Ashton's Liberal rival in the riding, Tina Keeper – analyzed above for the sex symbol frame used to report her candidacy – received similar coverage. Keeper was described as coming from "an accomplished aboriginal family," in which her "father [is] a member of the Order of Canada and her uncle the first native Anglican bishop in the country."[53] Providing more specific information, another article described her father as "a well-known elder from Norway House whose life work revolved around the impact of flooding from hydro dams on a handful of northern Manitoba First Nations."[54] This article made explicit connections between her father and her electoral prospects, asserting that "Ms. Keeper will arguably have an easier sell with aboriginal voters. If they don't know her from ... *North of 60*, they might have known her mother or her father, Joe Keeper." Interestingly, her mother was also mentioned in this

TABLE 2.13

Horserace vs. issue coverage of candidates, by sex (print news), 2006 election campaign

	Men		Women	
Type of coverage	n	(%)	n	(%)
Horserace	286	(50)	109	(63)
Issue	228	(40)	43	(25)
Neither	57	(10)	20	(12)
Total	571	(100)	172	(100)

Notes: Chi^2 = 12.81; df = 2; p = .00; Cramer's V = 0.13

article – she is a "well-known Anglican priest in Manitoba." Even though it is not only older, more prominent male relatives mentioned in the article, Keeper's ability to win the riding on her own merits and campaign was subtly questioned.

Representations of Viability

The general proposition in the literature that women receive more viability coverage than men is borne out in print news of the 2006 campaign. Focusing, in particular, on the distribution of horserace versus issue coverage, we can see that female candidates receive more horserace coverage than their male counterparts – 63 percent of women's stories versus 50 percent of men's are horserace stories (Table 2.13), a finding that is common in the literature (e.g., Kahn 1994, 1996).

Horserace stories focus, by definition, on competitive angles – on who is ahead and behind, who is likely to win an election, and so on – although it is important to remember that horserace coverage is not necessarily negative on its own. Indeed, in some cases, women are framed in a positive way, as the candidate to beat in a riding or as the likely winner, as was the case in a lot of the coverage of Rona Ambrose, for example. One journalist noted in a story about Ambrose that "it borders on the delusional to imagine Ambrose losing her seat."[55] As such, it matters a lot what is said or implied about women's competitive position in stories that focus on the horserace. Because tone is coded in the McGill Media Observatory's data set, I use this as a way of examining possible gender differences in the tone – positivity or negativity – of men's and women's horserace stories.[56] Negative tone in a horserace story would often be a signal that a story casts doubt on a candidate's competitiveness, and positive tone the opposite. Interestingly, there is no gender

TABLE 2.14

Tone of stories on candidates, by sex (print news), 2006 election campaign

	Men		Women	
	n	(%)	n	(%)
Neutral	503	(88)	152	(90)
Positive	27	(4)	11	(7)
Negative	43	(8)	5	(3)
Total	573	(100)	168	(100)

Notes: Chi^2 = 5.07; df = 2; p = .08; Cramer's V = 0.08

difference in tone for male and female candidates' horserace-focused stories (results not shown). For candidates of both sexes, 89 percent of their horserace stories were neutral in tone – as is the bulk of the news generally, particularly front-section news as opposed to editorials and columns. For both men and women, 5 to 6 percent of stories were negative and 5 to 6 percent were positive. According to these particular indicators, then, although women receive more horserace coverage than their male colleagues do, the tone of their stories is not measurably different from those of men.

Focusing a bit closer on the tone of stories – all stories, not just horserace stories – female candidates are not systematically disadvantaged on this indicator of news quality. Results are mixed, but the majority of analyses reveal either no gender differences in the tone of coverage or suggest that women sometimes receive slightly more positive coverage than men do. Looking at all print stories as a whole, women receive more positive- and neutral-tone stories than men, and fewer negative-tone stories (Table 2.14), although, as noted above, the bulk of news stories, regardless of gender, is neutral in tone, and where gender differences exist, they are not large.

Looking at candidates by level of experience, there are no gender differences in the tone of challengers' coverage, and female incumbents actually have fewer negative- and more positive-tone stories than do male incumbents (results not shown). Interestingly, the tone of incumbents' stories, regardless of candidates' sex, is overwhelmingly neutral (94 percent of both male and female incumbents' stories), perhaps because there is more in the way of rich information – a record in office, a well-developed public persona – on which to report. For challengers, a higher proportion of their stories slant positive or negative, rather than neutral. Fifteen percent of male challengers' and 10 percent of female challengers' stories contain negative or positive tone, a statistically significant gender difference. Turning to editorials and columns, the type of news items that are most likely to have tone, results are similar to other analyses: editorials and columns about women are judged by coders to be more neutral or positive than those about male candidates, and by a large margin, actually. Eighteen percent of editorials about male candidates have some positive or negative tone in them (and negative-tone stories account for 11 percent), but only 5 percent of women's editorials have tone in them, and most times it is positive.

All the evidence that women are not disadvantaged by the tone of their news articles is to be interpreted with caution, however. The Media Observatory team clearly engaged in rigorous training of its coders. However, it took a conservative approach to coding tone, which is probably the only sensible way to code this subjective aspect of the news. More specifically, the researchers note that their tone variables really only capture obvious tone in the news: "the default 'tone' for all party and leader mentions is neutral, and a mention has to be very clearly positive or negative in order to be coded as such. This means that our coding may miss some of the more nuanced positive and negative mentioned in articles. The tone we do capture is relatively clear, however – readily apparent to all readers, and also relatively reliable coding-wise."[57] In other words, some of the more subtle or encoded forms of tone that exist in gendered coverage of men and women may not be picked up by this measure.

Representations of Issues and Positions
Women receive less issue coverage than men do (Table 2.13), so the electorate is, therefore, offered fewer opportunities to become familiar with women's issue priorities and positions than they are for men's. This could be an important disadvantage for female politicians. The next question is how women's issue positions and priorities are covered. Analyses of television news of the 2000 election campaign found that coverage of McDonough associated her with "soft" issues more than with "hard" issues, and she was also the leader with the highest proportion of soft-issue coverage. Issue coverage of candidates in print news follows slightly different patterns, perhaps in part because candidates come in all political stripes, whereas my analyses of television coverage of leaders focus predominantly on a single female subject on the left wing of the political spectrum. As Table 2.15 shows, the nature of issue coverage in print news of the 2005-06 campaign was quite similar for both men and women. Broadly, most of their stories either did not mention issues, or mentioned issues that are not

TABLE 2.15

Issue coverage of candidates, by sex (print news), 2006 election campaign

	Men		Women	
Issues	n	(%)	n	(%)
Health care	21	(4)	2	(1)
Economic	82	(14)	13	(8)
Law and order	32	(6)	11	(6)
Social	92	(16)	25	(15)
Government and leadership	83	(14)	29	(17)
Other	270	(47)	92	(53)
Total	580	(101)	172	(100)

Notes: Chi^2 = 9.20; df = 5; p = .10; Cramer's V = 0.11.

Percentages may not total 100 because of rounding.

categorizeable according to larger, familiar themes. Coverage of government and leadership issues as well as social issues was similarly high for both male and female candidates, followed by economic issues, law and order issues, and health care. Indeed, the rank ordering of these issues in terms of the frequency, if not the actual levels, of their mention in candidates' coverage was virtually the same for men and women.

All this said, there were gender differences, although most of them small. Perhaps most significantly, men's stories were more likely to mention economic issues than women's, which corresponds to traditional gender stereotyping of issue priorities, as well as past literature on gender, media, and electoral politics. However, on the whole, women were not more likely than men to be covered alongside social issues or health care, both of which tend to be classified as "soft" issues. If we divide candidates into incumbents and challengers, the patterns change a bit on the challenger side. The pattern for incumbents was roughly the same as for candidates as a whole, except the gender gap in coverage of economic issues was even more skewed towards men, a result attributable, in large measure, to the fact that one of the important incumbents in 2006 was Finance Minister Ralph Goodale. Looking at challengers only, the stereotypical gender pattern in news coverage of men and women emerged (Table 2.16). Issues are categorized more broadly in this case to demonstrate the pattern. Hard issues are economic, foreign affairs, defence, and constitutional issues, largely, as outlined in detail in Appendix 1, and soft issues are those that deal with social policy, for the

TABLE 2.16

Issue coverage of male and female challengers (print news), 2006 election campaign

Issues	Men n	(%)	Women n	(%)
Hard	75	(33)	9	(20)
Soft	46	(20)	21	(48)
Other	108	(47)	14	(32)
Total	229	(100)	44	(100)

Notes: Chi^2 = 15.25; df = 2; p = .00; Cramer's V = 0.24

most part. One-third of male challengers' stories focused on hard issues versus 20 percent of female challengers' stories. The pattern was reversed for soft issues, which were the focus of nearly half of female challengers' stories versus only 20 percent of male challengers' stories.

The careful observer may wonder here whether partisan difference is the true driver of the issue-coverage gap between male and female challengers. Specifically, NDP candidates, who are more likely to focus on (or be associated with) social policy, make up a disproportionate share of the challengers, and, further, women make up a disproportionate share of NDP candidates. In other words, women are more likely to be both NDP and challengers than male candidates (see Table 3.4), producing a possible confusion of gender effects for party effects regarding the issue coverage of challengers. This is a logical concern, but it does not actually account for the difference in challengers' print coverage in the 2005-06 campaign. Even *among* NDP challengers, the gender-stereotypical issue coverage described above occurred (results not shown). Stories about male NDP challengers focused on the economy and public finances, as well as governance and leadership, more than did those about female NDP challengers; issue coverage of female NDP challengers focused more on health care and social issues.

Why does this pattern hold for challengers and not for incumbents? Because reporters are generalists with pressing daily deadlines, and they do not have enough time to gain expertise about every topic or politician on which they report (e.g., Ericson, Baranek, and Chan 1987, 1992). The constraints of the job, therefore, encourage reporters to rely on "low-information shortcuts" (Popkin 1991) to fill in the blanks. Zilber and Niven argue that the complexity of reporters' jobs encourages them to "categorize" politicians (2000a, 33). In turn, "categorizing members encourages the media to stereotype some as concerned about ... agriculture, some about taxes, and some about racial issues. In the process, members predominantly receive coverage only on 'their' issue and can come to be stereotyped as knowing or caring only about that issue" (33-34; see also Zilber and Niven 2000b).

Zilber and Niven (2000a) focus on African-American members of the US Congress and the tendency of their coverage to focus on racial issues. However, the pattern is general. Race is simply the most cognitively available cue from which to generate inferences in the case of visible minority legislators. In the case of female politicians, the distinguishing trait is sex, so women tend to be associated with issues commonly perceived as "feminine," such as education, health care, and welfare, and men are associated with hard issues like finance, defence, and foreign affairs. The key here is that journalists are less likely to be familiar with or have specific information about challenger candidates than about relatively well-known incumbents. Consequently, journalists may be more likely to rely on gender stereotypes in the issue and trait coverage of challenger candidates, resulting in gender-stereotypical issue coverage. The use of stereotypes to compensate for information gaps is a well-established topic in the voting behaviour literature, as well. Voters tend to use visible traits like race and gender to make inferences about the issue concerns and positions of unknown candidates (e.g., Burrell 1994; Huddy and Terkildsen 1993b; Kahn 1992, 1994; Leeper 1991; McDermott 1997, 1998; Sanbonmatsu 2002; Sapiro 1982). Plainly, this is a process that people use *generally* to compensate for information deficits.

Conclusion

Synthesizing the data presented in this chapter is straightforward, but leads to an ambiguous conclusion: the evidence on gendered coverage is mixed. On some indicators, female leaders and candidates are presented in television and print campaign news in fair or balanced ways in which their gender does not seem to have considerably affected their coverage. For example, news coverage of McDonough did not draw attention to her personal or family life; gaffes and problems in her campaign were not mentioned at a higher rate than for the other leaders; and her issue coverage, although focused on social policy, was a fair representation of her actual issue agenda in that campaign. For print news coverage of female candidates in the 2006 election campaign, significant attention was given to women's professional and personal credentials, including their occupations, educational backgrounds, political experience, past electoral victories, and the like, and professionalized coverage appeared in the same proportion of their stories as in those about male candidates. The tone in the news coverage of women did not seem to be more negative than in the news coverage of men – the opposite in some cases, perhaps as a result of the high quality of female candidates or focus on the positive content of feminine stereotypes. Issue coverage was similar for male and female candidates in the 2005-06 print news, and only when challengers were examined in isolation from incumbents did issue coverage follow traditional gender patterns linking female challengers with soft issues and male challengers with hard issues. In other words, once female candidates surmount the political-experience hurdle, their issue coverage is virtually identical to that of their male colleagues; it is among the inexperienced and relatively unknown candidates that political-issue coverage follows a more gender-stereotypical pattern, and not because of women's greater likelihood than men to be NDP challengers. In other words, it's not an effect that can be attributed to differences in parties' issue agendas.

There is, however, also considerable evidence to support the idea of gender effects in news coverage. McDonough was represented less often with symbols of power, her professional and political credentials were less prominent when compared with news coverage of the male leaders; features associated with strategic and competitive aspects of elections, such as polls, ads, and debates, were never the focus of her stories in 2000; and evidence offering for interpretive content was systematically lower for her than for her male rivals. McDonough and other female candidates were presented on the attack in a far greater proportion of their news stories than were political men, an illustration of the iron maiden stereotype that persists for powerful, ambitious women. For female candidates for the election in 2006, highly personalized coverage of appearances, family, and romantic lives was all too common in newspaper coverage – which contrasts with television coverage, perhaps owing to the greater "space" in print formats – and much of it was negative and trivialized women. The pet frame is apparent in how often women's success was subtly attributed to powerful men, particularly in the case of female newcomers. Also playing into representations of women's viability was the fact that they received more horserace coverage than men. In both television news and print news, there was a common finding that female politicians were regularly portrayed on the attack, even exaggerating their aggressive behaviours because of the value that the news places on that which is surprising and dramatic.

Combined with Chapter 1's conclusions about the signs of gender equality in news visibility, the result is clear: when the news does present women in gender stereotypical ways, it is quite visible to the electorate, rendering concern with responsibility and effects natural outcroppings of this insight. These are the subject matter of the remainder of this book. Although it has been tempting for scholars to interpret evidence of gendered patterns of news coverage as being the responsibility of the news and as having largely negative effects on female candidates and office holders, the chapters that follow attempt to grapple with difficult questions about both, and attempt to offer a careful, balanced perspective that suggests neither is universally true.

3

Who Is Responsible?
Explaining Gendered News

Explaining why gendered patterns emerge in the news is a challenging task, but a critical one. The news media constitute an important political institution in their own right, for the media are the primary conduit of political information, and therefore occupy a central place in processes through which public opinion is formed and political decisions are made, both by citizens and politicians. As such, the media are widely thought to have effects that contribute to the political under-representation of women (as well as other marginalized groups), a topic that is examined in the next two chapters. Recognition of the place of the media in modern democracy motivates the search for causes of other seeming distortions in news coverage as well, resulting in a tremendous literature debating the causes of ideological media biases (liberal and conservative), partisan media biases, biases in the coverage of visible minority candidates, and the like. Three factors account for gendered news coverage: culture, the operation of the news business, and politicians' provision of gendered behaviour for coverage, each of which is examined in detail here. The first two are identified as the primary causes by the gendered mediation thesis, and are well developed in the wider literature, but the last factor is virtually absent, not only from the theory, but from the gender, media, and political literature as a whole, for "political scientists generally have not taken account of how candidates' patterns of communication factor into media depictions of men and women" (Fowler and

Lawless 2009, 521). As such, the addition of provision-side considerations to our thinking about the quantity and quality of news coverage of female politicians is an important theoretical innovation.

In analyzing female politicians' participation in their own gendered mediation, there is no claim here that female politicians necessarily seek gendered coverage consciously and are to blame when it happens or when it has negative consequences for their public personas, electability, or political careers. However, neither is it accurate to portray female politicians simply as victims of media bias. Rather, there is a theoretical middle ground that recognizes both processes at work, acknowledging that gendered coverage is instigated sometimes by the media, and at other times by female politicians' own behaviour or political location. After all, the gendered norms that can give rise to the media's selective reporting and gendered framing of female politicians can also steer male and female politicians' own real-life gendered behaviour. Thus, what appears as gendered reportage can actually be fairly accurate reportage of gendered behaviour. For example, former Canadian Prime Minister Kim Campbell publicly joked about her weight, so can we blame the media for drawing attention to her appearance? To what extent can we critique the media for their gendered portrayal of US former Republican vice-presidential candidate Sarah Palin given that she presented a gendered public persona that made constant references to her role as a "hockey mom" and that joked about lipstick as the only thing that differentiates hockey moms from pit bulls? Lots of political women around the world have used gender strategically to bolster their visibility, their public approval, and their electability (e.g., Herrnson, Lay, and Stokes 2003; Kahn 1996; Niven and Zilber 2001a; Shames 2003; Thomas and Adams 2010), and in the context of elections it may make sense for them to do so when such opportunities appear. However, a gendered electoral strategy will produce gendered patterns of news coverage, even without the selective reporting and framing by news outlets.

Media content is always a combination of provision and presentation – of real-world events *provided* for coverage and of how those real-world events are selected, interpreted, and *presented* by newsmakers. News coverage can be gendered at the presentation stage (by the media) or at the provision stage (or both, in cases where gendered real-world behaviour is magnified or distorted at the presentation stage). This chapter has several tasks. Most importantly, however, in accounting for why gendered patterns of coverage of election campaigns exist in television and print news, it culminates in a conceptualization of the provision-presentation distinction,[1] including propositions about when, why, and how female politicians present gendered public personas.

Media Presentation

Gendered mediation theory is rooted in two core premises. First, news media reflect the culture in which they are situated, and from this tenet it is clear that gender schema and other culturally bound gender-role norms will deeply influence how politics is covered in the news. Second, the mechanics of the news media industry, which is dominated by men, reinforce the masculine character of the news. At every stage of the newsmaking process, there are multiple openings for newsmaker influence: selecting what will be presented as news, providing interpretive frames for stories, and packaging stories with graphics and other imagery. These represent just a sampling of the ways that real-world events are filtered in the news process. This process is not inherently undesirable. The myriad ways that reality is filtered by the news are simply a natural function of the facts that, first, condensing the range of daily events in the world is necessary and, second, the news is a human endeavour. The issue at hand is why media present gendered, often distorted, images of female candidates and politicians. Why is this the particular type of filtering we get?

Culture

Starting with the culture portion of the explanation, two insights are critical. First, men and women are portrayed according to culturally accessible gender stereotypes that derive, in part, from deeply rooted gender schemas. This is how the news may come to cover women's appearances and family lives in particular ways, relying on the mother frame, for example, and then implicitly or explicitly sending the message that female politicians face role tension as wives/mothers and as politicians. This is why women are assumed to gravitate towards soft issues and male politicians towards hard issues, a tendency that becomes more prominent in the news coverage of relative newcomers (e.g., Zilber and Niven 2000a). Indeed, low information about candidates increases journalists' reliance on gender stereotypes, which is then reflected in coverage. The influence of culture on news coverage is why male politicians can be implicitly or explicitly criticized in the press when they emote. Self-disclosure of emotion can be interpreted as more natural and acceptable from female politicians than from male politicians because of traditional stereotypes that regard such behaviours as natural or expected of women (e.g., Jamieson 1995). Former US vice-presidential candidate

Edmund Muskie's behaviour during the 1972 Democratic nomination process is an apt illustration of this claim. Early in the campaign, Muskie was the candidate favoured to win the nomination. During the New Hampshire primary, a New Hampshire newspaper published negative remarks about Muskie's wife. Responding to the article's claims, Muskie choked with anger and seemed to cry (Kendall 2000). The press reported that Muskie had "broken down," implying that he was weak and unmanly (e.g., White 1973). Muskie lost the Democratic nomination to South Dakota Senator George McGovern, and the crying incident is widely thought to have fatally damaged Muskie's campaign.[2] In contrast, Hillary Clinton received a boost in public approval after tearing up during the New Hampshire primary for the Democratic nomination in 2008, for it made her appear "softer" and more "human." That said, pundits and media debated at length whether the display was genuine or calculated, playing into stereotypes about women's strategic use of emotion to get what they want:

> When in trouble, girls cry. Although she is despised for being cold and calculated, whenever she breaks down crying, it must be more of the same cold and calculated moves performed in the unending search for power and notoriety. Had she been able to keep her cool, it would be yet another example of her inability to relate to common people. Either way, she loses. (Rossmann 2010, 248)

The news is a reflection, in short, of our gendered society, and thus naturally frames men and women within the boundaries of societal gender stereotypes.

Compounding the effect of gender schemas on how candidates are depicted is the fact that politics has been historically constructed as a male domain and the archetypical politician in the male image. This is another set of culturally bound codes that deeply affect how men and women are covered by the news. Put simply, masculinity sets the standards for political leadership. Attributes characteristically associated with the archetypical politician include strength, independence, autonomy, resolve, and competence (Huddy and Terkildsen 1993a; see also Funk 1997; Kinder et al. 1980; Shanks and Miller 1991; Mondak 1995), all of which are stereotypically male attributes. Huddy and Terkildsen (1993a) find that for a variety of political offices – from a president to a local councillor – a "good" politician is attributed with more masculine than feminine traits. Competence is consistently identified with political success, particularly ascension to political executive posts, and empathy is considered the least crucial attribute for this type of position (Kinder et al. 1980; see also Brown et al. 1988).[3] Examining Clinton Rossiter's (1960) classic list of presidential duties reveals the masculine bent of the position: chief of state, chief executive, chief diplomat, commander-in-chief, chief legislator, chief of the party, voice of the people, protector of the peace, manager of prosperity, and leader of the free world. For women, gender congeniality, the "fit between gender roles and particular leadership roles" (Eagly et al. 1995, 129), is low in the case of most political positions, and decreases the higher up a position is on the political ladder.

The disjuncture between traditional gender stereotypes and the cultural construction of politics as a masculine domain is one reason why women sometimes receive more viability coverage than men do, for their gender group is not historically associated with winning elections and holding public office, so this is a case where news coverage directly responds to culture-based norms that see office holding as more congenial to males, an account that is also consistent with a role incongruity theory of prejudice (e.g., Eagly and Karau 2002). The disjuncture is also partly responsible for women being written out of news stories framed using hyper-masculine imagery and metaphors associated with sports, games, and war. The alternative scenario is one that sees women written in, but accompanied by coverage that exaggerates or makes central to the story their aggressive or ambitious behaviour. Either way, the tension between feminine stereotypes and political role norms causes distortions in coverage – women are eliminated, or coverage encourages skepticism about their fitness for political life, or their counter-stereotypical behaviours become news in themselves because of the news value of drama and surprise.

The Gendered News Business

Structural and economic aspects of the news business buttress the effect of cultural factors described above: the norms and practices that pervade the profession and news organizations' commercial imperatives, as well as their organization and operation. Together, these are important causal factors in explaining gendered news. Sociologists have pointed out that the news is the product of predictable, uniform, routinized processes (e.g., Tuchman 1978; Schudson 1989), challenging the idea that the news is "objective" or "impartial." The sociological perspective on the production of the news is rooted in the sociology of work tradition and, more generally, in organizational or bureaucratic theory. Viewed through this lens, scholars have illuminated how the routines of journalism and the characteristics of news organizations influence news output.

Newswork operates according to a well-known creed or "occupational ideology" (Ericson et al. 1987, 120). Journalism has constituted itself according to norms of objectivity, impartiality, and independence. The profession defines good journalism according to procedural criteria; good journalism depends primarily on *how* news is collected and produced, not on the substantive content of reportage. Arguably, norms of objectivity, impartiality, and independence reflect a male conception of the profession and a decidedly masculine way of approaching news and the people who become news subjects. For example, detachment, impartiality, and the "fetishization of facts and factuality" are common journalistic practices (e.g., van Zoonen 1998). The journalist "assumes the role of a politically neutral adversary" because "journalists see adversarialism as an important counterpoint to becoming too close to their sources" (Bennett 2003, 194). Although it is desirable that journalists maintain professional distance from politicians and other official news sources, the need to project an appearance of politically neutral adversarialism is, arguably, part of the reason news frames focus on games, war, and sports, all of which emphasize conflict and competition. Journalism has pitted reporters against news subjects, particularly when the subjects are politicians. The news is written and spoken in a masculine language that focuses on conflict, drama, and competition, which reflects a masculine preoccupation with winning, according to a variety of scholars (e.g., Covert 1981; van Zoonen 1998).

The political economic structure of the news media industry also reinforces the masculine character of the news. Generally speaking, one of the unique economic aspects of most television media is its indirect financing, for "the product being sold is not programming to viewers but viewer exposures to advertising messages" (Hoskins et al. 2001, 19). Print news outlets, which must maintain both advertising contracts and circulation figures, face very similar pressures. Reliance on advertising revenues forces news outlets to pay close attention to the size and characteristics of their audiences, because news outlets' advertising fees are pegged to the size and makeup of the audience they can deliver to sponsors. It will come as no surprise that advertisers and marketers target their messages to high-income groups (James 2000, 36), so newsmakers must pay attention to their ability to deliver this audience segment to their advertisers. In turn, since the profile of the consumer "cream" is affluent, it is also disproportionately male, white, and older. Keeping ratings high among this segment of the news audience undoubtedly requires a certain approach to news topics and angles – presumably, an approach that avoids confronting the dominant societal assumptions about gender-role norms. Indeed, "no newspaper, magazine, or broadcasting outlet exceeds the boundaries of autonomy acceptable to those who meet the costs that enable them to survive" (Altschull 1997, 260). This is a subtle form of pressure, for companies and advertising executives do not tell newsmakers what stories to select or how to present their stories. Neither do newsmakers tell their reporters to cover a specific story simply to please advertisers. Rather, this form of journalistic control is exercised largely through the self-restraint and self-censorship of newsmakers, and it prefers (rather than explicitly requires) a specific form of news reporting that is quick, uncomplicated, dramatic, and adversarial. In other words, the political economy of the news media produces tendencies towards a particular type of coverage that is geared towards maintaining rather than challenging the status quo. Given conventional stereotypes about men and their interests, newsmakers have likely assumed that male viewers prefer conflictive, controversial, and quick-paced coverage that does little to challenge the notion that politics is a largely male preserve, at least in terms of the traits required to succeed in a political career. Clearly, culture and the operation of the news business interact in important ways, with culture defining important boundaries for profit-driven news organizations that must seek to satisfy advertisers and consumers.

In addition to the masculine ethos that pervades the news and the commercial pressures that contribute to the gendering of coverage, the news is also a decidedly regimented and hierarchical profession that has been and continues to be dominated by men. Most TV news organizations – and certainly all large mainstream outlets – operate according to strict hierarchies where production of the news is controlled tightly at the top and middle levels of the organization. A typical television newsroom is structured with a news director or editor-in-chief at the top, and the person in this role has ultimate authority over the news produced by the station (Schultz 2005).[4] Each news program an outlet offers usually has its own producer, and these producers work closely with the news director in planning news programming. For example, CBC's *The National* has its own producer, as does *Canada Now* and other news programs on the CBC. In turn, each producer is responsible to CBC's news editor-in-chief. In most cases, each program will have some hierarchy of producers including a senior or executive producer followed by one or more assistant producers, and so on.

TABLE 3.1

Status of men (x) and women (✓) in Canadian TV news, July 2011

Position	CBC	CTV	Global
Executive			
President and CEO	x	✓	x
News editor-in-chief	x	x	✓
Exec. producer flagship news program	x	x	x
Chief political correspondent	x	x	x
Anchors			
Morning	✓	✓/x	n/a
Midday	x	x	n/a
Flagship	x	x	✓
Weekend	✓	✓	✓
Bureau chief			
Ottawa	✓	x	x
Washington	x	x	x
London	✓	x	n/a
Beijing	x	x	n/a
Middle East	✓	x	n/a
Moscow	✓	n/a	n/a

After the producers come the assignment editors. An assignment editor is in charge of coordinating news coverage, which primarily means deciding on story assignments for reporters and videographers. According to the CBC website, "on any given day, the assignment editors must select from a blizzard of possibilities: news releases, stories from the news wires, suggestions from reporters and their own knowledge of what's happening on their 'beats.'"[5] The assignment editor decides "who needs to be dispatched to cover a story. Or whether it's worth covering at all."[6] Predictably, men tend to dominate all these influential positions, a manifestation in the news media of Bashevkin's (1993) "the higher the fewer" rule. Looking at the top levels of television and print news in Canada, only one of the three major TV outlets has a female president, only one has a female news editor-in-chief, and none of the three has a female executive producer for its flagship news programs (Table 3.1). In print news, there are no women at the top of five of the most important newspapers in the country, including Canada's two national dailies, the *Globe and Mail* and the *National Post*. All five

TABLE 3.2

Status of men (×) and women (✓) in Canadian print news, July 2011

Position	Calgary Herald	Globe and Mail	National Post	Toronto Star	Vancouver Sun
Publisher	×	×	×	×	×
President	×	×	×	×	×
Editor-in-chief	×	×	×	×	✓
Editor					
Managing	✓	✓	✓	×	✓
Editorial page	✓	×	✓	×	×
Business	×	✓	×	✓	×
Sports	×	×	×	×	×
Entertainment/ arts and life	✓	×	×	×	✓
Travel	✓	✓	n/a	×	n/a
International affairs	n/a	×	×	×	×
Local	×	✓	×	×	✓

papers listed in Table 3.2 have male presidents and publishers, and only one of the five has a female editor-in-chief. However, four of the five dailies have female managing editors, so women are often fourth in command at daily newspapers, and they are obviously successful in obtaining operational leadership positions.

Increasing women's representation in news outlets is often touted as a prescription for gendered coverage (e.g., Chambers, Steiner, and Fleming 2004; Liebler and Smith 1997; Mills 1997). In line with "difference" theorizing (Gilligan 1982), which suggests that women tend to have different issue priorities and unique styles of inter-relation and communication, scholars have argued that more women, and especially more women in positions of power, may result in less masculinist reporting, for a uniquely female way of doing the news – one that is more sensitive to gender issues and the portrayal of political women – may gradually emerge. In its conceptualization of the impact of women on the news system, this argument is very similar to the claim that a critical mass of female legislators alters both the tone of legislative debate and its policy output. Although perhaps intuitively appealing, both of these claims are quite optimistic given the powerful macro forces at work. Indeed, given that culture defines the boundaries of acceptable coverage; that female journalists, like their male counterparts, are socialized into professional norms and practices that contribute to masculinized news; and that all news organizations must attend to the preferences of advertisers and consumers in content decisions, increasing the number of women in the profession is probably not sufficient by itself to instigate widespread change in news coverage. News imbalances or distortions are endemic throughout the system, and women's under-representation in the profession, particularly in powerful positions, is more aptly viewed as a *symptom* or effect of the news media's masculine character than as one of its causes. By extension, this suggests that the remedial effect of increasing women's numbers in the profession, particularly in rank-and-file positions, is limited. The causes of gendered news are too deeply ingrained and complex for staffing reforms to be an effective solution.

Even if some individual female journalists do prioritize different work values or journalistic practices that would produce more gender-balanced coverage – and this is an important assumption – the different factors described so far in this chapter work against them "feminizing" newswork, for "organizations with male-dominated power structures and political climates may promote social interactions in which female employees are expected to act and perform much like their male counterparts, perhaps to avoid exclusion or gain promotion" (Rodgers and Thorson 2003, 662). In general, professions that are dominated by men encourage women to conform rather than confront prevailing workplace norms and routines. This is part of the reason why numerous studies report no sex-of-journalist differences in news coverage (e.g., Chambers, Steiner, and Fleming 2004; Henningham and Delano 1998; Liebler and Smith 1997; Rakow and Kranich 1991; Ross 2001; Weaver and Wilhoit 1996), a pattern that largely characterizes coverage of the 2000 federal election campaign in Canada as well. As Figure 3.1 illustrates, there was no difference between male and female reporters in the political issues that received priority in their stories of the 2000 election campaign. Likewise, there was little difference in male and female reporters' use of news techniques that highlighted the horserace frame (Figure 3.2), such as a focus on leaders over parties and reporting of polls. There was no sex-of-reporter difference in the extent to which politicians' attack-style behaviours are mentioned in news stories (results not shown).

Not only do male and female journalists seem to produce consistently similar coverage, in fact reportage from female journalists can be more

FIGURE 3.1

"Hard" versus "soft" issues, by sex (2000 election campaign).

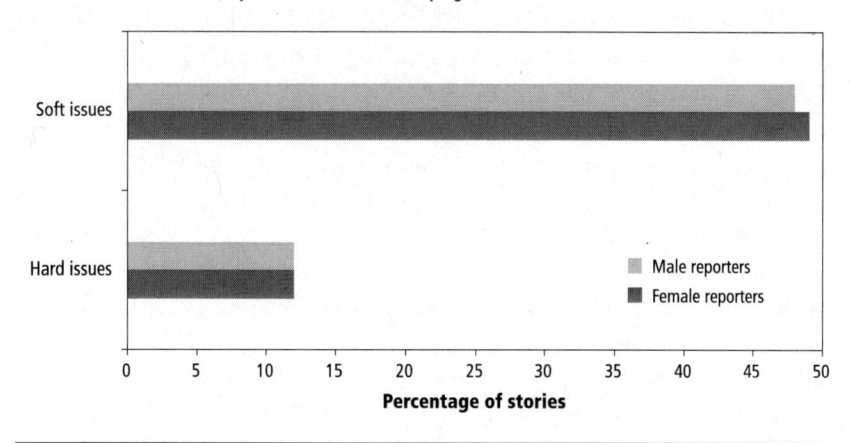

Note: Each group of bars for the division of male- and female-reported stories is derived from tabular analysis. The test of statistical significance used in all analyses is the Pearson's Chi-square.

FIGURE 3.2

Evidence of horserace coverage, by reporter sex (CBC, 2000 federal election coverage).

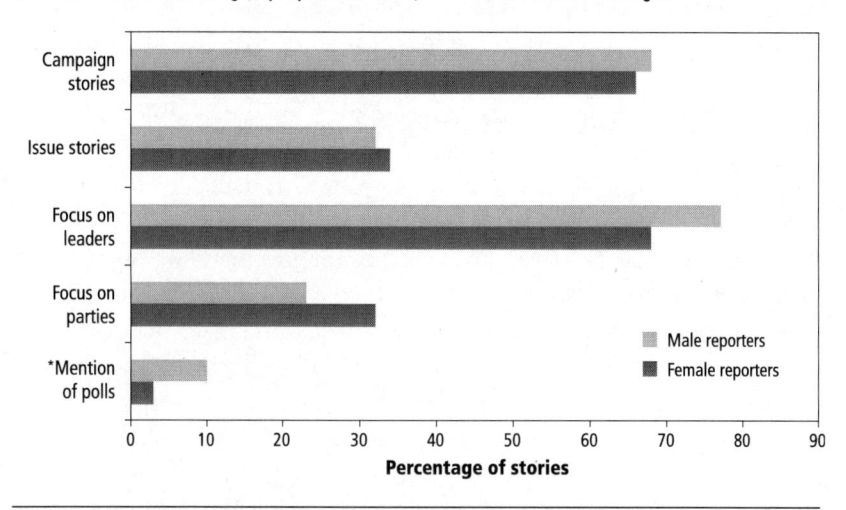

Note: Each group of bars for the division of male- and female-reported stories is derived from tabular analysis. Statistically significant differences between male- and female-reported stories are indicated by an asterisk (*) next to the heading on the vertical axis. The test of statistical significance used in all analyses is the Pearson's Chi-square.

aggressive or negatively charged than that of men. For example, female journalists used more stereotypically masculine imagery than male journalists in covering the televised leaders' debate for the 2000 federal election (Gidengil and Everitt 2003a) and more negatively charged verbs, such as "blasted" and "mocked," to report the entirety of the campaign during the 1993 federal election in Canada (Gidengil and Everitt 2003b). A "hard-hitting" reporting style may be attractive for female journalists, many of whom must feel as though they have to "prove their professional mettle" in this realm that is historically dominated by men (Ross 2002, 108). As will be discussed in the next chapter, women in traditionally masculine workplaces, such as politics, business, and journalism, often confront pressure (either real or perceived) to conform to masculine styles of speech, behaviour, and interaction. This can result in a "damned if you do, damned if you don't" dilemma. In the news realm, women who eschew "hard-nosed" reporting styles may leave the impression that they are not serious journalists. Meanwhile, aggressive female journalists may be viewed as unconventional, hard to get along with, or anomalous. Either way, female journalists are not all that well placed, in the main, to revolutionize the media system.

There is a fundamental problem with the claim that a reporter's sex influences news content, because it focuses on the individual. The problem is the same for other individual-level traits such as journalists' ethnicity or class, for that matter. In many ways, the idea that news biases occur at the individual level, as opposed to the aggregate or systemic level, is incongruent with common wisdom about the news industry. As Craft and Wanta astutely observe, "Much of the newsroom sociology literature suggests that the individual journalist is unlikely to be able to inject much personal perspective into the news – news culture and routines dampen most of the differences in viewpoint or experience workers bring to the newsroom" (2004, 127; see also Reese and Ballinger 2001).

Strictly speaking, the sociology of newswork argument does not deny that a journalist's gender *could* influence how and what she reports; rather, the sociology of newswork argument holds that there are relatively few openings for gender to exert its potential impact. The structure and operation of news outlets, the financial imperatives of the media environment, and the culture and practice of journalism tend to subdue individual-level influences on the news such as a journalist's gender, ethnicity, or ideology. In other words, the idea is that there can be tensions between the individual- and the system-level influences on the news, and in most cases, the system-level influences will prevail.

Clearly, newsmakers and the news system more broadly play a fundamental role in the creation and dissemination of gendered news coverage of female politicians. We know that the news plays a role, and the processes through which gendered mediation occurs are well theorized in the literature. The news reflects a gendered culture and, as a profession, the news is controlled and defined by men and masculine conceptions of politics. The political economic structure of the news and the sociology of newswork reinforce the status quo and create disincentives for presenting more balanced, less gendered portrayals of political women. Yet, this is only part of the story. Gendered news is not universally attributable to the news media, and such claims can produce only a partial understanding of how the news comes to depict male and female politicians differently. A comprehensive explanation must also incorporate the differences in the behaviours of male and female politicians in real life, for these, too, result, naturally, in differences in coverage.

Politician Provision

This brings us to provision. Media content at any given time is a combination of provision and presentation. Provision is what the politicians provide in terms of the substance of speech, the manner of speech and behaviour, and the staging of the event that is being covered. Some individuals speak more articulately or have more publicly appealing mannerisms, for example, and this quite naturally makes for better news coverage, irrespective of how newsmakers edit and package news stories. A politician who has the ability to state an issue position in an articulate or clever way likely gets more sound bites in the news than her comparatively less articulate colleagues, because it is easier for newsmakers to extract good sound bites from footage. The point is that how a politician acts and speaks, as well as what a politician says to journalists, influence the resultant coverage she receives. All politicians bear some individual responsibility for the quantity and quality of their news coverage. This should be regarded as a positive aspect of the politician-journalist relationship, because it suggests that politicians have some control over how they are covered in the news. By the same token, it follows that politicians are sometimes responsible for gendered coverage. These observations do not mean that politicians exercise unfettered agency over the presentation of their own behaviour to the public and to news outlets. Gender can never be absent; politicians cannot choose to present ungendered representations of themselves to audiences and newsmakers, and this complicates thinking about agency in gendered provision of news. In addition to the impossibility of eliminating gender, there are a host of scenarios in which politicians may be put into gendered positions or roles by other political actors – for the purposes of campaigns or as a result of ministerial appointments, for example – further diminishing personal agency over the provision of their own behaviour, a point that is taken up in greater detail later in this chapter. In the end, however, all real-world behaviours that occur prior to news coverage of them are provision. Whether agentic on the part of a politician or not, behaviours are what is available for newsmakers to use as coverage, and the principal point for this section is that gendering of female politicians often occurs at the provision stage independently of what occurs at the presentation stage.

News content is a combination of provision and presentation, and this complicates the study of political communications. In the context of news coverage of female politicians, it is difficult to gauge the extent to which differences in men's and women's news coverage accurately reflect reality. Measuring gender differences in news coverage of men and women is relatively straightforward; yet, we cannot determine with absolute certainty which portion of gender differences in coverage is due simply to real-world differences in men's and women's behaviours and which portion of the observed male-female differences is attributable to the way that the news media report stories. This line of thought is seldom explored in analyses of women, media, and politics. A sizeable portion of the published work assumes that gendered news coverage of politicians is attributable to the media. Although failure to engage appropriately with this assumption is a weakness in the literature, there are notable exceptions. For instance, Gidengil and Everitt's work (1999, 2000, 2003a, 2003b) systematically compares politicians' behaviours in leaders' debates with post-debate coverage, a relatively rare example of a research design that permits comparison of provision and presentation. Their evidence is quite compelling that the media exaggerate female leaders' aggressive behaviours in post-debate coverage.

There are at least three scenarios, each amply documented in various literatures, in which the behaviours of female politicians are gendered at the provision stage, prior to and independently of media presentation. These cases of gendered provision occur as a result of (1) the fact that we are all gendered beings, (2) the strategic use of gendered speech or behaviours by candidates, and/or (3) the gendered division of political labour. Each is presented below as distinct, although they overlap in various ways, most obviously in the fact that culture plays a role in all three scenarios, particularly as it manifests itself in pressure to conform to gender stereotypes.

Gendered Beings

The first type of gendered provision results from the fact that we are all gendered beings, a fact that is commonly reflected in our actions, attitudes, and traits. Stated plainly, we know that men and women tend to have different behaviours or outlooks on certain matters. The large and well-developed literature on gender gaps in attitudes and behaviours is one example, for it shows the persistent differences in men's and women's political issue positions and issue priorities. Although there is variation in the size of the gap over time, over the past three decades or so, women have tended to veer to the left of men on social and economic issues (e.g., DeVaus and McAllister 1989; Everitt 1998, 2002; Gidengil 1995; Gidengil et al. 2003; Gilens 1988; Mueller 1986; Norris 1988; Inglehart and Norris 2003; O'Neill 2002; Shaffner 2005; Shapiro and Mahajan 1986). Women tend to be more supportive of social spending and an activist welfare state and, conversely, less optimistic about market economics, deregulation, and free trade (e.g., Erie and Rein 1988; Gidengil 1995; Gidengil et al. 2003; Shapiro and Mahajan 1986), a pattern that Gidengil (1995) captures well in her analysis of how "social woman" and "economic man" responded to the options presented to Canadian voters during the 1988 free trade election.

To be clear, these are generalizations. There are many right-wing women and many left-wing men in every electorate, and cross-pressures exert an important influence on behaviours and public opinion on every possible dimension. Gender is not the only or even necessarily the most salient political characteristic for most voters. The extent to which gender structures political attitudes or behaviours fluctuates across time and space, variations that can be explained, in part, by differences in political environments, particularly the availability of cues that prompt gender-based thinking or action. Work on the 1992 "Year of the Woman" election – which saw an unexpectedly large cohort of women elected to the US Senate – often attributes the women's electoral success, in part, to a fertile environment that had sensitized the electorate to the vital gender issues of the day: the highly publicized Hill-Thomas hearings highlighted the sexual harassment many American women continued to face (e.g., Dolan 1998; Paolino 1995); abortion issues had once again re-emerged at the US Supreme Court; and a spirited public debate had materialized around the Family and Medical Leave Act (Dolan 1998), a statute drafted by the National Partnership for Women and Families that required employers to provide twelve weeks of paid leave for employees because of new parenthood, illness, or care for someone with an illness. Cue taking was also an important part of Gidengil's

(1995) account of the gender gap in differences on the issue of Canada-US free trade. In such cases, not only may gender-based thinking be cued within the electorate – leading voters to choose women in greater numbers or reject the free trade deal – but a gendered electoral environment may encourage female candidates to strategically use gender-based appeals, by campaigning "as women," for example, a possibility that relates to the next scenario in which gendered provision can occur.

Gender gaps in public opinion exist in domains other than social policy and government intervention. Gender differences in attitudes towards military force "are some of the largest and most consistent in the study of political psychology" (Sapiro and Conover 1993, 1095). Women tend to be less "hawkish" than men on war and defence. Women tend to be less supportive of the use of military force, in general, and this has been true from the Second World War to the Vietnam War to the Gulf War (e.g., Clark and Clark 1993; Eichenberg 2003, 2005; Sapiro and Conover 1993; Shapiro and Mahajan 1986; Smith 1984; Wilcox, Hewitt, and Allsop 1996). Some studies find that gender is the single largest predictor of attitudes towards military intervention (e.g., Wilcox, Hewitt, and Allsop 1996). In terms of the principal objectives of military action, when survey questions present military force as a means of alleviating humanitarian crises, gender gaps tend to decrease, because women's support increases (Eichenberg 2003). When survey questions mention casualties, gender gaps tend to widen, because women's support for military force declines. Women are also less supportive of increased defence spending and nuclear weapons development (Sapiro and Conover 1993; Eichenberg 2003, 2005), a finding that may be related to their greater support for spending on social policy.

Beyond gender gaps in issue positions and issue priorities, convincing evidence exists that men and women tend towards different modes of inter-relation and moral reasoning (e.g., Gilligan 1982; Noddings 1984). Women tend to gravitate more than men to intersubjective reasoning (an ethic of care), while men tend to focus on rules, hierarchy, and justice (an ethic of justice). This finding tends to be explained by gender differences in socialization experiences – the field's most famous thinker, Carol Gilligan, is a developmental psychologist – not as a result of natural or innate differences in men and women. Moreover, the literature is clear that these are tendencies or patterns. Women are not unconcerned with competition, justice, or individual rights, just as men are not uncaring; the point is that each gender group tends to rely disproportionately on one of these lenses over the other. Differences in fundamental values, in fact, are part of the reason why gender gaps in public opinion emerge, although other factors are important too, such as women's greater economic vulnerability and the effects of gender consciousness.

Like attitudes and opinion, there are often important differences in men's and women's political behaviours, as well. These include differences that can emerge in men's and women's campaign styles and legislative behaviours, both of which speak directly to the provision side of news coverage of politicians. As candidates, we know that women sometimes self-present differently than their male colleagues do, although it is important to remember, again, that this is a generalization that cannot be extended to all women and to all political contexts. Indeed, much of the time, male and female candidates emphasize the same types of issues and traits in their campaigns, a trend that seems to be on the increase (e.g., Bystrom et al. 2004; Dolan 2005; Sapiro et al. 2011). When there are differences, one of the more frequent patterns sees women campaigning "as women" by highlighting their stereotypically feminine traits and/or issue competencies (e.g., Kahn 1996; Shames 2003; Herrnson, Lay, and Stokes 2003; Niven and Zilber 2001a), even if partisanship and incumbency are larger influences on campaign style and content (e.g., Mueller 2008).

Once elected, gender differences in politicians' speech and behaviour can carry over into legislative work. In some contexts, female legislators tend to adopt more cooperative, rather than competitive, legislative styles (e.g., Kathlene 1994; Thomas 1991, 1994; Thomas and Welch 1991), a finding that is echoed in studies on management and organizational behaviour (e.g., Eagly and Johnson 1990). The claim that women tend to exhibit legislative styles different from those of their male colleagues is bolstered by the fact that this gender difference has been found across levels of office holding from national to state/provincial (e.g., Trimble 2000) to municipal politics (e.g., Weikart et al. 2006), as well as in different countries and regions (e.g., Childs 2008; Schwindt-Bayer 2006). As legislators, there is also evidence that women are more likely than men to prioritize so-called soft issues such as health care, education, social welfare, and especially women's issues (e.g., Bratton 2005; Niven and Zilber 2001a; Schwindt-Bayer 2006) and that they also tend to hold more liberal welfare policy preferences than their male counterparts hold (e.g., Poggione 2004; Thomas and Welch 2001), findings that echo patterns of public opinion.

The point is that we know men and women sometimes think, speak, and act differently – whether for reasons connected to biology, socialization, or both, an argument that is not necessary to resolve in this book. A branch of work on gender and political representation anchors arguments for equity in legislative representation to the idea that women have unique policy concerns, positions, and life experiences that are best represented by other women. Literature on the critical mass concept and some work on quotas make complementary claims about the different experiences, skills, and representational considerations female office holders bring to the job. All these arguments rely heavily on claims for the existence of a set of politically relevant traits, attitudes, issue priorities, issue positions, and experiences that are shared by members of one gender group and not shared by members of the other gender group. Arguments are made in favour of increasing women's presence in legislatures and institutions based on the claim that women are different in politically relevant ways.

Following this same logic, we need to take seriously the idea that men and women are reported differently in the news, in part, because they behave differently in politics. This is not to say that gender differences in coverage are fully accounted for by male-female differences in behaviours, but that some *portion* of gendered coverage must be due to real-world male-female differences. Indeed, it is hardly surprising that the news tends to present female politicians as more compassionate, other-oriented, or liberal given what we know about some of the gendered patterns of women's behaviour as candidates and legislators compared with their male counterparts. This is a fact we should be quick to recognize in collective efforts to understand, explain, and predict patterns of news coverage.

Strategic Use of Gendered Behaviours
A second form of gendered provision occurs when female candidates and politicians *strategically* present themselves to voters and newsmakers using gendered traits and/or behaviours. The difference between this form of gendered provision and the first form is that the first form is conceptualized here as more "genuine" or "unaffected," in the sense that the provision of gendered behaviours is not employed as a means to an electoral or political goal. In contrast, this second form of gendered provision *is* instrumental; it is undertaken as part of a strategy to gain electoral advantage, to capitalize on an opportunity. Gender stereotypes thoroughly pervade electoral politics, and not just in news coverage, but as a force guiding how voters, parties, and the media think about male and female candidates, a point emphasized in the earlier discussion of the impact of culture on news coverage. Given an electoral environment infused with gender dynamics, female candidates are often presented with two choices: they can work to

"dispel stereotypes" or they "may adopt strategies that exploit voters' stereotypes" (Kahn 1993, 483).

Using stereotypes to their advantage by presenting gendered personas to the public may be particularly attractive when the political climate favours stereotypically feminine traits, issues, or behaviours – such as the US Senate races in the 1992 "Year of the Woman" – and when the context is right, this strategy can benefit female office seekers (e.g., Herrnson et al. 2003). Consider electoral climates where governance and political corruption are important campaign issues – as was the case in Canada in the campaigns for the 2004 and 2006 federal elections as a result of the Sponsorship Scandal. Female politicians are often perceived by voters and newsmakers as less likely to engage in political corruption than their male counterparts (e.g., Burrell 1994), and this "fairer sex" stereotype can be electorally useful when strategically cued or invoked by female politicians themselves. Female candidates may benefit from strategic self-presentation "as women" in order to capitalize on stereotypes that depict women as a group as altruistic, trustworthy, ethical, and other-oriented (e.g., Eagly and Crowley 1986; Huddy and Terkildsen 1993b).

In other contexts, female politicians sometimes strategically draw attention to their status as "outsiders" (e.g., Gulati 2004; Shames 2003), which may be particularly effective if the public is in an anti-incumbent mood. Examples of the above are apparent in Michelle Bachelet's and Ellen Johnson Sirleaf's successful bids in 2005-06 for the presidencies of Chile and Liberia, respectively. Both women confronted important barriers as women, but they also seized opportunities to use gender to their advantage on the campaign trail (Thomas and Adams 2010). In Chile, Bachelet argued that she would be able to strengthen democracy through her inclusive and cooperative leadership style, which she attributed, in part, to her experience as a woman. Similarly, Liberia's Johnson-Sirleaf regularly said that being a woman meant that she was better able than her male campaign rival to combat corruption and promote a peaceful transition out of the civil strife that had plagued her country for decades. Both women campaigned "as women" by highlighting stereotypically feminine traits and issue priorities.

In other contexts, women may benefit from highlighting their relative novelty in the political sphere. For example, in my own experience interviewing Canadian members of Parliament on the topic of their media coverage (see Goodyear-Grant 2009), sentiments like this were expressed by a couple of the twenty-seven interviewees. One Liberal female politician noted (with what might be called a slightly tongue-in-cheek tone) that she had greatly benefited from "all the fuss" about women in politics. This interviewee was not a cabinet member, nor prominent in the party or the legislature. Through the course of our conversation, it became clear that she thought she would have received less media coverage if she had been a similarly unexceptional male MP. The word "unexceptional" here is not meant to be understood in a derogatory or evaluative sense, but to highlight the fact that objectively, and by her own description, this interviewee was relatively junior and had not occupied any elevated role in the party or the legislature beyond that of rank-and-file backbencher. Obviously, that she was an MP and, thus, a member of the political elite, made her exceptional by most standards. The overarching point here is that female politicians' approaches to the media are multifaceted in that they have identified potential pay-offs from the way that the public and the news media focus on them as gendered individuals, a point that van Zoonen (2006, 289) makes as well when she identifies the "opportunities that the personalization of political culture produce for female politicians" (see also van Zoonen 1998, 2000a, 2000b, 2005).

In cases where enhanced visibility is a function of "difference," it may be rational for politicians to view this as advantageous, because candidates commonly prefer more coverage than less coverage given that their careers depend on re-election. In fact, because visibility is a fundamental objective of politicians, it is not difficult to imagine scenarios where female politicians might decide to strategically draw attention to their gender in order to gain coverage. It is important to keep in mind that the primary goal of many female politicians, like their male colleagues, is re-election, not revolutionizing the political system, let alone the media industry. Put differently, it is important to interpret politicians' actions and attitudes in light of their chosen priorities and goals. Although many of the Canadian MPs that I interviewed expressed serious dissatisfaction with gendered and racialized coverage, the issue is complex, for there are benefits to being different in a news environment that rewards the anomalous and the surprising with greater attention.

Gendered Division of Political Labour
A third form of gendered provision occurs as a result of the gendered division of labour that exists in many legislatures and governments, where policy "pink-collar ghettos" have been common since women entered formal politics. The appointment of women to cabinet positions, for example, tends to be disproportionately to low-power, low-prestige portfolios, often

FIGURE 3.3

Percentage of female candidates and MPs, by election year and political party

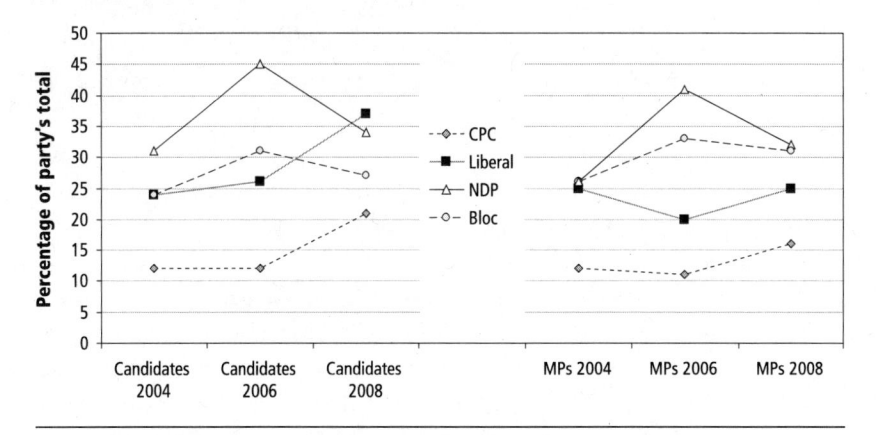

in "feminine" ministries such as health, education, and culture. This pattern holds for a variety of political appointments from legislative committee assignments to cabinet appointments (e.g., Bashevkin 1993; Bittner and Goodyear-Grant 2013; Childs 2008; Davis 1997; Escobar-Lemmon and Taylor-Robinson 2005; Goodyear-Grant 2013; Heath, Schwindt-Bayer, and Taylor-Robinson 2005; Krook and O'Brien 2010; Moon and Fountain 1997; Reynolds 1999; Studlar and Moncrief 1999), although some of these authors note an upward trend in women's success at "cracking the inner circle" over time (e.g., Escobar-Lemmon and Taylor-Robinson 2005, 838). Across Canada, the United States, Western Europe, and Australia, female politicians have been disproportionately located in "feminine" policy spheres, which gives rise to the provision of gendered information about female candidates and politicians to newsmakers and the public. When women are disproportionately located in soft policy arenas in government, whether by their own choices or as a result of political appointment, they are linked with stereotypically feminine issues and traits, such as compassion and warmth, which is then reflected in the coverage they receive in the news.

Gendered patterns in cabinet appointments, candidacies, and the like characterize politics at all levels in the Canadian setting, leading to substantial potential for gendered provision of information about women's issue expertise and political traits to both the media and to the public. As Figure 3.3 demonstrates, the left-wing NDP was more likely to nominate female candidates than Canada's party of the right, the Conservative party, from

2004 to 2008, and as a result was also more likely to elect female MPs, a pattern that characterizes the distribution of women's candidacies across time and space in Canada, with few exceptions. Female candidates, therefore, are strongly associated with political parties that focus on social policy and other stereotypically feminine policy fields, while fewer women are associated with political parties that focus on fiscal issues and other stereotypically masculine policy fields. This is not to say that the NDP does not focus on fiscal issues or the CPC on social issues; rather, the point is that voters form stereotypes about political parties regarding their policy positions and the traits that their candidates tend to demonstrate (e.g., Rahn 1993; Hayes 2011). Work on issue ownership demonstrates that political parties actually claim specific policy fields as "theirs," and these party-issue associations tend to be enduring in the minds of citizens once established (e.g., Ansolabehere and Iyengar 1994; Bélanger 2003). The Canadian national political party associated with masculine policy fields simply tends to have fewer female candidates and MPs.

Once in government, a similar pattern persists regarding cabinet appointments. Following the 2006 federal election, for example, Conservative Prime Minister Stephen Harper appointed only six women to his twenty-seven-member cabinet, and none of these were in the prestigious, stereotypically masculine positions of finance, defence, or foreign affairs. Rather, women presided over the following portfolios: environment (Rona Ambrose), human resources and skills (Diane Finley), social development (Diane Finley), Canadian heritage (Bev Oda), status of women (Bev Oda), national revenue (Carol Skelton), international cooperation (Josée Verner), and La Francophonie (Josée Verner). Over the course of the Conservative party's first term in office, the number of women in cabinet declined to five at one point, and two of these women (Diane Ablonczy and Helena Guergis, both of whom joined the ministry in 2007) were in less important secretary-of-state roles. Part of the problem facing Harper was that he had a small group of female MPs from which to select cabinet members in 2006, a situation directly related to the fact that the party elected the fewest female MPs among the major national parties. Harper appointed a larger proportion of women to cabinet following the 2008 election – in fact, numerically, this was the most gender-equitable federal cabinet in Canada to date, being 29 percent women. However, portfolios were still assigned according to the typical gender pattern (see also Goodyear-Grant 2013). Like the partisan distribution of women's candidacies, the assignment of cabinet portfolios creates conditions in which political women come to publicly represent stereotypically feminine issues more than men do, who are more evenly distributed across parties and political assignments. This results in gendered provision of political information not only about women's issue priorities, but also their traits and political competencies, to the media and to the public.

Compared with the previous two forms of gendered provision, this third form is distinguished by the fact that women are often *assigned* to gendered roles *by other political actors*. This is not to say that the other two forms of gendered provision (gendered beings and gender strategy) can necessarily be viewed as the result of female politicians' genuinely free choices, to be contrasted with the effects of political appointment. Indeed, women may project gendered personas or even strategically use gendered behaviours for electoral advantage because of the paucity of other options for self-presentation. Female politicians may gravitate towards "soft" issues or the presentation of gendered traits because this is what is stereotypically expected of female politicians or because they fear negative press if they adopt stereotypically masculine traits and behaviours, which can result in coverage that uses the iron maiden frame. Remember, gendered mediation theory tells us that counter-stereotypical behaviours on the part of female politicians can be magnified and distorted at the presentation stage by the media. This may result in coverage suggesting that women who behave as assertively as their male colleagues, for example, are overly aggressive. In the case of former federal Liberal cabinet minister Sheila Copps, her assertiveness time and again resulted in media coverage that suggested she was "loud," "shrill," and sometimes downright "bitchy" (Copps 1986, 2004). Therefore, female politicians may present gendered personas to the public and to newsmakers as a result of self-censorship of their behaviours in order to avoid negative press. Although the gendering of the behaviours occurs at the provision stage, it is apprehension about the presentation stage that largely motivates the original behaviours. It is fear of how the news media and the public will perceive them that pushes female candidates towards the projection of conventionally feminine personas.

To complicate the agency or choice issue further, the gendered division of political labour can be the result of female politicians' own choices, not political appointment. Sometimes, female cabinet members, for example, are located in soft portfolios because they specialize in this policy arena and have themselves chosen to focus their legislative work on a soft policy field such as health or education, so it is not always a matter of women being shunted into soft policy fields by others. By the same token, this "choice" may be motivated by pressure to conform to gender stereotypes, or out of apprehension that their expertise will be undervalued in "harder" policy fields. Obviously, it will sometimes be challenging to differentiate, both conceptually and empirically, between (1) women genuinely choosing to adopt gendered political personas, (2) women ostensibly choosing to project gendered personas, but mostly as a result of pressure to conform to gender norms, and (3) women being assigned to gendered roles by other political actors and having gendered personas projected on them as a result. These three represent a gradient of choice or agency, from most to least autonomous.

The Provision-Presentation Distinction Applied

Looking back to the previous chapter's analysis of party leaders' issue coverage in the 2000 federal election campaign, provision on the campaign trail is important to explaining the seeming gender difference in this indicator of gendered news coverage (Table 2.7). McDonough garnered the highest proportion of soft-issue coverage, and by a large margin; she also trailed by about the same margin in hard-issue coverage, a pattern that reflects traditional gender stereotypes. The pattern also reflects ideological stereotypes of left and right parties – McDonough led the left-most national party in that campaign – as well as party leaders' own real-life behaviours, for the NDP released the largest proportion of press releases about health care and the second largest about social issues generally (Blais et al. 2002a, 27, Figure 1.2). A closer look at the press release data set reveals that the NDP distributed no press releases on job creation, the debt or deficit, crime, or national defence, all important issues in the "hard issue" category (results not shown). Based on the distribution of press releases focused on hard versus soft issues,[7] the NDP leader did not warrant a higher proportion of hard-issue coverage than she received, because this simply was not what she spent the campaign talking about (Table 3.3). Seventy-eight percent of the NDP's releases focused on soft issues. By comparison, the balance between soft and hard issues in the other parties' press releases was more even. For none of the other parties did soft issues comprise even half of the parties' press release topics, although the Liberal and Alliance came close to half (48 percent and 45 percent soft-issue press releases, respectively). In short, McDonough's high proportion of soft-issue coverage in television news coverage compared with that of the male leaders seems to be largely the

TABLE 3.3
Issues addressed in political parties' press releases, 2000 election campaign

Type of issues	Liberal n	(%)	Alliance n	(%)	PC n	(%)	NDP n	(%)	BQ n	(%)
Soft	33	(48)	25	(45)	8	(30)	25	(78)	19	(30)
Hard	24	(35)	23	(41)	8	(30)	6	(19)	26	(40)
No main/uncodeable	12	(17)	8	(14)	11	(40)	1	(3)	19	(30)
Total	69	(100)	56	(100)	27	(100)	32	(100)	64	(100)

Note: Chi^2 = 30.71; df = 8; p = .00; Cramer's V = 0.25

result of gendered (and ideological) provision caused by the parties' different issue agendas in the actual campaign.

That McDonough led a party of the left and was, therefore, associated more heavily with soft rather than hard issues is not necessarily a manifestation of the "gendered beings" account of gendered provision, although this should not be ruled out, for gender gaps in public opinion on a wide variety of issue dimensions provide a reasonable explanation, at least in part, for the fact that political women tend to be more numerous in left-wing rather than right-wing parties. However, the "gendered division of labour" variant, discussed below, may be an equally compelling account of why women tend to be disproportionately located in parties like the NDP, which has been less electorally competitive at the federal level, historically, than its rivals. Bashevkin argues that we must take into account the condition of the political parties that women lead, and these tend to fall disproportionately into two categories: "wilderness parties that had long been far from power" or once-competitive parties that "had reached a critical condition – and had entered ... an irreversible slide – some time before female leaders ever got the keys to the corner office" (2009, 44). In the Canadian context, this pattern results in gendered provision of political women's behaviours given that the NDP, a party of the centre-left that focuses on soft issues more than the others, has been the long-standing third party at the national level.

Looking at the print news of the 2005-06 campaign, the party-based explanation for differences in men's and women's issue coverage provides little traction in uncovering any potential provision of gendered information for news coverage. As noted in the previous chapter, female challengers, but not female incumbents, in the 2006 race were associated in news coverage with

TABLE 3.4

Male and female challengers by political party, 2006 election campaign

	Men		Women	
	n	(%)	n	(%)
Liberal	137	(26)	50	(26)
Conservative	190	(36)	26	(14)
NDP	185	(35)	103	(55)
BQ	15	(3)	10	(5)
Total	527	(100)	189	(100)

Note: Chi^2 = 38.32; df = 3; p = .00; Cramer's V = 0.23

soft issues more and hard issues less than their male counterparts were (Table 2.16). Intuitively, observers may be quick to point out that this pattern may be attributable to the fact that female challengers were far more likely to run for the NDP and far less likely to run for the Conservatives than were male challengers (Table 3.4); 55 percent of female challengers ran for the NDP compared with 35 percent of male challengers, and only 14 percent of female challengers ran under the Conservative banner compared with 36 percent of male challengers, differences of 20 percent or more in both cases. Comparing incumbents, in contrast, there were no statistically significant differences in the partisan distributions of male and female candidates (Table 3.5). The natural conclusion may be that female challengers are portrayed alongside soft issues more than male challengers because of this gender gap in the distribution of challenger candidates across parties. However, this is not the case. Even *among* NDP challengers, the gender gap in issue coverage persists (results not shown). This does not mean that the gendered-beings explanation or strategic deployment of gender on the campaign trail are not possible explanations for this finding, for male and female NDP candidates may have different issue priorities, a question these data cannot settle. Rather, it does tell us that party effects are not masquerading for gender effects here, and that party is not the reason for any possible gendered provision. In the end, it may be that these results are a function of gendered presentation on the part of the press rather than gendered provision, a finding that would be consistent with work on news coverage of inexperienced candidates about whom the press has little prior information.

TABLE 3.5

Male and female incumbents by political party, 2006 election campaign

	Men		Women	
	n	(%)	n	(%)
Liberal	91	(41)	27	(49)
Conservative	78	(36)	11	(20)
NDP	13	(6)	4	(7)
BQ	37	(17)	13	(24)
Total	219	(100)	55	(100)

Note: Chi^2 = 5.10; df = 3; p = .16

Even women who run for parties of the right – which emphasize hard issues more, and which are stereotypically associated with these issues to a greater extent – can end up with high volumes of soft-issue coverage by virtue of becoming spokespersons for those issues. For example, the fact that Rona Ambrose, a Conservative incumbent in the 2006 race, was associated heavily with child care in coverage of the campaign[8] is largely because she was involved in the formulation of the party's child care policy and became the policy's chief spokesperson during the campaign, and because she was the party's social development critic at that time. In other words, provision, not the news media's presentation, accounts for the link. This sort of scenario may reflect the genuine policy interests of female candidates, or it may be the result of parties' strategic use of female candidates and MPs to pitch soft policy issues to the electorate, or it may reflect a situation in parties where opportunities for women – whether involvement in policy formulation or appointments to cabinet – are structured in some ways according to traditional notions of men's and women's policy strengths. Such intra-party dynamics pose challenges for uncovering provision of gendered information to news media.

Provision explains some patterns; however, for other aspects of gendered news coverage presented in Chapter 2, gendering does not seem to occur at the provision stage. Evidence points, instead, to media presentation. The prevalence of attack-style coverage in female candidates' news coverage compared with their male counterparts is one such example. Television coverage of McDonough and the male leaders in the 2000 race illustrates the claim. Previous work has made the case that McDonough's attack-style behaviour

TABLE 3.6

Attacks in parties' press releases, 2000 election campaign

Attack	Liberal n	(%)	Alliance n	(%)	PC n	(%)	NDP n	(%)	BQ n	(%)
Yes	45	(65)	50	(89)	23	(85)	28	(87)	48	(75)
No	24	(35)	6	(11)	4	(15)	4	(13)	16	(25)
Total	69	(100)	56	(100)	27	(100)	32	(100)	64	(100)

Note: Chi^2 = 13.65; df = 4; p = .01; Cramer's V = 0.23

in leaders' debates was exaggerated in post-debate coverage (Gidengil and Everitt 2003a), a pattern also identified in post-debate coverage of Kim Campbell and Audrey McLaughlin (ibid.). Gidengil and Everitt's analysis of the 1997 and 2000 English-language leaders' debates reveals that McDonough was actually less aggressive in the debates than were her male rivals, but the news portrayed her as more aggressive than the male leaders. For the 1997 debate, "there was not a single indicator of confrontational behaviour on which McDonough ranked first or even second," and the authors contend that McDonough switched to an even more "low-key style of debating" in 2000 (566). In other words, McDonough's level of aggressive debate behaviour, which was relatively low to begin with, was even lower in the 2000 leaders' debate compared with earlier campaigns.

Examining the parties' press releases during the 2000 campaign provides another indicator of the incongruence between actual and mediated attack-style behaviours. The CES press release data set codes whether parties' press releases contained an attack on another party or leader (Table 3.6). Naturally, this is not a direct indicator of leaders' behaviours, for press releases are party communications; however, leaders personify parties for the electorate in the Canadian system generally, and they are the central figures in the parties' campaign strategies. Looking at the distribution of attack-style communications from political parties, several important patterns emerge. Most press releases contain attacks, and these tend to be personalized attacks directed at a rival party leader (Blais et al. 2002a). Critically, the NDP had a lot of attack-style press releases (87 percent) in 2000, but the proportion of attacks in its releases was virtually identical to the other challenger parties, particularly the Alliance (89 percent) and Conservatives (85 percent). This indicator of real-world behaviours is inconsistent with news coverage of the leaders' aggressivity, for McDonough's coverage contained a far higher proportion of attack-style behaviours than coverage of Clark and Day (Figure 2.1). Like Gidengil and Everitt's analysis of McDonough's debate behaviour, this points to gendering at the presentation stage. Compared with the male leaders, McDonough's attack-style behaviours are far more prominent in her news coverage than in her party's press releases. In contrast, something that was accurately portrayed in the news was the difference between Chrétien and his rivals in terms of the proportion of attacks each party made. A far lower proportion of Liberal press releases attacked compared with those of other parties, and this is reflected in the fact that Chrétien had the lowest proportion of attack-style coverage among the leaders. On the offensive, the challengers launched more attacks than the incumbent, and this was reflected in news coverage.

Naturally, that candidates present gendered personas to the media and the public also means that some may be motivated to consciously avoid the presentation of gendered personas through self-regulatory behaviours. Indeed, if women strategically present gendered personas at some times, it holds that they strategically avoid gendered provision at other points. This is discussed in greater detail in Chapter 5, which presents politicians' own reflections on their experiences with media coverage, with journalists, and with the challenges of obtaining beneficial coverage. A good illustration of self-regulation for the avoidance of gendered coverage is female politicians who shield their personal lives from media scrutiny. This may discourage news coverage from focusing on them as wives and mothers, as divorced women with failed marriages – which is often presented so negatively, like hard evidence of instability – or as public officials whose attention and time will be divided between personal, domestic responsibilities and public service. Another example of provision that attempts to minimize gendered coverage is when female candidates emphasize their political identities first, and then their gender identities secondarily. In the 2008 US presidential election, for example, both Hillary Clinton and Sarah Palin made reference to themselves as "candidates who happen to be women," not as "women candidates," although "both clung to stereotypical portrayals of women when it appeared to suit their needs" (Carlin and Winfrey 2009, 327).

Discussion and Conclusion

Explaining and attributing responsibility for patterns of gendered coverage is highly challenging, although it is clear that newsmakers are not solely responsible for the gendered reportage of female politicians. What is difficult is sorting through the details of when, where, and under what conditions gendered provision and gendered presentation occur. Gendered provision can occur in at least three scenarios: (1) when female politicians speak or behave differently as a result of genuine gender gaps in politicians' issue positions, issue priorities, traits, or behaviours; (2) when female politicians speak or behave differently as a result of presenting *strategically* gendered personas; and (3) when the gendered division of labour in legislatures and governments means that female politicians are disproportionately in positions of acting as spokespersons for soft policy fields. As a result, when we see gendered reportage of female candidates and politicians in news coverage, we must endeavour to investigate whether the gendered coverage is the result of provision or of presentation. Indeed, as the chapter has illustrated, there is always a possibility that what appears as gendered reportage can actually be accurate reportage of gendered behaviours.

The question that naturally arises at the end of this chapter is this: How can the provision-presentation distinction be useful for individual researchers and the gender, media, and politics research agenda as a whole? First, and most importantly, attention to the provision-presentation distinction will enhance our explanatory (and thus predictive) power. Systematic attention to the provision stage in our analyses of gender and media coverage will inevitably result in fuller, more nuanced accounts of how, when, and why news coverage is so deeply gendered, in no small measure because taking provision seriously requires researchers to incorporate other gendered institutions, such as political parties and presidents/prime ministers, and structures, such as culture, into analyses in the search for causes of gendered provision. This will encourage us all to keep sight of the powerful contextual forces at play in the production of gendered news coverage on the provision side. Moreover, engaging with the provision stage of political communications will also permit researchers to more fully grasp and elucidate the complex and dynamic relationships that exist between news subjects, newsworkers, and their audiences. The relationship between politicians and newsmakers is not straightforward or static. It is dynamic and symbiotic. The relationship is one of constant negotiation, as Ross (2002) has aptly pointed out. Indeed, often, women's participation in their mediation involves self-censorship of speech, dress, and behaviours in order to *discourage* journalists from focusing on their gendered identities, a theme developed further in Chapter 5 (see also Goodyear-Grant 2009). In some cases, female politicians avoid events or behaviours because they fear negative coverage that might exploit particularly damaging gender-role stereotypes; this self-censorship follows from the reality that women's speech, appearance, and behaviours tend to be selectively presented, or misrepresented, in the news.

Second, and relatedly, this chapter gives rise to practical guidance for researchers in that it underscores the importance of studying politicians' real-world behaviours alongside media coverage of the same, and doing so in a systematic manner. A handful of researchers have been doing this for some time (e.g., Gidengil and Everitt 1999, 2000, 2003a, 2003b), but these treatments do not theorize the issue or analyze the types of circumstances that lead to gendered provision. Attention to the provision-presentation distinction will encourage scholars to adopt research designs and methodological tools that facilitate comparisons between provision and presentation.

Finally, greater attention to the provision-presentation distinction may be of practical advantage for female politicians and campaign practitioners. Researchers who are careful to separate provision and presentation in a systematic way in their work on political communications may be positioned to offer useful advice to female (and male) politicians about how the provision of gendered information affects media presentation, as well as the implications, both positive and negative, of the provision of gendered information for politicians' public personas, electoral prospects, and political careers. A driving force behind research on gender, media, and politics – indeed, behind work on gender and representation generally – is a belief that women's political under-representation is both unjust and undesirable. Given that the traditional barriers to women in formal politics, such as party gatekeeping, fundraising, and the like, are being dismantled (or at least diminished), researchers have increasingly focused on how the media affect demand for and supply of female candidates. Greater attention to provision as distinct from presentation may allow us to not only better explain mediated representations of female politicians, but also to offer practically useful generalizations on how provision and presentation interact.

Although it is important to sort provision from presentation in terms of responsibility for gendered news, the fact remains that there are differences in coverage that may harm female candidates' electoral prospects and, in the long term, the representation of women in political life. The patterns matter on their own, regardless of which forces are responsible for producing them, for the effects of gendered coverage span both the short and long term, and can be quite negative for political women, although not universally so. Analyses of the effects of gendered news coverage tell us not only which of the patterns are harmful, but also which of them may offer opportunities for women seeking office to capitalize on their status as women.

4 Backlash or Boost? The Effects of Attack-Style News

A fundamental concern of this book is whether gendered news matters – whether it affects public perceptions of female politicians and, by extension, their electoral prospects and political careers. This chapter focuses primarily on the first component: public perceptions and electoral prospects, with an emphasis on attack-style news coverage. News about politics generally is quite adversarial – and understandably so, given that drama and conflict are important criteria of newsworthiness. Evidence has accumulated that female politicians receive more combative news coverage than their male colleagues do, even though female politicians tend to be less conflictive in reality (e.g., Gidengil and Everitt 1999, 2000, 2003a, 2003b), a manifestation of the iron maiden frame that is pervasive in news coverage of political women. The evidence suggests there are imbalances in reportage of men and women. Chapter 2 demonstrated that campaign news often presents female politicians as more confrontational and aggressive than their male counterparts. For example, both Alexa McDonough and the other female candidates in the 2000 federal election campaign were more likely than male leaders and candidates to be shown on the attack in television news of the campaign. Chapter 3 went on to demonstrate that combative depictions of the NDP leader were exaggerated, according to a comparison of the prevalence of attacks in the party's press releases versus in McDonough's campaign coverage, a finding that is supported by past work comparing female leaders' behaviour in leaders' debates with post-debate coverage (Gidengil and Everitt 1999, 2000, 2003a, 2003b). Questions about the effects of attack-style news coverage are critical, then, for the news is generally combative, and female politicians' coverage is particularly so.

This chapter moves to the next step. It starts from the observation that political success turns more and more on candidates' personality traits, and in Westminster systems, it is the leaders that play the key role (e.g., Bartels 2002; Bean and Mughan 1989; Bittner 2011; Johnston 2002). This is an inevitable by-product of the heightened personalization that comes with the celebritization of politics. Although traits have become more important, not all traits are equally valued, and some traits are evaluated differently in male and female politicians.

Electoral advantage is often thought to be gained by male politicians who adopt tough, aggressive personas, and who are presented as such in the news media. George W. Bush, for example, successfully cultivated a Texas, "straight-shooter" (Safire 2005) image, and during the early days after 9/11, described the administration's response to the attacks using "the metaphor of 'the hunt' and the mythic notion of the 'Old West'" (Coe et al. 2007, 32). In Russia, Vladimir Putin "from the beginning ... distinguished himself from Yeltsin – in his youth, vigor and especially over time, his masculinity" (Wood 2011). Aggressive, masculine, attack-style politics are frequently demonstrated through photo opportunities where male politicians engage in the world of sport – Putin in martial arts, former California "Governator" Schwarzenegger through his bodybuilding career, former Canadian Alliance leader Stockwell Day as he rode to a press conference on a Sea-Doo in the fall of 2000, and others. Such displays have been performed for centuries. "Chivalric society," for example, "was built on the idea of a completed circle in which the power of the ruler was confirmed through his demonstrations of strength using his body and the bodies of others" (Bonde 2009, 1550).

The literature is clear about two points: first, voters use masculine stereotypes to attribute traits, beliefs, and issue competencies to male politicians and feminine stereotypes to attribute traits, beliefs, and issue competencies to female politicians (e.g., Alexander and Anderson 1993; Burrell 1994; Huddy 1994; Huddy and Terkildsen 1993a, 1993b; Lawless 2005; Leeper 1991; McDermott 1997, 1998; Rosenwasser and Dean 1989; Rosenwasser and Seale 1988; Sanbonmatsu 2002, 2004; Sanbonmatsu and Dolan 2009; Sapiro 1982), and, second, in the minds of voters, politics is more strongly associated with masculine traits than with feminine traits, or masculine traits are deemed more important to politics than are feminine traits (e.g., Huddy and Terkildsen 1993a, 1993b; Kinder et al. 1980; Lawless 2005;

Lawrence and Rose 2009; Rosenwasser and Dean 1989). For example, in Lawless's (2005) study of attitudes towards candidate traits in the post–September 11th era, three of the top four traits identified as most important in politics are stereotypical masculine traits (self-confidence, assertiveness, and toughness). Compassion was the only stereotypical feminine trait in the top four list. In sum, therefore, the literature tells us that voters believe that men are masculine and that masculine traits are more integral to politics than feminine traits.

Where the literature is less clear is on what all this means for voter responses to the behaviours of male and female candidates. The literature does not offer much formal testing of the benefits that male candidates are assumed to gain from going on the offensive or acting aggressively in politics; however, the data that have been reported suggest that men accrue the expected advantages from acting tough (e.g., Ansolabehere and Iyengar 1991, 1995; Hitchon et al. 1997). The idea that displays of masculinity may positively affect public perceptions of male politicians is no surprise in light of the congruence between stereotypical masculine traits and political traits.

What happens when women go on the offensive, or when they are depicted by the news media as aggressive, often in a way that demonstrably exaggerates their attack-style behaviours? To assess the effects of attack-style coverage on perceptions of female politicians, this chapter analyzes voters' responses to media coverage of male and female party leaders' attack-style behaviours in the context of the 2000 Canadian federal election campaign using a unique combination of data that matches media content with voters' responses to that content. This is the last Canadian federal election in which a woman led a competitive party. The chapter tests two possibilities, which are not compatible:

> *Backlash*: Female politicians are penalized more (or gain less) from attack-style behaviours than male politicians.
> *Boost*: Female politicians are penalized less (or gain more) from attack-style behaviours than male politicians.

Essentially, the question is: do women profit or lose with attack-style coverage?

Backlash or Boost?

The gender-conditional effects of aggressive, attack-style political behaviours are important for several reasons. First, this style of behaviour is prevalent in political campaigning (e.g., Ansolabehere and Iyengar 1995; Brooks 2010, 2011; Geer 2006; Sigelman and Buell 2003), and it tends to be central in media coverage (e.g., Geer 2006; Soroka and Andrew 2009). Women do engage in this type of behaviour, and at the same rate as male candidates, by some estimates (e.g., Bystrom and Kaid 2002).

Second, exaggeration of women's aggressive behaviours regularly occurs at the presentation, rather than provision, stage. The media distort by exaggerating women's counter-stereotypical attack-style behaviours. As such, analysis of this type of gendered coverage reveals whether the news media act as an indirect barrier to women's political representation by consistently presenting coverage that harms public evaluations of them. In either case, whether backlash or boost is the dominant effect, the media would be a significant influence on voters' orientations towards female candidates and politicians, and thus play an important if indirect role in women's electoral prospects.

Finally, existing literature does not offer a clear guide about the effects of attack-style behaviours, and their exaggeration in media, for political women. Boost or backlash? Both effects are supported by theoretically sound and intuitively appealing accounts, as well as confirmatory empirical evidence, in the literature. The duality of these predictions evokes Mandel's (1981) idea of the "double bind" whereby aggressive women are seen as unfeminine, but feminine women are seen as unsuitable for office (e.g., Bystrom et al. 2001; Bystrom et al. 2004; Jamieson 1995; Lawrence and Rose 2009).

How does the electorate react to women on the offensive, and how do these reactions compare with those towards male politicians who engage in the same behaviours? There are three possible outcomes: a backlash effect, a viability boost, and of course, no effect.[1]

Gender stereotypes, which have both descriptive and prescriptive content, are central to both the backlash and boost effects. The backlash account focuses on the potential negative consequences for women who defy traditional gender stereotypes, while the boost account focuses on the potential positive consequences for women who are seen to conform to traditional political leadership stereotypes.

Focusing first on the story predicted by the backlash hypothesis, gender stereotypes link women and femininity with modesty, cooperation, sympathy, kindness, and orientation towards others, while masculinity is linked with independence, aggression, forcefulness, and decisiveness (e.g., Best and Williams 1990; Broverman et al. 1972; Eagly and Steffen 1984; McKee and Sheriffs 1957). Prentice and Carranza (2002) demonstrate that aggressiveness is one of the traits that most differentiates men from women in the minds of the public, for men are thought to possess this trait far more than women, and aggression is seen as more socially desirable for male behaviour than female behaviour. What may make the adoption of stereotypical masculine traits appealing to female candidates, however, is that these are the traits most closely associated with politics (Kinder et al. 1980; Lawless 2005; Lawrence and Rose 2009; Rosenwasser and Dean 1989). Candidates of both genders use "gendered adaptive" strategies (Banwart and McKinney 2005) in an effort to create broad-based appeal or balance their public personas, particularly in mixed-gender races. It may not even be a matter of "adopting" masculine traits; the women who self-select or are recruited into candidacy may be more likely to possess traits associated with men and masculinity than the female population more generally, because such traits are prized for office holding.

The critical component of the backlash account is the idea that female politicians are punished for defying gender stereotypes, on both cognitive and normative levels. Psychologists have demonstrated that people react negatively to disagreement between existing knowledge (stereotypes) and new information. People seek congruence between their cognitions. Counter-stereotypical behaviours by female politicians contradict existing knowledge about typical female behaviours, producing a tension. A normative tension is also produced, for "gender stereotypes ... are also prescriptive. That is, they denote not only differences in how men and women actually are, but also norms about behaviours that are suitable for each – about how men and women *should* be" (Heilman 2001, 659). Okimoto and Brescoll (2010) actually measure the emotions triggered, and they find that "moral outrage" towards counter-stereotypical behaviours is in large measure responsible for backlash effects.

Backlash against female politicians could assume different forms, but of central importance are two possibilities: voters may like aggressive female politicians less and they may vote for them less,[2] effects that are certainly related. Analyses of the work world, focusing in particular on female managers, show that when women act aggressively or self-promote in order to display their professional acumen and competence, a decline in their social and professional attractiveness tends to result, leading to professional and economic repercussions (Rudman 1998; Rudman and Glick 1999, 2001; Rudman and Fairchild 2004; Rudman and Goodwin 2004; Phelan and

Rudman 2010). Women in historically male-dominated roles are evaluated differently from their male counterparts, and this can lead to the punishment of women for defying stereotypes. Compared with identically presented men, assertive women are judged to be less hireable in corporate settings (e.g., Rudman 1998; Janoff-Bulman and Wade 1996), lacking in social skills (Rudman and Glick 1999, 2001), and less nice or likeable in work and social settings (e.g., Eagly et al. 1992). Moreover, women are judged to be less persuasive when they use forceful speech compared with tentative speech (Carli 1990) or "task-oriented" speech compared with "people-oriented" speech (Carli, LaFleur, and Loeber 1995). In group settings, women who verbalize intellectual forcefulness – by arguing in favour of an idea, for example – provoke negative facial expressions, while the same behaviour by a man provokes positive facial expressions (Butler and Geis 1990). Clearly, there are circumstances in which women are penalized for assertive and forceful behaviours, and in the corporate world, these would relate to women being seen as less nice, less hireable, and less promotable, effects that have direct parallels to female seekers of political office.

Turning squarely to the political sphere, the number of studies that provide evidence for the backlash effect against women who act aggressively is small – much smaller than the volume of confirmatory evidence in the psychology literature on ordinary men and women and in the business literature on men and women employed in the corporate world, as Brooks notes (2011). In a study examining affect towards news media coverage of party leaders in the 1993 and 1997 Canadian federal election campaigns, Gidengil and Everitt (2003b) found that people reported lower affect towards counter-stereotypical women who were reported using aggressive rather than neutral verbs, but male leaders were not similarly affected. Aggressive verbs of reported speech include "attack," "argue," and "hammer home." Neutral verbs of reported speech included "say" or "tell," whose usage is far more common than usage of aggressive verbs. Interestingly, female participants reacted in a particularly negative way to aggressive verbs, a finding the authors deemed "consistent with work on the perception of anger expression: Women perceive the same behaviour to be more aggressive and less appropriate than men do" (219). That female politicians' speech was more likely than that of their male counterparts to be reported using negative verbs – a chief finding of the article – therefore, produced a combined sex-of-politician and sex-of-participant effect that diminished the appeal of female candidates among female voters, in particular.

Hitchon and her colleagues (1997) have demonstrated that neutral political ads are seen as more desirable for women than emotional ones, whether the content of the appeals is positive or negative, and the same study also demonstrated that female politicians are penalized more than their male counterparts for going negative (see also Ansolabehere and Iyengar 1991, 1995), a result consistent with Gidengil and Everitt's findings.

Female politicians who run for high-level office – female party leaders, in parliamentary systems, and presidential and vice-presidential candidates – may be particularly vulnerable to backlash effects on account of their visibility and relative novelty. According to Kanter (1977a, 1977b), token status can magnify negative evaluations of women. Tokens receive considerable attention, and are usually under heightened pressure to perform. Tokens may be susceptible to even harsher disapproval when the positions they occupy have been considered sex inappropriate (Yoder 1991).

There is evidence to support the idea of a backlash against female politicians who go on the offensive; however, the opposite effect – the "viability boost" – offers an equally compelling account and ample empirical support. Huddy and Terkildsen's work (1993a, 1993b), for example, suggests that female candidates can reap the benefits of adopting masculine personality traits while not sacrificing the benefits that female candidates obtain from being stereotyped as compassionate, honest, and ethical (see also Huddy 1994), and they ultimately recommend that female candidates emphasize masculine traits. Gordon and her colleagues (2003) found similar results in an experiment with undergraduate participants. Students viewed negative campaign advertisements of male and female candidates. The ads were not real; they were scripted in order to manipulate the sex of the candidate and the tone of the ad. One of their key findings was that when ads showed women acting in stereotypically masculine ways – such as going on the attack – or emphasizing stereotypically masculine characteristics such as leadership and independence, the women were viewed more favourably by participants. Gordon and her colleagues conclude by noting (2003, 49) that their data "do not support the conventional wisdom that female candidates will be penalized more than male candidates for using negative advertisements" (see also Hitchon and Chang 1995). Leeper's (1991) findings are complementary, for the results of his experimental work show that women are not punished for adopting tough issue positions or masculine-style demeanours. "If women vying for executive posts stress unambiguous masculine themes," states Leeper, "they can expect voters to still assign to them a battery of feminine traits – possibly giving them the edge over their one-dimensional male opponent" (256).

What processes could account for these results? Historically, women have been viewed as less competitive and less competent than men generally (e.g., Broverman et al. 1972), and voters tend to make automatic assumptions that women are less viable candidates for office than men are (e.g., Sapiro 1982). All this is unsurprising given that politics is associated most strongly with masculine traits (Huddy and Terkildsen 1993a, 1993b; Kinder et al. 1980; Lawless 2005; Lawrence and Rose 2009; Rosenwasser and Dean 1989). As a result, a female candidate's ability to win elective office and perform the job of a politician is often in doubt, regardless of her background and credentials. Low-information contexts are particularly troublesome for female candidates, because voters tend to rely more heavily on stereotypes to fill in the blanks (e.g., Kahn 1992; McDermott 1997, 1998; Sanbonmatsu 2002, 2004; Sapiro 1982). Thus, coverage highlighting a woman's ability and willingness to act aggressively could send a compelling signal that women are suited to the political world, information that may counteract gender stereotypes, producing a boost to her attractiveness as a candidate.

Aggressive political behaviours may also indirectly boost women through effects linked to assumptions about policy expertise. Domains of policy expertise thought necessary for political leadership are those most stereotypically tied to men/masculinity such as defence and military issues (e.g., Alexander and Andersen 1993; Huddy and Terkildsen 1993b; Leeper 1991; Mueller 1986; Rosenwasser and Dean 1989; Rosenwasser and Seale 1988; Sanbonmatsu 2002; Sapiro 1982, 1983; Shapiro and Mahajan 1986). Predictably, political issues and traits are related. "Instrumental" traits, such as assertiveness and mastery, are linked with military, defence, and economic management, while "communal" traits, such as warmth and expressiveness, are related to health, education, and other "compassion" issues (Huddy and Terkildsen 1993b, 141). Voters tend to assume that female candidates possess communal traits and are expert in compassion policy fields, while male candidates are assumed to possess instrumental traits and expertise in military, defence, and similar policy fields (see also Burrell 1994; Kahn 1996; Matland 1994; Matland and King 2002; Sanbonmatsu 2002, 2004). Therefore, news that depicts women as possessing stereotypically masculine traits, such as aggression and assertiveness, may encourage voters to implicitly attribute expertise in hard policy issues to women as well. This effect may offer the greatest viability boost to relatively unknown female candidates, for the tendency to attribute sex-stereotypical traits and policy competence is even stronger in low-information contexts, as noted previously.

Voters' Characteristics

Voters are not expected to respond uniformly to actual or mediated attacks by political women, so the sources of variation in voters' responses constitute an important matter for this study. Two factors are of particular interest: gender and gender ideology. Starting with the former, research demonstrates that women are more perceptive than men with regard to both verbal and non-verbal communication (Argyle et al. 1970; Hall 1984; Rosenthal et al. 1979). Women are also more likely than men to react adversely to hostile or aggressive behaviours (Brooks 2010; Gidengil and Everitt 2003b; Smith et al. 1989; Wiley and Eskilson 1985), regardless of the sex of the aggressor, a phenomenon Brooks calls a "negativity gap" (2010). Additionally, women's reactions can be particularly negative when the aggressor is herself female. Rudman's experiments show (1998, 640) that women, but not men, "found ... self-promoting women less competent, less socially attractive, and subsequently less hireable than self-promoting men" (see also Rudman and Glick 1999; Powers and Zuroff 1988), perhaps as a result of the "queen bee" syndrome (e.g., Derks et al. 2011). The strongest backlash against counter-stereotypical women can come from women, not from men. This finding is contested, however. Other studies show no such effect (e.g., Carli 1990; Carli, LaFleur, and Loeber 1995; Schultz and Pancer 1997).

In addition to gender, participants' gender ideology may be an important mediator of their responses to news depictions of female politicians' attack-style behaviours. Gender ideology is a concept that refers to one's orientations towards "a division of paid work and family responsibilities that is based on the notion of separate spheres" (Davis and Greenstein 2009, 88; see also Tolleson-Rinehart 1992). In other words, gender ideology refers to one's view of the appropriate gender arrangements in the public and private spheres, and focuses, in particular, on social, political, and economic structures. Gender ideology can be conservative, which would indicate acceptance of traditional gender arrangements in the public and private spheres – acceptance of inequalities in political and economic power favouring men, and emphasis on traditional ideas about women's place in the family and home. On the liberal or egalitarian end of the spectrum, gender ideology would reject traditional arrangements, and hold to greater equality in the division of roles and in political and economic power, and acceptance of the idea that men and women do not have "natural homes" in either the public or private spheres. Like any belief spectrum, there is considerable space between the two poles for more middle-of-the-road positions. For the analyses at hand, gender ideology may play an important role in mediating responses to political women who engage in aggressive behaviours. For participants of both sexes, an egalitarian gender ideology may diminish the impact of the prescriptive component of gender stereotypes which says that women and men *should* behave in largely traditional ways: women as warm, compassionate, and cooperative and men as tough, aggressive, and decisive, for example. Among gender egalitarians, there may be no backlash against women who are reported on the attack, because such respondents view men and women as equal, and do not hold to traditional views on men's and women's relative spheres and strengths. However, even if the judgmental or evaluative aspect of counter-stereotypical behaviours were eliminated – and that is itself a tentative proposition – the descriptive content of stereotypes would remain, and stereotypes are notoriously difficult to resist.

Electoral Context, Data, and Methods

This chapter looks for evidence of backlash and boost in the context of news coverage of leaders of the four major national political parties in the 2000 Canadian federal election campaign. As discussed in earlier chapters, the parties' campaign platforms were typical fare and reflected their positions on the ideological spectrum (Blais et al. 2002a). The NDP and the BQ both campaigned in favour of a nationally funded prescription drug plan, social programs, and environmental protection. The PCs and the Alliance – both on the right – paid attention to crime, and the Alliance put special emphasis on fiscal issues, and ignored environmental issues. The Liberal Party heavily emphasized health care, and so did all the other major parties given the issue's lasting importance in Canadian electoral politics. Nothing of great note happened during the campaign in terms of significant leader gaffes. All of the leaders had political experience, although they varied in the levels and durations of office holding. Alexa McDonough was the sole female party leader in the 2000 race, and as such, investigation of the gender effects of aggressive behaviours in the pages that follow relies on comparisons between her and the three male leaders identified above.

To assess the question of whether voters react differently to male and female politicians on the offensive, I use a combination of data: content analysis data of CBC television news stories of the 2000 Canadian federal election campaign that code for party leaders' attack-style behaviours, which were analyzed in detail in Chapter 2; ratings provided by participants in a media reception study ($N = 56$, all from Toronto, the country's largest city) of how these stories reflected on the major party leaders; and variables for several key characteristics of the participants of the media reception study. The three data sources were combined to form a single, stacked data set[3] that integrates the three components.

In a series of binary logistic regressions, this chapter tests whether male and female leaders' stories are evaluated differently when they are depicted as aggressive in news compared with when they are not. The dependent variable in all models codes participants' ratings of how a news story reflected on the political party that was the focus of the story, as either good (coded 1) or bad (coded 0).[4] Arguably, given the prominence of party leaders in Canadian politics, generally, and the fact that in Canada, political campaigns and their coverage in the news are dominated by the party leaders, the dependent variable used here is a reasonable test of how voters respond to portrayals of leaders in the news. However, the set-up does have limitations. The news rating variable is not a direct test of voters' responses to the media coverage of leaders, but rather an indirect one that measures voters' assessment of whether the content of a story is good or bad for the political party. Moreover, the dependent variable measures affective response, not whether respondents would (or did) vote for a leader or party. In other words, it measures perception, not behaviours. The second limitation is likely more easily overcome than the first. Although there is debate about the issue, convincing evidence demonstrates that perceptions of leaders have important and predictable effects on voting behaviour (e.g., Bittner 2011; Johnston et al. 1992; Johnston 2002).

Several independent variables are included in the analyses. Leaders' aggressive behaviours in each news story are coded into three categories: no aggressive behaviour (coded 0), *either* verbal attack or aggressive bodily gestures, but not both (coded 0.5), and *both* verbal attack and aggressive gestures (coded 1).[5] A verbal attack indicates that a party leader was shown in a story attacking another party or leader verbally. Coders were instructed that "attack" was not equated simply with criticism or negative evaluation, as discussed in Chapter 2. Citizens accept that politics is about conflict (Mutz and Reeves 2005), and civilized disagreement is generally expected of political elites. Verbal attack refers, rather, to the following types of behaviour: instances where untrue or unsubstantiated allegations were made; or where the tone was unduly harsh, rude, or confrontational; or where name calling and mud slinging that go beyond mere criticism were depicted.

In addition to verbal attacks, politicians' body language was also coded according to its level of aggressivity. A powerful form of communication, some researchers estimate that non-verbal cues have up to four times the impact of verbal cues when they are used together (Argyle et al. 1970; see also Argyle, Alkema, and Gilmour 1971), because people trust non-verbal cues. Body language is unconscious or involuntary, for the most part, so we generally assume that non-verbal cues do not lie. Of the different types of body language coded in this study, three are counted in these analyses as aggressive: finger pointing, fist clenching, and hand chopping, a classification consistent with psychology, communications, and linguistics research on how these three types of gestures are typically interpreted (Argyle et al. 1970; Argyle et al. 1971; Henley and Freeman 1995), as well as previous research on gendered mediation of politicians (e.g., Gidengil and Everitt 2000, 2003a).

Other independent variables included in models are the following: participants' sex, gender ideology, party identification, and baseline feelings about each of the leaders. Sex is coded 1 for female and 0 for male participants, and is included primarily because gender may have independent effects on news story ratings irrespective of leaders' levels of aggressive behaviour in the stories. For instance, male and female voters sometimes have baseline preferences for candidates of one gender over the other (Sanbonmatsu 2002), which may lead them to rate stories about same-sex leaders systematically higher than those about opposite-sex leaders.

Gender ideology is operationalized with a variable that codes participants' responses to the statement: "Society would be better off if more women stayed home with their children."[6] Respondents who agreed or strongly agreed with the statement (coded 0) are traditionalists, and those who disagreed or strongly disagreed are egalitarians (coded 1). The variable is incomplete in the sense that it does not measure some of the important dimensions within the concept of gender ideology. Nevertheless, this indicator is certainly appropriate given that it asks respondents to make a direct judgment about the worth of assigning women primarily to the domestic sphere, and thus, indirectly about women's relationship to activities outside the home – if women are not in the home, where else would they be but the public sphere?

Party identification is coded 1 when participants' party identification matches that of the leader portrayed in a story, and 0 if there is no match.

TABLE 4.1

Ratings of news story, by party leader, 2006 election campaign

	Chrétien		Day		Clark		McDonough	
Rating	n	(%)	n	(%)	n	(%)	n	(%)
Bad	1,014	(48)	1,195	(59)	337	(29)	192	(19)
Good	1,116	(52)	826	(41)	828	(71)	807	(81)
Total	2,130	(100)	2,021	(100)	1,165	(100)	999	(100)

Weak identifiers are coded as having no party identification, so are always coded 0 for this variable. Party identification per se is not expected to influence how participants perceive politicians' aggressive behaviours in news stories; what matters is the match between personal partisanship and that of the leader shown in a given story. When a match occurs, an increase in story ratings should result. Likewise, leader-feeling thermometers are also included, because they should correlate positively with ratings of leaders' stories, independent of the content of coverage. Rescaled 0 to 1, these thermometers were originally 100-point thermometers, where 0 represented "really dislike" the leader and 100 represented "really like" the leader.

Results

Stories about McDonough received the highest mean rating: 3.5 on the original 5-point scale from "very bad" (score of 1) to "very good" (score of 5) (results not shown). Clark followed McDonough closely, with a mean rating of 3.3, and Chrétien and Day trailed with mean ratings of 3.0 and 2.8, respectively. Day was the only leader to receive a mean rating below a score of 3. With the recoded variable used here, ratings are put into two categories, "good" or "bad." The distribution of leaders' stories into those categories is shown in Table 4.1. Again, McDonough had the highest proportion of good ratings, and Day the lowest.

The participants in the media response study were all from the Toronto area, as noted above, so this distribution of mean ratings likely reflects Day's unpopularity among Ontarians relative to the other leaders (e.g., Blais et al. 2002a, 167). The point here, however, is that ratings were generally good, and the female leader in the campaign had the highest mean rating, which reflected her likeability among the electorate more generally. A question in the 2000 Canadian Election Study (CES) asked respondents which party leader they viewed as most trustworthy, for example, and McDonough and

TABLE 4.2

Determinants of leaders' news story ratings (selected by party that was focus of story, binary logistic regressions), 2006 election campaign

	Respondents' ratings of news stories on			
	Chrétien	Day	Clark	McDonough
Respondent is female	−0.17 (0.09)	0.08 (0.08)	0.27 (0.20)	0.26 (0.17)
Respondent has same party ID as leader	1.00*** (0.09)	−0.31 (0.23)	0.09 (0.13)	0.39* (0.22)
Respondent has positive feeling for leader	0.90*** (0.17)	1.44*** (0.17)	1.32*** (0.26)	0.64* (0.37)
Respondent has egalitarian gender ideology	0.34*** (0.11)	−0.14 (0.10)	0.23 (0.16)	0.11 (0.17)
Leader depicted as aggressive in story	2.06*** (0.51)	−0.14 (0.50)	0.97 (0.59)	−1.14** (0.56)
Pseudo-R^2	0.12	0.03	0.04	0.04
Constant	−1.36*** (0.24)	−0.74*** (0.25)	−0.33 (0.29)	1.60*** (0.37)
N	2,010	1,913	1,101	949

Note: Results are divided by leader, so each column represents a separate model for each leader's news story ratings. Within this, the variable names in the far-left column provide information on the determinants of leaders' news ratings. Cells contain logits, with robust standard errors in parentheses.

* $p < .10$; ** $p < .05$; *** $p < .0$

Chrétien were tied as the top choice with an equal plurality of respondents (23 percent for each, results not shown).

Keeping in mind, then, that McDonough's news ratings were generally high, and she was well liked and respected by the electorate, the critical question is whether depictions of her on the attack in television news harmed or helped her. Did going on the offensive result in backlash or boost compared with her male counterparts? Starting with the first set of models (Table 4.2), the results suggest that news depictions of McDonough on the attack harmed her. Participants in the media response study rated her stories lower when she was depicted on the attack. Compared with the other models in the table, which estimate the effects of male party leaders' aggressive behaviours on ratings of stories about their parties, McDonough was the only leader for whom a negative effect is obtained (logit of −1.14). Incumbent Prime Minister Chrétien's aggressive behaviour had a positive effect on ratings of stories about his party, and the aggressivity of the other two male leaders' behaviour had no significant effect on their ratings.

The substantive effects of McDonough's and Chrétien's aggressive behaviour on their ratings are depicted in Figures 4.1 and 4.2, respectively. These figures show the results of post-estimation predicted probabilities of positive news ratings for different levels of leader aggressivity.[7] Looking at Figure 4.1, if all McDonough's stories had no aggressive behaviour in them, the predicted probability of assigning her a positive rating rather than a negative rating would be about 0.9[8] (keeping in mind that the neutral rating option was excluded from analyses). In other words, when she was not on the offensive, her ratings were nearly universally good. On the other end of the spectrum, if all McDonough's stories featured verbal attack with aggressive body language, the predicted probability of judging McDonough's stories to be good rather than bad for the party would be about 50 percent, a very large decline, indeed.

The substantive impact of Chrétien's aggressive behaviour tells a different story (Figure 4.2). There is obviously a non-linear relationship occurring whereby no aggression caused a lower probability of positive news ratings; *some* aggressive behaviour boosted Chrétien's ratings; yet, the *combination* of verbal and non-verbal aggression lowered his news ratings again. In other words, participants responded well to Chrétien when he was on the offensive using *either* verbal attack or aggressive body language like finger pointing and fist clenching, but not when he did both. The probability of a positive news rating when he used one or the other was about 0.7, versus 0.45 when he used no aggressive behaviour or combined both kinds of aggressive behaviour. This suggests that not only are citizens perhaps intolerant of aggression on the part of political women, but they may be intolerant of aggression generally when it reaches too high a level. Indeed, a male politician can go on the offensive, but Figure 4.2 suggests there may be a limit or a point of diminishing returns, as it were. It is particularly interesting that

FIGURE 4.1

Predicted probabilities of positive news ratings, by McDonough aggressivity

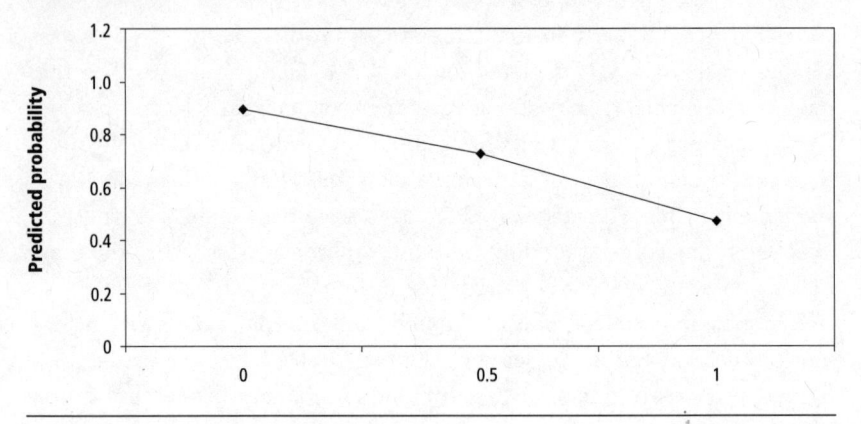

FIGURE 4.2

Predicted probabilities of positive news ratings, by Chrétien aggressivity

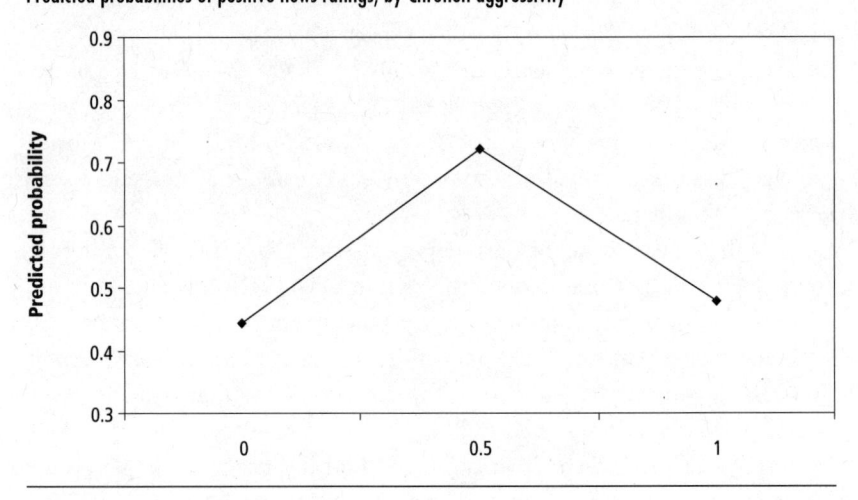

Chrétien was the only one of the three male leaders who derived a boost from aggressive behaviour, for he was the incumbent prime minister in that election.[9]

In terms of the other variables in the models presented in Table 4.2, predictably, positive feelings towards party leaders boosted their news ratings across the board, although some leaders gained more (Day and Clark) than others (McDonough and Chrétien). For Chrétien and McDonough, participants rated stories higher when their own partisan affiliations matched those of the leader in the story, but the same was not true for Day and Clark. Gender itself did not have much impact on news ratings of the leaders – only for Chrétien's stories, to which women were less likely than men to attach positive ratings. Finally, gender ideology likewise had little impact in the models; those with egalitarian rather than traditional gender ideologies were more likely to assign positive ratings to Chrétien, but there were no effects for the other leaders. Neither participant sex nor gender ideology had any independent influence on ratings of the female leader's news stories.

The next question is whether the sex or gender ideologies of respondents have indirect effects, as conditioners of respondents' reactions to news stories depicting attack-style behaviours by party leaders. Do women respond differently than men when leaders go on the offensive, particularly when female leaders do so? Do those with egalitarian gender ideologies have more tolerance for female counter-stereotypical behaviours? In both cases, the answer seems to be "No." Table 4.3 presents two more sets of models for each leader's stories: first, with a variable interacting respondent sex with leader aggressivity, and, second, with a variable interacting gender ideology with leader aggressivity. None of these interaction variables is statistically significant.

Discussion and Conclusion

The overall conclusion of these analyses is that McDonough did not experience a boost from aggressive behaviours in the 2000 campaign. News stories that showed her on the offensive were far less likely to be rated positively than those in which she was more subdued, consistent instead with the backlash hypothesis. The three male leaders were not penalized for their attack-style behaviours; attacks either failed to affect leaders' ratings (Day and Clark) or actually boosted their ratings (Chrétien). Even for the male leaders, however, there seems to be a tolerance threshold. As Figure 4.2 demonstrated, the relationship between Chrétien's aggressive behaviour and his news ratings was not linear. Moderate aggression seemed to be the best strategy for him, and may well be for other male politicians, too. Although citizens expect politics to be conflictual – at its core, politics is a struggle over the distribution of scarce resources, after all – tolerance wanes when behaviours breach norms of civility (e.g., Mutz and Reeves 2005). Perhaps this is why Chrétien's ratings declined when he combined both forms of aggressive behaviour – perhaps he went too far.

TABLE 4.3

Determinants of leaders' news story ratings, testing interactive effects of sex and gender ideology (selected by party that was focus of story, binary logistic regressions), 2006 election campaign

	\multicolumn{8}{c}{Respondents' ratings of news stories on}
	Chrétien		Day		Clark		McDonough	
Respondent is female	−0.15 (0.11)	−0.17* (0.09)	0.07 (0.10)	0.08 (0.08)	0.23 (0.29)	0.27 (0.20)	0.45 (0.40)	0.26 (0.17)
Respondent has same party ID as leader	1.00*** (0.09)	1.00*** (0.09)	−0.31 (0.23)	−0.31 (0.30)	0.09 (0.13)	0.09 (0.13)	0.40* (0.22)	0.39* (0.22)
Respondent has positive feeling for leader	0.90*** (0.17)	0.91*** (0.17)	1.44*** (0.17)	1.45*** (0.17)	1.32*** (0.26)	1.31*** (0.26)	0.64* (0.37)	0.62* (0.36)
Respondent has egalitarian gender ideology	0.34*** (0.11)	0.28** (0.12)	−0.14 (0.10)	−0.09 (0.12)	0.23 (0.16)	0.29* (0.18)	0.11 (0.17)	0.48 (0.34)
Leader depicted as aggressive in story	2.14*** (0.54)	1.84*** (0.50)	−0.15 (0.50)	0.02 (0.45)	0.93* (0.51)	1.10 (0.67)	−1.02* (0.59)	−0.76 (0.51)
Female * leader aggressive	−0.10 (0.39)		−0.02 (0.23)		0.11 (0.58)		−0.30 (0.41)	
Egalitarian gender ideology * leader aggressive		0.40 (0.38)		−0.18 (0.27)		−0.20 (0.66)		−0.59 (0.52)
Pseudo-R^2	0.12	0.12	0.03	0.03	0.04	0.04	0.04	0.04
Constant	−1.37*** (0.24)	−1.32*** (0.25)	−0.74*** (0.26)	−0.77*** (0.24)	−0.31 (0.29)	−0.37 (0.28)	1.52*** (0.39)	1.37*** (0.34)
N	2,010	2,010	1,913	1,913	1,101	1,101	949	949

Note: Results are divided by leader, so each column represents a separate model for each leader's news story ratings. Within this, the variable names provided in the far-left column provide information on the determinants of leaders' news ratings. The last two variables are interaction terms to gauge whether the effects of leader attacks are conditional on or mediated by 1) the sex of respondents and/or 2) gender ideologies of respondents. Cells contain logits, with robust standard errors in parentheses.

* $p < .10$; ** $p < .05$; *** $p < .01$

The analyses presented in this chapter have important strengths. I have used a powerful and novel combination of data that tests how real news stories (not those designed for experimental treatments) affect male and female voters' perceptions of politicians and their news stories. The data were not collected from student respondents, which is common in other published work on the topic, and is on this dimension generalizable to the real world of electoral politics.

At the same time, it is important not to lose sight of the limitations of the data when considering implications or generalizations across time and space. My analyses have been conducted on a Toronto-based sample, which requires cautious generalization to other contexts. All my models control for important variables such as party identification, gender ideology, and baseline feelings about each of the leaders of national parties in the 2000 campaign, which together likely account for much of the regional variance that may exist in ratings of leaders' news stories. Nonetheless, region of residence as well as whether one lives in an urban or rural area may have independent effects (or even interactive effects) on how one rates news, news of men and women leaders, and, most importantly, news of men and women leaders shown on the attack. Research on regional and provincial political cultures in Canada suggests that there are genuine value differences as well as different attitudes towards government from one part of the country to the next (e.g., Henderson 2004; Simeon and Elkins 1974). Some of this work also identifies intraprovincial or intraregional cultures, especially along urban-rural lines (e.g., Henderson 2004), suggesting that urban-rural differences can lie over regional or provincial cultural differences. In short, these are the sorts of considerations that must be borne in mind when generalizing from a small and geographically restricted sample.

Most importantly, in terms of limitations, is the fact that the results are based on a single election and four leaders, only one of them female. A key question raised by the preceding analyses is whether there were other factors, not accounted for here, that influenced McDonough's ability to successfully act aggressively. One possibility that comes immediately to mind is political party. McDonough led a party of the left, the New Democratic Party. Early in this chapter, a great deal of space was allotted to the effects of gender stereotypes on reactions to female politicians' behaviours, but these are not the only types of stereotypes that affect voters' thinking. Of particular interest, in light of the results presented here, is whether party stereotypes condition voters' responses to female politicians who go on the offensive? Although "research on gender stereotypes and partisan stereotypes has proceeded on separate trajectories" (Sanbonmatsu and Dolan 2009, 485), recent work suggests that attention should be paid to the interaction between party and gender (e.g., Brians 2005; Dolan 2004; Hayes 2011; Huddy and Capelos 2002; Matland and King 2002; Sanbonmatsu and Dolan 2009). Examinations of US voters' stereotypes of Republican and Democratic women's issue competencies, for example, suggest there is important variance across parties (e.g., Sanbonmatsu and Dolan 2009); a parallel question arises regarding how voters sort through evaluations of candidates' traits and behaviours when gender and party stereotypes both provide relevant guides. In particular, the question of whether women from right-wing parties are better able to gain from aggressive behaviours than their left-party counterparts seems an obvious avenue for future inquiry. An important extension of Hayes' recent work (2011), for example, is that partisan stereotypes that ascribe more masculine traits to right-wing partisans and more feminine traits to left-wing partisans may mitigate voters' negative reactions to aggressive or tough political women if those women belong to right-wing parties. Although their behaviours defy traditional gender stereotypes, they fit with partisan stereotypes, and depending on which stereotype is most cognitively accessible for a voter, the gender-norm violation may be less salient. Thus, aggressive political women on the right of the political spectrum may not only "get away with" attack-style behaviours, but they may benefit from them. For women on the left, like Alexa McDonough, attack-style behaviours violate gender and partisan stereotypes, a worrying outcome for many political women, perhaps, given their concentration in centre and centre-left parties. In the end, the particular question coming from the preceding analyses is whether McDonough would have suffered backlash if she had led a right-wing party? The answer may be no. If she had led a party of the right, the effects of aggressive behaviour on her news ratings may have been closer to those of her male counterparts.

A natural question arises in responses to my findings about all the aggressive women in politics who have made it – who have had tremendous political success. Famous examples include Margaret Thatcher, the "Iron Lady"; Ellen Johnson Sirleaf, the "Iron Lady of Liberia"; Benazir Bhutto; Golda Meir; Indira Gandhi; and others. If women are punished for attack-style behaviours, how is it that tough women succeed? Clearly, aggressive women are not universally punished or shunned in politics. The chapter has not presented evidence that can settle the question; nevertheless, speculation on the matter must be directed not only to partisan stereotypes, but also to the political context in which such women operate. The political climate or issue agenda may modify which of the two effects (backlash or boost) is most likely in response to female politicians' aggression. In political atmospheres where war, national security, and foreign policy top the political agenda, the "iron maiden" frame may help women's electoral prospects, producing a viability boost when they are depicted as tough or aggressive. In such contexts, voters place even greater emphasis on stereotypically male traits, as Lawless's work (2005) on the post-9/11 American electorate has demonstrated, and women who can demonstrate "toughness" may convince voters that they can govern in such climates. Voters may be so focused on the traits necessary for presiding over such issues that the tension between women's toughness and feminine stereotypes becomes less salient than the need for office seekers to conform to (masculine) standards of political leadership. Conversely, when military and security issues do not define the political agenda, as was the case in the 2000 Canadian federal election campaign, the response may be different. When women go on the attack, voters may focus more on or be more likely to notice the tension produced between women's behaviours and stereotypical expectations. In the end, future research on this topic should build on the strengths of these data by studying not only a greater number of women leaders and/or candidates and similarly situated male comparators in order to produce more robust generalizations, but also to include a diversity of leaders and/or candidates from different parties, particularly women from different parties, and across different electoral contexts.

In light of what we know about the electoral environment, the results presented in this chapter are not good news. Findings suggest that women can lose when they are depicted behaving as political leaders are expected to behave: hard-hitting, tough, and willing to engage in critique of opponents and their records. This may be particularly true for left-wing women and women who find themselves in electoral climates that highlight "soft" issues. One further feature of political life must be recalled to fully grasp the negative implications. There is obviously variation in female politicians' behaviour. Some are aggressive, and some are not. However, the news media tend to exaggerate the attack-style behaviours of female politicians, largely because such behaviour is unexpected and, therefore, quite newsworthy. As discussed in Chapter 2, 33 percent of McDonough's stories showed her on the offensive, compared with only 5 percent, 10 percent, and 12 percent for Chrétien, Clark, and Day, respectively (Figure 2.1). The fact that McDonough's ratings were consistently high, whether she was on the attack or not, misses the point. The crucial point is that her ratings would have been higher had 33 percent of her stories on the CBC news not shown her combining verbal attack with aggressive body language. Therefore, not only does the news fail to depict reality accurately by distorting its representation of political women, as well as contribute to greater aggression on the whole in the political sphere, but also this practice can have negative effects on female politicians' political careers. If attack-style behaviours harm perceptions of female politicians – and in some cases, they clearly do – the news media's exaggeration of women's aggression magnifies that harm and creates an electoral liability.

This chapter has focused on short-term effects of the news on public perceptions, and has found negative consequences for the lone woman leader in the 2000 election campaign in Canada. The next chapter addresses themes similar to those explored here, but from a politician-centred perspective, and with a much longer-range perspective on how the news media affect men's and women's political careers. Research on the effects of the media tends to focus on how audiences react to the content and style of the news, and only rarely do scholars consider how men and women politicians themselves understand and navigate their interactions with the news media. Indeed, this chapter has demonstrated empirically what women politicians seem to know implicitly: the way the news tends to portray them can harm their appeal.

5

Media Effects on Politicians' Experiences of Their Political Careers

In 2000, a wetsuit-clad Stockwell Day, former leader of the now-defunct Canadian Alliance, roared to a beachside press conference in the Okanagan Valley on a Sea-Doo. This was his first press conference as a sitting member of Parliament, and it was a strategy designed to contrast Day's youth, athleticism, and energy with the advancing age of incumbent Prime Minister Jean Chrétien. Would a female politician have contemplated the same move? Would a woman consider doing a press conference with wet, stringy hair, dressed in neoprene, riding a motorized watercraft? The answer, in most cases, would be "No." Admittedly, the stunt did not work in Day's favour, for it appeared contrived and silly. In the case of female politicians, however, if the stunt appeared silly, it would have been precisely *because* the rider was a woman. In other words, unlike Day, female politicians would fear appearing unnatural holding such a press conference, and they would anticipate gendered media coverage of such an event. Self-regulation of speech and behaviours, therefore, is heavily influenced by views about anticipated coverage.

This chapter turns to the longer-term consequences of the news media on women's political careers, and adopts a perspective in which male and female politicians' own experiences are central. The chapter presents evidence that female politicians' gendered experiences of the media have become less negative with time, presumably reducing obstacles to women's political participation. All the same, media portrayals continue to generate unique challenges for female office seekers. Women face an uneven media playing field, which, in turn, contributes to their continued political under-representation. Not only that – female politicians are keenly *aware* of the situation they face regarding their coverage, their relationships with newsmakers, and how both affect their political careers.

The Sea-Doo press conference is an example of gender differences in how male and female politicians present themselves to the news media. Not all differences are so blatant, but they exist, nonetheless. This chapter takes up this theme and presents evidence that male and female politicians' experiences of the news media environment – from coverage to relationships with newsmakers – differ in consequential ways. Using data gathered in interviews with Canadian members of Parliament, this chapter demonstrates that female legislators experience news coverage in distinctly gendered ways. Among the chief concerns for female candidates is how to position themselves in order to obtain fair, balanced, or positive news coverage. Male and female MPs have different expectations of how the media will cover them, which, in turn, produce divergent self-presentation styles. Self-presentation is a key theme in this chapter. By focusing on how female politicians try to position themselves for reporters, including efforts to minimize what they regard as harmful coverage, this chapter demonstrates that political women engage in significant and careful self-regulation of their behaviours as a result of their expectations of gendered mediation, which is the equivalent of saying that they participate in their own mediation. Female politicians self-censor their speech, dress, and behaviours. All politicians engage in self-regulation along these lines; however, political women do so, in many cases, in order to discourage journalists from focusing on their gendered identities. Sometimes, female politicians avoid events or behaviours because they fear negative coverage that might exploit particularly damaging gender-role stereotypes. All of this self-censorship follows from the reality that women's speech, appearance, and behaviours are often selectively presented, or misrepresented, in the news; and the patterns of self-censorship are not unique to Canada, but are pan-national (see Ross 2002; Ross and Sreberny 2000; Fox 1997; Jamieson 1995; Niven and Zilber 2001b).

Few scholars have examined how female politicians understand their mediation and what strategies they adopt to navigate news coverage (see Bystrom and Miller 1999; Bystrom et al. 2004; Ross 2002; Ross and Sreberny 2000). A blind spot in the literature has resulted, parallel with the scarcity of work on gender and political leadership more generally. Given that few citizens have first-hand knowledge of politicians, news organizations constitute important political actors connecting ordinary citizens with the political sphere. Therefore, how politicians perceive their treatment in the media is crucial to understanding this field.

Research shows not only that the news media play an important macro-level role in contemporary politics, but also that that they matter to the decision making of individual citizens, a point that has been discussed at various places throughout this book. Political decisions, including how people vote and evaluate political candidates, are reached on the basis of personas that are reflected through the media, and ample work demonstrates that the selective presentation of female candidates in news stories can raise doubts about women's viability or suitability for leadership positions, thereby contributing to women's chronic under-representation in politics at all levels. News showing politicians on the attack – which tends to constitute an unduly large portion of female politicians' coverage – can negatively affect perceptions of women, as the previous chapter's analysis of news ratings in the 2000 election campaign demonstrated. This effect was not found for the male politicians in the race.

Methodology

This chapter presents the results of twenty-seven semi-structured interviews conducted in 2005 with current and former Canadian members of Parliament. My method of targeting interviewees combined theoretical or purposeful sampling with "snowball" or convenience techniques (Warren 2001). With theoretical sampling, "the interviewer seeks out respondents who seem likely to epitomize the analytic criteria in which he or she is interested" (87). All MPs possess the primary criteria of being federal-level politicians who have fought an election campaign and, therefore, have experience dealing with a variety of news media. Since all MPs were possible interviewees, the most important task was to decide which types of MPs to target. My primary goal was to obtain interviews with MPs of both sexes from all three nationally competitive political parties, namely, the Liberal, Conservative, and New Democratic parties. To a lesser extent, I also targeted MPs by region, experience in federal politics, age, and visible minority status. Ultimately, the objective was to ensure the participation of MPs with diverse characteristics, since "the philosophy of responsive interviewing suggests that reality is complex; to accurately portray that complexity, you need to gather contradictory or overlapping perceptions and nuanced understandings that different individuals hold" (Rubin and Rubin 2004, 67).

In other words, my general selection strategy was to target MPs so that comparison and control were built into the sample (King, Keohane, and Verba 1994).

A priori research designs provide good frameworks, but qualitative interviewing often poses sampling challenges because of time and access limitations. In this study, gatekeeping was a general obstacle, particularly for Liberal MPs who were government members at the time. Telephone and email communications with MPs were never direct; instead, my interview requests were routed through administrative staff. I used a combination of contact methods, always combining phone calls with follow-up emails, and in most cases, repeated contact was necessary to obtain responses from MPs or their staff. Many of the MPs I contacted never responded to the requests for interviews, and many others denied access, usually because of overburdened schedules. Although my approach was to target MPs according to specific primary (sex and party) and secondary (region, age, experience, minority status) criteria, the reality was that I interviewed whoever agreed to participate. As it turns out, I had more success securing interviews through MPs' own personal recommendations – that is, when one MP I had interviewed personally requested a fellow MP (usually a member of the same party) to also grant me an interview. This style of participant recruitment is known as the "snowball" or convenience method.

Of the twenty-seven interviewees, several had served as cabinet ministers and one – Kim Campbell – as prime minister. The sample included eighteen women and nine men, which permits direct comparison of men's and women's experiences of mediation. Among interviewees, there were nine Liberals (in government at the time), twelve Conservatives, and six New Democrats. Kim Campbell is counted as a government member because she served on that side of the House of Commons during her time in federal politics. My sample, thus, includes ten government and seventeen opposition MPs (eleven of the twelve Conservatives plus six New Democrats).

Interviews were conducted in a semi-structured style, meaning a list of broad topics or questions was used to guide, though not determine, the course of the interviews. This style provided room for each interview to vary, including in terms of the order of questions or specific follow-up queries. Ultimately, I aimed to give interviewees an opportunity to choose their own topics of discussion, since what respondents chose to talk about often revealed a great deal about their experiences with the media.

Six of the twenty-seven interviewees agreed to be identified in this research. Among the twenty-one who chose to remain anonymous, seventeen agreed to include any part of their comments in this chapter, while the other four indicated through the course of the interview what could or could not be reported. It is noteworthy that of the eighteen women interviewed, only two (Kim Campbell and Alexa McDonough) agreed to be identified in this research. By contrast, nearly half of the men interviewed (4 of 9) said they could be identified, which suggests female politicians may be more guarded than their male counterparts, possibly because of negative experiences with the media.

Interviewees were informed that this research project focused on media coverage of elections and politicians. No specific mention was made of the treatment of women versus men, to avoid priming interviewees towards certain topics or positions. If, by the end of their interviews, MPs had not mentioned any type of gender issue, they were asked a specific question about the presence of stereotypes or biases in Canadian televised news. Of the eighteen female interviewees, twelve spoke spontaneously about how being a woman had influenced their news coverage, while the other six did not. When asked at the end of their respective interviews whether gender played a role in their news coverage, all six of these women responded affirmatively, and most gave short examples of how being a woman had either hindered or helped their coverage.

Perspectives on Media Presentation

Like their Australian, British, and South African counterparts (Ross 2002; Ross and Sreberny 2000), Canadian politicians distinguished among different media formats. Former Prime Minister Kim Campbell was unequivocal in her preference for print and radio over television,[1] arguing "TV is difficult, because they take a five-second sound bite and end up presenting none of your points and often you are presented out of context." Campbell was sensitive to misrepresentation issues; in her view, Liberal leader Jean "Chrétien was repeatedly let off the hook with off-the-cuff comments and blunders." She explicitly stated, "This is a gender thing." Echoing several female MPs at Westminster (see Ross 2002), Campbell maintained, "Radio is the best of all, because you can talk and get your points out, and people can hear the tone, pitch and variety in your voice, but without the distraction of the visuals." Campbell spoke in detail about the fast pace and visual focus of TV that, in her view, drew voters' attention away from the sometimes complex messages of politicians.

Media format preferences are not just a function of gender. This is not the whole story. Certainly, given Campbell's autobiography, *Time and Chance*, and her personal discussion with me, not only was Campbell annoyed at the tendency of the media to take her speech out of context, she was at times uncomfortable with the media's focus on her clothes and weight during her political career. Highly visual media certainly do emphasize physical appearance; however, there were other factors at play. Campbell's reasons for preferring print and radio over television included a view that "this may be an age thing." Gender was, therefore, not the only factor that affected her preferred media format. Campbell's preference for print and radio as an "age thing" contrasted with the views of Conservative MP Rahim Jaffer, whose preferred news coverage was television: "TV is key ... A second best is a print story with a picture accompanying it, preferably in colour."[2] Age thirty-three at the time of our interview, Jaffer was one of the youngest MPs in the House of Commons.[3] He grew up in the era of personalized, "candidate-centred" politics (Wattenberg 1995) and felt comfortable with the visual media. Moreover, his comments about print media expressed a clear preference for visual content, since he said a print story must have a picture to accompany it, and ideally, a picture in colour.[4]

Other MPs tended to share Jaffer's perspective. One Conservative woman believed local or, less often, national television news coverage of her participation in Question Period was "by far" the best way for constituents to see her. Subscribing to the view that "there's no such thing as bad publicity" – a position disputed by evidence presented in an earlier chapter – she aimed to be very visible to the public and especially to voters in her district. When this same sentiment was expressed by British and Australian legislators, Ross and Sreberny (2000) concluded that "in an era of presentation politics and an apathetic polity, many women feel their constituents only believe they are actually doing their job and representing their interests when they see them 'live' on television" (86).

In short, conversations with Canadian MPs revealed a generational dimension to media format preferences. Some older interviewees, notably, former NDP leader Ed Broadbent, observed that back when newspapers had more reporters in Ottawa, journalists could develop clear areas of expertise. He noted specifically that newspapers used to have more specialist reporters, including reporters who focused on labour issues, which would have obviously been of great interest to the left-of-centre NDP. Past difficulties with different media formats also played a role in politicians' preferences. Believing that she faced critical coverage of her physical appearance as well as misrepresentation in television coverage, Kim Campbell preferred the medium of radio interviews, which isn't a visual format. In her view, this format offered more time for articulating complex points.

In addition to preferences for types of media, many female politicians prefer live interviews to pre-recorded news stories, because live interviews leave much less room for "creative editing" (Ross 2002, 103). At the same time, live appearances carry particular risks. All politicians must carefully manoeuvre live appearances. Interviewers can ask difficult questions, and claims made "off-the-cuff" can beleaguer politicians, particularly during campaigns. In some cases, speaking spontaneously seems to have more damaging consequences for female politicians, as Kim Campbell expressed regarding her experience of the 1993 federal election campaign. There were several instances during the campaign where Campbell's words were quoted out of context in a way that made for negative media coverage. Early in the campaign, she told reporters, "You can't have a debate on such a key issue as the modernization of social programs in 47 days [because] serious, honest and realistic changes to our social programs require and demand extensive consultations with the provinces and more importantly with every Canadian" (Dougherty et al. 1993). Plainly, her point was that election campaigns are not long enough to discuss complex political issues, a point that is difficult to refute. A number of media reports put their own spin on Campbell's remark, portraying her comments as arrogant and elitist. An op-ed piece after the 1993 campaign noted, "Until she made her disastrous statement about campaigns not being the place to discuss serious policies, Kim Campbell was in contention to be prime minister."[5] The op-ed continued with the claim that "the statement convinced others that Ms. Campbell was an arrogant intellectual who felt ordinary voters were incapable of informed debate on such issues as the future of social programs."

Campbell was dogged frequently in this manner. At the very beginning of the 1993 campaign, Campbell made a statement about employment prospects: "I think realistically all the developed industrialized countries are expecting what I would consider an unacceptable level of unemployment for the next two, three or four years."[6] She continued by noting that she "would like to see, certainly by the turn of the century, a country where unemployment is way down." Across the country, the early to mid-1990s were marked by a stunning recession that was pegged as the worst economic downturn since the Great Depression of the 1930s. Within this context of economic malaise, and knowing that it takes time to tackle joblessness, Campbell's remarks were honest and reasonable. A campaign post-mortem portrayed her comment as cold: "Ms. Campbell was supposed to persuade Canadians who had seen their expectations dashed that she would create new opportunity for them. Instead, she told them not to expect work for the rest of the decade."[7] Another piece claimed that her remark about jobs exhibited "about as much sympathy for job-seekers as a Zurich banker has for overdrafts."[8] Again, Campbell's comments were portrayed in a simplistic manner and as evidence of her alleged arrogance and elitism.

Interestingly, off-the-cuff remarks made by Chrétien during the 1993 campaign did not attract the same type of negative attention. During the campaign, Liberal leader Jean Chrétien was asked whether he would raise taxes to meet his deficit-reduction target. Chrétien snapped back, "Don't ask me. I cannot make a budget for three years from now."[9] Several days later, he told reporters, "Let me win the election and after that, you come and ask me questions about how I run a government."[10] Chrétien's comments were not interpreted as arrogant or menacing, unlike those of his rival, Kim Campbell. According to the Fraser Institute's National Media Archive, "Campbell was portrayed as confused, and often having to explain and re-explain her statements ... In contrast, Jean Chrétien was rarely asked to clarify his statements."[11] Imbalances in the treatment of Campbell and Chrétien became so evident that journalists themselves remarked on the seeming double standard in media reports, noting "would Tory leader Kim Campbell be allowed to make such a statement without being accused of arrogance?"[12] and "Let's see if we've got this straight. Kim Campbell says something that everyone acknowledges to be true, and it's a 'gaffe.' Jean Chrétien vows to do something that everyone knows will accomplish nothing, and it is said to offer 'hope.'"[13]

Regardless of media format, female members of Parliament raised the common theme that reporters focused on their physical appearances and personal lives. Several of the women noted that the print media, not televised news, were the worst offenders in this respect. Part of the explanation, although none of the women identified this as a factor, is that televised news actually has sparser content than newspapers. Discounting the time used for opening credits, commercials, and closing credits, the average televised newscast is fairly short. This is why newspapers are often said to produce more in-depth coverage than televised news. During our interview, former NDP leader Alexa McDonough recalled a story in the *Ottawa Citizen* during her early years in Ottawa.[14] After an aide called excitedly to tell her about page one coverage, McDonough opened the paper to see a large photo of herself above the headline, "Alexa McDonough, Call Your

Dry-Cleaner."[15] The main point of this front-page column was that she had worn the same dress to two different events in the same week.[16] Although McDonough was angered at the time, she saw over the years that this type of coverage was "par for the course." Comments about her appearance and that of other female MPs were made with sufficient frequency that they could not be ignored. According to McDonough, the amount of writing about women's physical appearance was not matched by similar coverage of men in the House of Commons, a view that is consistent with analyses of male and female candidates' press coverage in the 2005-06 election campaign examined in Chapter 2. Referring explicitly to the *Ottawa Citizen* story, she wondered how many male MPs did *not* wear the same suit twice in one week. "Could you imagine a story," she asked, "with the following headline: Jean Chrétien wears same suit twice in one week? No man has ten suits, and no one expects him to, but a woman is supposed to have a closet full of clothes." Audrey McLaughlin, McDonough's predecessor as NDP leader, recounts a similar story in her autobiography. Two PC female ministers went to an event wearing the same outfit, causing a minor media stir. "Whatever for?" asks McLaughlin, "The papers could as easily have run the following headline: 'Two Hundred and Fifty Male MPs Appear in Commons Wearing Same Dark Blue Suit'" (1992, 92).

Ross and Sreberny's (2000, 87) consultations with female MPs in Britain resulted in similar findings. They quoted Labour member Dawn Primarolo, who said:

> I don't know whether it is deliberate or it's so ingrained, but a woman's appearance is always commented on. That never happens to male politicians, ever, unless they have made a particular point about their style, but then they are presented as extreme, exceptions that prove the rule. Women are never the right age. We're too young, we're too old. We're too thin, we're too fat. We wear too much make-up, we don't wear enough. We're too flashy in our dress, we don't take enough care. There isn't a thing we can do that's right.

Frustration over the attention reporters paid to physical appearances was, therefore, not peculiar to female politicians in Ottawa.

Female MPs interviewed for this study believed that the media are intrusive in their treatment of women's personal lives. One interviewee argued that the fact that many women in the House of Commons were divorced or single was disproportionately prominent in news coverage, and she went on to note that print outlets were particularly likely to mention the divorced or lone-parent status of female MPs. This view is confirmed by a number of empirical analyses conducted outside Canada (see, e.g., Bystrom, Robertson, and Banwart 2001; Kahn 1992, 1996; Kahn and Goldberg 1991; Robertson et al. 2002; Muir 2005). As Carmen Lawrence, the first female premier of an Australian state, noted, "When I became Premier, all this stuff came out, [using my] first name, wanting images of me shown in domestic situations and references to my family and all that stuff that comes out with women ... you rarely see a man described as Joe Bloggs, 54, father of three" (Ross 2002, 87). Similar evidence was presented here in Chapter 2's analyses of print news coverage of the 2005-06 campaign, for Belinda Stronach's status as a divorced woman and single mother was mentioned regularly, Olivia Chow's connection to Jack Layton was mentioned in all her stories, and Rona Ambrose's childlessness was likewise considered newsworthy.

Given the attention paid to their personal lives, many female politicians retreat from media scrutiny. Kim Campbell noted that endeavouring to keep their "love lives" out of the public eye followed from a realistic sense that this type of coverage can harm women's careers – even if parallel coverage of bachelorhood and single fatherhood can glorify men's lives. Alexa McDonough said she made concerted efforts throughout her political career to keep her personal life out of the public spotlight, including by shielding her children from media scrutiny.[17] McDonough was concerned that her status as a divorced woman could – and would – be used in a negative way, particularly if members of the general public absorbed ideas from the media and elsewhere that her leadership and policy abilities were questionable because she was divorced.

Female politicians outside Canada share the view that care must be taken to shield one's personal life from media scrutiny (e.g., van Zoonen 1998, 2000a, 2000b, 2005, 2006). Legislators as diverse as German Chancellor Angela Merkel, former Finnish Prime Minister Tarja Halonen, former US Senator and Secretary of State Hillary Clinton, and former Dutch Green leader Femke Halsema all became "reticent about opening up their private personae to the scrutiny of the media and public" (van Zoonen 2006, 297). Shielding partners and spouses from media attention is important for two reasons: first, few are willing to jeopardize the privacy and security of their families, particularly their children, by exposing them to media scrutiny; and second, keeping family members out of the picture helps discourage the use of traditional "wife" and "mother" designations in media coverage that can be part of mother framing. Shielding their private lives is also a way for women to circumvent or at least minimize media attention to role conflict in news coverage.

In contrast, it is commonplace to see family members of male politicians. Jean Chrétien, Paul Martin, Brian Mulroney, Stephen Harper, and others have often brought their wives to political events. In the 2000 Canadian federal election campaign, Joe Clark travelled the country with his daughter, Catherine Clark, who became a focal point of media attention. News reports explicitly claimed that Catherine Clark's involvement was intended to add youth, beauty, and "pizzazz" to the PC leader's campaign tour.[18] Quite aside from the fact that Joe Clark saw no liability in bringing his family into the campaign, media treatment of Catherine Clark was interesting in itself. Reporters automatically assumed that she acted as "window dressing" for Joe Clark's campaign, even though she was, in fact, a public relations specialist for one of the largest such firms in the country, Hill + Knowlton, and acted as a campaign advisor for her father during the 2000 campaign.

Canadian female politicians have additional reasons to be concerned about news framing of "unconventional" aspects of their personal lives. If they are unmarried or unattached, or if they are not regarded as "feminine" in the stereotypical sense of the term, then questions about their sexual orientation tend to follow. Journalists have hinted about lesbianism in their coverage of a number of federal MPs including Audrey McLaughlin, Sheila Copps, and Deborah Grey (see Sharpe 1994, 31-32). In the US, innuendos about Clinton-era Attorney General Janet Reno were so frequent that Reno told a number of reporters, "I am just an awkward old maid with a very great affection for men" (Reno as quoted in Jamieson 1995, 73). Analysts can debate the wisdom of replying to such rumours, particularly, in the candid manner employed by Reno, but it remains a fact that female politicians often believe they need to present themselves explicitly as heterosexual.

Not all the women I interviewed were critical of the media's interest in women's private lives. One Liberal MP, for example, believed female politicians sometimes invited this sort of commentary. Referring specifically to Belinda Stronach's decision to cross the floor to join the Liberal cabinet in 2005, she said too much coverage of this story focused on the reaction of Peter McKay, Stronach's former partner, and all the "jilted lover garbage." Yet, in her view, Stronach should have expected this kind of attention because she had engaged in an "office romance"; for women to be taken seriously, according to this interviewee, they need to keep personal and private lives separate. This MP maintained that it was foolish to expect reporters to turn down headline-grabbing information, since news is a business and political gossip sells. This interviewee suggested implicitly, then, that gendered provision was part of the reason for the focus on McKay when Stronach crossed the floor. Stronach had mixed her personal and professional lives, making her personal life relevant to (or, at least, closely associated with) her professional life. This is not to say that media presentation is not a large part of the story regarding how Stronach's floor crossing was covered. Indeed, the media were guilty of bringing the jilted McKay up in most of the stories about the floor crossing, making it an issue again and again.

In contrast to the female interviewees, the men did not have much to say about their families or personal lives. One of the two male MPs who mentioned this dimension was Gurmant Grewal, a Conservative MP from British Columbia. Grewal spoke in some detail about the fact that his wife, Nina Grewal, also held a Commons seat. He noted with some pride that they were the first married couple to serve as MPs at the same time and that they had received considerable media attention as a result. This was presented as a positive and uncomplicated part of his public persona in the legislature, not as something that was problematic. The second mentioned family in the context of his wife's view that party events were boring and that, as a result, she did not usually accompany him to "official events." Clearly, men and women in Parliament perceived media scrutiny of their personal lives differently. Women cited endless pitfalls while men revealed little concern, let alone pressure for strategic self-presentation. Kim Campbell seemed particularly troubled by this obvious double standard; in her words, "Look at Trudeau, for example, whose love life was a mess. It didn't hurt him. Quite the opposite – media and the public thought he was dashing and sexy."

Political women are keenly aware of the terrain they confront in obtaining positive news coverage, and so, too, are politicians with other markers of difference. Visible minority women face unique dilemmas, as their sex intersects with their ethnicity, provoking further anticipation that the media will focus on their appearance, in this case, highlighting their minority status as well as their gender. A growing body of literature highlights the gendered and racialized aspects of the news (e.g., Carter et al. 1998; Fleras and Kunz 2001; Gershon 2012; Henry and Tator 2002; Law 2002; Saunders 1991; Terkildsen and Damore 1999; Tolley 2012; Zilber and Niven 2000a, 2000b). Work on media representations of black women contends that "sexualized and servile images of Black women are widely disseminated in popular culture" (Lawson 2002, 199), regardless of the fact that "racist discourse is increasingly coded with more 'acceptable' signifiers of difference" (203). Gershon's (2012) recent work on members of the US Congress demonstrates, moreover, that minority women are disadvantaged on both visibility and the quality of their coverage in the news compared with all other members. In her autobiography, Rosemary Brown – the first black woman to be elected to a legislative body in Canada, in 1972, and a candidate for the federal NDP leadership in 1975 – shares reflections on media coverage of her during her political career. Referring specifically to her bid for the national NDP leadership, Brown has this to say in her autobiography:

> I believe that [reporters] hoped I would win so that they could conduct endless research on "the impact of a Black female immigrant socialist on the political landscape of Canada," and they hoped that I would lose to demonstrate the accuracy of their political forecasting. I imagine that even as wild and bizarre headlines were zipping through their heads – "White Canadian Party Elects Black Leader," "One of the World's Largest White Countries Led by Radical Black Feminist Socialist," "Shocked Canadians Appeal to the World for Help After Black Leader Elected," "White No More," "Brown Is Beautiful says Black Leader to White Country," "Country Falls to Feminists" – tantalizing them, they were hoping that in the end the party would choose a staid, sensible leader in the Canadian mould. (1989, 172)

In much of Brown's book, references to her gender or to sexism are intertwined with discussion of race and ethnicity in Canada. Similarly, in the National Film Board documentary *Sisters in the Struggle* (1991), an interviewer asked Brown whether it was racism or sexism that she fought hardest against. Brown's response, to paraphrase, was that it was neither, because she could not separate her feminism from her efforts to combat racism.

Among my interviewees, one male MP also highlighted media focus on his ethnicity. Gurmant Grewal said that his coverage regularly includes reference to his ethnicity and/or religion.[19] He said that stories tend to open with "the Indo-Canadian Member from ..." or "Gurmant Grewal, a non-practising Sikh, said yesterday ..." Grewal explicitly questioned what relevance his religion has to his activities as a member of Parliament. He continued by noting that the media do not report on the religious affiliations of other MPs, presumably meaning MPs from Judeo-Christian backgrounds. He said that the media do this because he is different. Reference to ethnicity and religion signify the same message as references to gender: this person is different, this person is novel, this person is an outsider, as work on racial mediation has pointed out (e.g., Tolley 2012).

The population of visible minority members of Parliament was – and is currently – small, and the sample of visible minority members that I interviewed was even smaller. Thus, it is difficult to discuss the conversations I had with interviewees who chose to be unidentified in this study, because factors such as partisanship, the province or region they represent, and, in some cases, the nature of their comments could conceivably identify them. In general terms, the small number of visible minority MPs I interviewed tended to think that their ethnocultural identities were often mentioned in news coverage, even in cases where this was irrelevant to the policy fields or committee work they tend to do. In one case, an interviewee did mention that being linked to ethnic heritage could be a positive factor for candidates, like him, who run in ridings with a sizeable concentration of people from the same ethnic background. Nevertheless, this interviewee mentioned that it is not necessary for the media to explicitly mention a candidate's ethnicity in such cases, because voters are aware of the identifiers of shared ethnic background, such as surnames.

There was only one case where a visible minority MP interviewed did not mention his ethnocultural heritage in any context: Conservative MP Rahim Jaffer. I did not ask him about his heritage or his experience as a visible minority MP, and neither did he mention these. Perhaps Jaffer did not feel they were relevant to his work in Ottawa, and perhaps he did not notice or did not mind if the media drew attention to his background.

Quality and Quantity of Coverage

Party connections played an important role in distinguishing among MPs. NDP and Conservative members on the opposition benches criticized the media for focusing too much on the Liberals, who were in power at the time we met. New Democrats claimed it was particularly hard for them to attract attention, although Ed Broadbent saw it as "appropriate for media to pay more attention to government." Six of the eighteen female interviewees mentioned party or region before gender as a factor in their coverage, which reminds us of the variety of factors that shape press attention.

Several female politicians mentioned reporters' lack of knowledge about them; one, for example, claimed that unless you are a "high-profile" candidate (e.g., a veteran MP or cabinet minister), you tend to be ignored. In her experience, journalists did not take the time to "do their research" since they asked questions about children of childless candidates. This may result from a history of female candidates running in unwinnable seats, which leads journalists to expect that female nominees will lose on election day, and to them women are, therefore, less worthy of media attention.

Do political women have the sense that they are taken as seriously by reporters as men are? Alexa McDonough recalled that when she first came to Ottawa, in 1995, and through the 1997 federal election campaign, she was routinely addressed by journalists as "Audrey." Audrey McLaughlin was McDonough's predecessor as federal NDP leader; both were social workers, had two children, were divorced, and shared the initials "A. Mc." However, McDonough insisted this treatment did not befall men in politics. During the 1980s, she pointed out, several men named John served as MPs, including John Turner, John Crosbie, and Jean Chrétien, but reporters did not confuse them. Many men named Bill and Mike participated in Canadian politics, shared the same professional background, and had the same number of children, but they were not mixed up with each other. An important factor to keep in mind here, though not mentioned by McDonough, is that both she and McLaughlin led the national third party, which was never in a competitive position over the tenure of either of their leaderships. As such, journalists had fewer incentives, I suppose, to avoid mixing them up, unlike the numerous Johns, Mikes, and Bills around Parliament in that era who sat on the Conservative or Liberal sides of the House.

McDonough claimed that women such as herself and McLaughlin were "interchangeable" in the minds of reporters, a view consistent with cognitive psychology research on "outgroup homogeneity bias" (e.g., Mullen and Hu 1989). This perspective leads individuals to perceive members of other groups as more alike or "interchangeable," in McDonough's words, than members of their own group. The dynamic at play renders members of marginalized groups, such as women in politics, homogeneous and essentialized. McDonough admitted that other than wearing a name tag to press conferences and media scrums, she could do little to avoid being confused with McLaughlin. She often asked an assistant to introduce her to journalists at formal events including press conferences and speeches, but she could not use the same strategy in situations when a journalist just "puts a microphone in your face."

Kim Campbell linked reporters' lack of knowledge to their assumptions about female politicians. In her view, journalists implied she slept her way to the top because they found it difficult to grasp that women could achieve success through "intelligence, political know-how, and hard work." She noted that reporters repeatedly called her a "rookie" even though she was one of the most experienced politicians to work in the Prime Minister's Office; Campbell had held a variety of federal cabinet portfolios including national defence and justice (the first woman to hold these posts) as well as positions at all three levels of government before becoming national Conservative leader. By way of comparison, Pierre Trudeau had one year of cabinet experience before becoming prime minister, while Brian Mulroney and Joe Clark had none. Campbell's point, ultimately, was that "the media could have called me a moron or an idiot, which is a matter of opinion, but the facts just did not support the use of the adjective 'rookie' to describe me." When asked how she dealt with this aspect of her coverage, Campbell submitted that although a politician can do a lot to cultivate favourable coverage during non-election periods, "there is little a politician ... can do about damage control" in the midst of a campaign.

Other female interviewees were more optimistic about their ability to influence coverage during a campaign, including four who had attended campaign schools earlier in their careers. All four said this training had markedly improved their media skills. That three of them were Liberals may indicate a greater commitment of resources to that activity by some parties than others. One woman who had participated in campaign training after her first nomination as a Liberal candidate said running a campaign and, in particular, dealing with the media are "not intuitive," since both require specialized public speaking and networking skills. No male MPs mentioned campaign schools or other forms of campaign and media training.

The campaign comments of both male and female MPs suggested that many were more concerned with the quantity rather than the quality of media coverage. Some had learned, for example, that campaign events had to be timed for maximum visibility so that nightly television stories were based on morning or early afternoon appearances. Less high-profile appearances in hospitals or seniors' homes could take place at the end of the day, and receive local newspaper coverage.

Marked gender divides can be discerned in the ways MPs assessed Question Period in the House of Commons, a topic that came up frequently in response to my questions about news coverage between elections. Neither Kim Campbell nor Alexa McDonough mentioned Question Period or the media coverage it attracts, which was interesting considering that both are former party leaders, and Campbell is a former prime minister. Ed Broadbent and Stockwell Day – two male former party leaders – both mentioned Question Period and its coverage in the media. In general, it was not surprising that so many MPs mentioned Question Period, because it is the only aspect of parliamentary activity that receives habitual news coverage. Lacking in drama and conflict, legislative debates and points of order do not make for enticing news stories. Question Period is a different matter, for it is exciting, fast-paced, and conflictive. Most of the interviewees did mention Question Period and its coverage, and of these twenty (11 women, 9 men), women tended to focus on their dislike of these sessions – including ways they had found to avoid them by retreating to caucus lounges.[20] A woman on the Liberal side of the House, in fact, said that if you can survive Question Period, dealing with the media is a "piece of cake." The same woman said that in her opinion, it could be particularly challenging to go through Question Period, and then have to meet the media scrum in the House lobby directly afterwards. She said that one never really leaves Question Period or a media scrum feeling that the interaction has been good, because even if one really nails a question or a sound bite, the atmosphere is unbelievably chaotic.

This is not to say that all female politicians are uncomfortable with the raucous atmosphere of Question Period. Some female politicians have excelled in this environment – maybe even revelled in it as many of their male colleagues do. Former Liberal MP and cabinet member Sheila Copps, for example, was a member of the so-called Rat Pack[21] that was famous for its relentless piercing critique of Mulroney and the PC governments both in the House of Commons and to the media. During her political career, Copps was typically quite comfortable with adversarial politics (Copps 1986, 2004); at the same time, Sheila Copps grew up in a political household,[22] which likely acclimatized her to and prepared her for the exigencies of politics more than is the case for many other female (or male) politicians (e.g., Lawless and Fox 2005, 2010).

Among my particular interviewees, only one man, former NDP leader Ed Broadbent, expressed dissatisfaction with the tone of Question Period. Other male MPs focused their comments on using Question Period to attract news coverage. This was particularly the case for Conservative Rahim Jaffer, who spoke at length about his adversarial talents in "going over the top, getting theatrical in QP" as part of a three-man "hit squad" that attacked the governing Liberals.

When asked for their thoughts on how reporters cover Question Period, women tended to maintain that because these sessions were rowdy, so was the media coverage of them. In other words, provision plays an important role in how Question Period is covered. None of the female MPs shared

Jaffer's comfort with the conflictual style of Question Period. Even Jaffer recognized this gender angle, since during his interview, he mentioned "hit squad" attacks on Immigration Minister Judy Sgro that were presented in the media as "all-male aggressors harass woman in the House who is just trying to work on social issues." Jaffer noted the Conservative caucus worked right away to "re-tool" their Question Period strategy so that the next day, all of the party's questions were assigned to women. From then on, Jaffer said, the Conservatives tended to assign female caucus members to "go after" female ministers in the government.

This story sheds light on how gendered norms can challenge and constrain men. Jaffer's comments, as well as changes to the Conservative party's Question Period strategy, show how men's attacks on female politicians can backfire because they breach norms of "gentlemanly" conduct. US research in this area identifies a common tactic for male politicians, which is avoiding direct attacks on women (e.g., Kahn 1993). As Kahn's analysis of campaign commercials reveals, men are less likely to run candidate-centred attack ads when their rivals are women because they do not want to be seen as "beating up on" women (1993, 491). At the same time, the fact that male politicians often avoid direct attacks on or verbal arguments with their female rivals may further trivialize female politicians. Although none of my interviewees framed the issue in such terms, the unavoidable implication is that female politicians do not possess the mettle to defend their policy platforms, political decisions, or simply, to verbally spar with their male counterparts. The suggestion is that female politicians are weak or timid.

Although women tend to be more critical of the adversarial style of politics, particularly Question Period, gendered reportage hinting that mixed-sex political sparring is an unfair fight precisely because one of the politicians is female is problematic for any politician, irrespective of sex. In addition, the Conservatives' revision of their Question Period strategy to pit Conservative women against government women can also raise problems – as the following paragraphs illustrate – because media often depict woman-to-woman conflict using a "catfight" frame. In fact, female politicians are often wary of appearing too aggressive at all, regardless of the sex of opponents. Former Prime Minister Kim Campbell's autobiography makes this point very clearly. The format of the 1993 leaders' debate was not the traditional series of one-on-one confrontations, "which enabled leaders to argue without struggling to be heard" (Campbell 1996, 278). Rather, the format took the form of discussion among all the participants "which would make it extremely difficult for one leader to contradict or question another if it was his or her turn to speak. In theory, there was to be a certain amount of open give and take, but in reality, it meant we would often be talking over one another." Reflecting on her preparation for the debates, Campbell notes, "If I wanted to respond to an attack – and I was to be the recipient of the lion's share of the attacks – I ran the risk of appearing too aggressive, and aggressiveness is seen as less attractive coming from a woman." Throughout her analysis of her time in office, Campbell repeatedly returns to the idea that the media's inflexibility to move beyond gendered stereotypes constrains politicians, men and women alike.

How do media accounts frame conflicts *between* women in politics? Five of the eighteen female MPs noted their purposeful avoidance of situations that could be portrayed as "catfights." Alexa McDonough recalled that as a member of the Nova Scotia Legislature and leader of the Nova Scotia NDP, she was invited to join the provincial delegation to the Charlottetown constitutional discussions. Although much of the Canadian women's movement under the umbrella of the National Action Committee on the Status of Women (NAC) mobilized against the accord that came out of those talks, McDonough supported the deal. She chose not to participate in a televised debate, however, with NAC president Judy Rebick on account of fear that it would be portrayed as a catfight. McDonough found the situation regrettable because a debate would have drawn public visibility to the Charlottetown Accord, NAC, and individual political women including Rebick and McDonough.

A bright spot in female MPs' views on their news coverage was the knowledge that members of rare species tend to attract attention. Several Canadian women commented on how the relative novelty of female politicians increased their media visibility and positively shaped the content of coverage. One Liberal noted, tongue in cheek, that she had greatly benefited from "all the fuss" about women in politics (see the discussion in Chapter 3, p. 126). In cases where enhanced visibility follows from women's minority status in legislatures, it is understandable that politicians will view this situation as advantageous. Given that immediate career prospects including re-election benefit from more rather than less coverage, one can imagine scenarios in which female politicians might decide to strategically, and subtly, draw attention to gender as a marker of difference, in order to attract press attention. It is important to bear in mind that the primary goal of many female politicians, like that of their male colleagues, is re-election, not revolutionary change in the political system or the journalism profession. Put differently, we must interpret the statements of interviewees in light of their chosen priorities and goals. Many female MPs I interviewed expressed serious dissatisfaction with biased media coverage, at the same time as they recognized the benefits of their outsider status. Multiple markers of difference, however, can be used to marginalize and discredit "outsider" women, thus neutralizing any advantage that might have accrued from greater press attention because they were unusual political participants.

On the issue of visibility or quantity of coverage, several MPs interviewed, men and women both, expressed some variant of the old saying "there's no such thing as bad press." Seven of the twenty-seven expressed this attitude, although not necessarily in direct or explicit terms. Interestingly, none of the party leaders seemed to put stock in the sentiment. This was something that male and female leaders shared in common. If they had led parties, they did not believe that visibility was the overarching priority in terms of news coverage. Former NDP leader Alexa McDonough was very direct: "I get more respect from media now that I'm not leader anymore."

The likely explanation for the difference between those who had served as party leaders and those who had not is that party leaders had personally experienced (or, at the very least, witnessed) the worst forms of news coverage: mud slinging; highly unflattering photos and camera angles; unwanted attention to one's past, one's personal life, or one's family; and the inevitable attacks from columnists and pundits about one's ineptitude for leadership or uninspiring policy vision. Leaders are always subject to intense media scrutiny and large volumes of coverage, so naturally, experience as a party leader would lead one to adopt a more measured attitude towards the idea that "there's no such thing as bad press."

Relations with Reporters

Sharp differences existed between men and women, as well as among women, in the degree to which MPs built personal relationships with journalists. Except for Ed Broadbent, every male legislator I interviewed talked about efforts to forge ties with reporters. Stockwell Day spoke at length about his experiences in the Alberta provincial legislature, where friendly relations with local reporters produced favourable media coverage.[23] Day noted that these relations extended beyond the workplace, since MLAs and reporters often socialized together at charity functions, party events, and so on.

Female politicians with provincial experience maintained that relations with the media were more cordial at that level. Alexa McDonough, for example, claimed she never felt uncomfortable or marginalized by Nova Scotia journalists during her provincial career; in fact, both MLAs and reporters shared a sense of intimacy and of working towards the "same goals." Kim Campbell believed the "Ottawa press pack" was tightly knit, often caught up in a political "who's who game" that excluded her and many other women. Campbell maintained that outside Ottawa, regional "reporters do not focus exclusively on national politics, and they would listen to my policies on the wheat trade, for example." She argued that regional reporters cared about issues affecting their area – such as the wheat trade in the Prairies – while members of the Ottawa press corps were narrowly preoccupied with partisan politics and gossip.

Conservative politicians from western Canada viewed the challenge of winning favourable media coverage in Ottawa as particularly difficult. Stockwell Day said that as a westerner, leader of the Canadian Alliance, and purported "right-wing nut-job" and "Christian fundamentalist," getting Ottawa journalists to "warm up" to him was far from easy. He talked at length about how the documentary, *The Fundamental Day*,[24] an in-depth examination of Day's religious beliefs that aired on CBC's *The National* during the 2000 election campaign, sank his image. Yet, he worked at rehabilitating his image with journalists, who tended to preface his coverage with "the Christian fundamentalist leader" or "the right-wing leader," which is parallel to Grewal's comment that descriptors such as "the Indo-Canadian member" were regularly used in coverage. Some male politicians also feel negatively stereotyped in the media. Rahim Jaffer shared the view that bias against westerners and politicians on the right wing of the spectrum was a reality, but said the trick was to bring journalists into "your fold." He organized frequent social events where politicians and journalists met for drinks or dinner.

No female MPs talked about cultivating personal relationships with journalists, nor did they mention participating in events, receptions, or dinners with members of the press. When asked about ties with reporters, women tended to be either negative or ambivalent. Comments along the former lines emphasized the conflictual nature of journalist-politician relations. One Liberal woman termed the parliamentary press corps a "shark tank," and another characterized it as having a "barracuda mentality" because of reporters' reliance on questions that aimed "straight for the jugular." McDonough was less harsh than these respondents; she was struck most by how "impersonal" relations were between MPs and the Ottawa media. McDonough believed journalists were doing their jobs, trying to sell their stories to editors and readers. These relatively neutral views contrasted with those of the two Liberal women, likely because McDonough had long served as an opposition member in Halifax and Ottawa, while the two Liberals sat on the government side. Government MPs, whether men or women, may find themselves disproportionately on the defensive with reporters, while opposition MPs seem inclined to appreciate whatever coverage they receive.

Some female MPs voiced particularly intriguing views of female journalists. Two spontaneously mentioned this subject. McDonough said that at several points throughout the years, she had felt supported by female journalists. She and a Liberal MP singled out Julie Van Dusen, a senior journalist with the CBC. The Liberal MP saw Van Dusen as the best reporter in Ottawa, one who was willing to tell male journalists to "back off" or "get real" when a "sexist" question was posed. This Liberal remarked that in the midst of a media scrum on a rough day, a shared sense of fairness among women made a world of difference.

When I asked the other sixteen female MPs about their experiences with female journalists, most recalled incidents where the latter had been sensitive or supportive, either in person or in their reporting. A minority viewed male and female journalists as indistinguishable. Kim Campbell pointed out that not only are female journalists expected to conform to standard journalistic modes of writing, which tend to be adversarial and masculine in style, but also "women are not making the editorial decisions" in media organizations. She noted, "The media culture is another barrier, because there is a certain way of getting and writing stories, and it is pre-defined, and it is hard for any individual to buck this." These are the same insights made in earlier chapters about the powerful constraints imposed on female journalists – indeed, all journalists – by the sociology of newswork and the political economy of the news business. Moreover, Campbell noted that "women are not always sympathetic and do not always feel a solidarity with other women." Campbell noted that even when women are in positions of power, such as female hosts of political talk shows in the United States, you do not see more women on their shows or more attention to topics that are specifically regarded as important to women.

Discussion

At the same time as news coverage helps to shape how voters in a democracy perceive political figures, for politicians, the news is the most unpredictable form of political communication. They have virtually no control over how information is presented and interpreted. Public figures try to predict how audiences will react to their self-presentations – including their style, speech, ideas, interpersonal manner, and gestures – but also they need to anticipate how newsmakers will portray these same characteristics to the public. Moreover, they must do all this while maintaining the appearance of spontaneity, which is one of the key ingredients in a successful presentation of self (Goffman 1959).

This chapter has examined how Canadian MPs understand the news media and, further, how they tailor their presentations of self in light of these perspectives. Both men and women viewed press coverage as distorting reality, notably, as focusing on or even exploiting stereotypes. Many female MPs mentioned gender stereotypes as a defining feature of their coverage. One man, former Alliance leader Stockwell Day, reported stereotypical coverage of his religious and political beliefs (e.g., "Fundamental Day" and "right-wing nut-job"). Given that the comparative literature reveals similar findings, we know dissatisfaction of this kind is hardly unique to Canadian politicians (see Ross 2002; Ross and Sreberny 2000).

In our interview conversation, Kim Campbell took this analysis one step further. She viewed stereotyping as a widespread problem that is not necessarily a function of media coverage. In her words, it is difficult for women "to act in a naturally feminine way given that politics is defined by men. Disempowered people never know what it is like to be themselves in politics. Women CEOs have the same problems ... Women leaders have to hold back and cannot be their true selves, because their true selves do not mesh with the definition of leadership." Campbell ended this observation with a question: "What is the professional and psychological price of holding back?" A phrase like "psychological price" refers to the personal cost to female politicians of adopting a neutered or masculine public face. Campbell believed this practice was harmful because "you forget to be true to yourself," perhaps one of the intangible reasons why women are more reluctant than men to consider running for office (e.g., Lawless and Fox 2005, 2010), contributing to the notable supply problem of female candidacies.

Former NDP leader Audrey McLaughlin offered a similar perspective in her autobiography: "The danger in all this is that you will lose track of who you really are, that your public persona will no longer reflect your private self" (1992, 204). Amid debates about whether voters use stereotypes to ascribe traits or policy positions to female candidates or whether "acting tough" harms or helps women at the polls, we may have overlooked another important issue: how do the adoption of neutered or masculine political personas affect female politicians personally? This is a consequential question, since women's individual decisions to enter or remain in political office are highly personal considerations. The political mask may be unappealing to many highly qualified women.

It is clear that the understandings of media coverage held by Canadian women MPs resemble those of their counterparts in Australia, the United Kingdom, South Africa, and the United States. If generalizations are to be made, my analyses suggest the following: first, female political leaders *do* confront disadvantages in their media presentations and, second, these disadvantages hold clear consequences for their chances of winning and retaining elected office, and perhaps for the decision to run at all.

Conclusion

A serious consideration of the changes that have occurred in women's lives including their access to education and professional careers, their financial independence, and their political, economic, and social rights over just a few generations would predict a much more equitable distribution of formal political power than currently exists. Women care, obviously, about the full range of political issues that confront the modern world, and women have the skills, backgrounds, and qualifications for taking leadership roles in formal politics – as legislators, party leaders, prime ministers, and presidents – to tackle the big issues of the day. Why, then, do women still comprise only a quarter of the members of Parliament in Canada, and why has women's representation failed to grow measurably since the early 1990s? Why are women still in many ways at the margins? The factors responsible are complex and intertwined, to be sure. Important barriers exist on both the demand and supply sides of the matter including gatekeeping at the nomination stage, inadequate efforts to identify and recruit female candidates, the effect of electoral rules that do not permit ticket balancing, and women's own uncertainties about their qualifications for elected office. Some of these barriers are being dismantled, making the persistence of women's political under-representation all the more puzzling.

Accounting for inequities in representation requires us to look at the news media. The news media constitute the information system for modern government, and the news media are the venue through which most citizens experience politics. Modern encounters with politics are largely mediated ones, whether via the traditional media – television, radio, and print news – or new media, much of which are citizen generated and fundamentally altering the political world and the way citizens experience it. The news media powerfully condition the way that candidates and politicians are presented to the electorate and, in turn, how the electorate responds to those who aspire to political office. Yet, what is seen, read, or heard in political news media is all too often gender imbalanced. Female candidates' visibility in the news does not seem to be the problem it was just a few decades ago. Today, men and women are regularly present in the news in roughly equal proportions to their share of candidacies, and sometimes female candidates receive more coverage, or more prominent coverage, than male candidates do. Political women are aware of this, and very few of my interviewees talked at any length about problems with attracting coverage. Western Canadians and opposition members, for example, perceived visibility imbalances, but women, typically, did not.

The quality of that coverage is another matter. There are still reasons to be concerned. Women remain disproportionately presented in the sex object, mother, pet, and iron maiden frames that Kanter (1977a, 1977b; see also Robinson and Saint-Jean 1991, 1995) described decades ago, all familiar gender tropes that are constraining for women. Women's attack-style behaviours are persistently exaggerated in news coverage. Issue coverage of politicians reflects traditional gender stereotypes. Women receive more horserace coverage than do their male counterparts. Women are linked less with symbols of political power. Women's appearance, private lives, and parental status are often treated as relevant to their political roles or to their seriousness as politicians. In short, the patterns of news coverage examined in this book uphold the ideas that compared with their male counterparts, female candidates' looks and private lives are disproportionately relevant to their political roles; that women are generally less viable as candidates for office; and that women are very aggressive political competitors, more so than their male counterparts. All of these are misguided.

At the same time, careful and nuanced thinking on the matter is required. The evidence does not point universally in a single direction. There are aspects of the news – patterns revealed in this book – that are not gendered, at least, not in the sense of producing differentiated coverage for men and women. There are indicators of both quantity and quality of content in which coverage of men and of women is nearly identical. The differences in issue coverage between male and female challengers that were discovered in print news of the 2006 election campaign, for example, were missing in news coverage of incumbents. What accounts for the mixed findings? Why do gendered patterns of news coverage emerge on some indicators, but not on others? The most intuitive answer is that "the 20th-century shift toward gender equality has not ceased but is continuing" (Eagly 2007, 9). We are in an era of transition for women. Substantial change in women's public and private roles has occurred (and is occurring). At the same time, this change is accompanied by the persistence of traditional norms and patterns of behaviours that continue to work against women. There has been a partial embrace of political women – when they "prove" themselves as incumbents, for example – and some of the barriers have been dismantled, but old ideas are sticky.

Ideas, norms, beliefs, attitudes – all of these relate intimately to culture. This is where the primary root of gendered coverage is found, for it is the antecedent to all the other factors that produce the differences in coverage. Indeed, it is culture – ideas, norms, and beliefs – that poses the most formidable, least malleable obstacle to gender equity in political representation. A serious consideration of the effect of culture on newswork, as well as on political behaviours, has the advantage of advancing our ability to explain why gendered patterns in the news emerge. Critically, we are forced to confront the provision-presentation distinction, a framework that recognizes that both can initiate gendered patterns of coverage. Sometimes media are to blame, for the operation and political economic imperatives of the news business privilege representations of female politicians that fall comfortably within society's current understandings of women's public and private roles, as well as dominant gender-role stereotypes. The ways that journalism, as a profession, defines newsworthiness also hinges on what our culture defines as the unexpected, the dramatic, or the surprising – women behaving contrary to conventional gender-role norms, for example, which then tends to be reported excessively as a result.

Sometimes, gendered patterns of coverage accurately reflect the reality of female politicians' speech and behaviours. Yet, if men and women self-present differently to the public and to the media, this too, is largely the result of culture (although, certainly, there are arguments to support the idea that some differences are more hardwired). Women may strategically campaign "as women" because the electoral climate favours social issues, which allows women to draw on stereotypes that associate them with compassion and communality. Or, women may campaign "as women" because they think this is how voters best relate to them.

The effects of gendered news are myriad, and care is required in thinking about effects. It may be tempting to quickly assert that all the gendered patterns in coverage have negative consequences for female politicians and gender equality in political representation more generally. This would be hasty. Things are not so simple. Granted, all gendered patterns of coverage may be said to treat female politicians as gendered beings first, and public officials second, which is negative in light of the fact that the archetypal politician possesses decidedly masculine traits and behaviours. Gendered coverage divides men and women implicitly into two categories of politicians: those who defined the mould and those who have adapted to it. This aspect of gendered news can always be criticized. At the same time, however, it is difficult to deny the reality that gendered coverage can work for female politicians. For example, in contexts where the political agenda turns to health care, education, social programs, and the like, news that presents women as particularly suited to these issue domains can increase their appeal among voters. This is not the same as saying that women are better suited to certain policy domains, or that they invariably present themselves to voters as such. Rather, this is simply to say that this type of coverage may benefit women electorally, which is why political women might engage in the strategic provision of gendered behaviour.

Effects can be quite negative, as well, damaging public attitudes towards and the electoral prospects of female candidates. Responses to attack-style coverage of the party leaders in the 2000 federal election campaign made this clear. McDonough lost ground when presented attacking another party or leader (Table 4.2 and Figure 4.1), but the male leaders did not, and the incumbent prime minister, Jean Chrétien, gained from his attack-style coverage. His news stories were more likely to be rated good when he went on the attack, and bad when he did not (Table 4.2 and Figure 4.2). That women's conflictive behaviours tend to be magnified in news coverage can, therefore, be quite detrimental to their careers, for it would compound the negative effects of such coverage. Female politicians are quite aware of the dangers posed to their political aspirations by this kind of negative coverage, and they seem to devote a fair amount of attention to negotiating mediation in order to prevent it.

The book has demonstrated that the news can affect the third step in the three-stage path to elected office: selection by voters. What about the other two stages? Women have to volunteer to run, and they have to be nominated, a process that is governed with very few exceptions by political parties.

With the candidate supply issue, it is clear that the negative effects of gendered news create echoes that undermine prospects for equal representation in the future. The effects on the supply of political women may actually be quite devastating. Based on some of the patterns identified here, portrayals of political women in the news can signal to women in the pool of eligible candidates that a run for office would mean facing intense scrutiny of the most private aspects of their lives and being framed in stereotypical ways using sexist tropes that offer limited understandings of women's political skills. It sends the message that their candidacies may not be treated as seriously as those of similarly qualified men. For some, it would send the message that a run for office is to be avoided. For girls and young women, growing up watching Belinda Stronach portrayed as a pretty bimbo or Hillary Clinton as a calculating ice queen can leave a lasting impression. The media are a powerful socializing influence, perhaps more so for today's youth than for any other generation. Some of the patterns of gendered news examined in this book may actually cause negative role-model effects for young women that cue them to not only avoid political careers themselves, but perhaps even to disengage from politics, which continues to be portrayed, in many ways, as a male realm. Given that progress in women's representation requires a greater number of highly qualified female candidates, these longer-term impacts are serious impediments to the goal.

Gendered news may also affect the middle stage in the three-part selection process: recruitment and nomination by political parties. The knowledge that women can receive unfavourable coverage may cause party power brokers, at both the local and national levels, to avoid recruiting female candidates. It may also encourage political parties to pay undue attention to prospective candidates' private lives in an effort to weed out women who would be particularly grilled by the press – divorced women, for example, whose coverage often hints at a supposed instability, flightiness, or inability to commit, not only to a man, presumably, but also to a party, to a policy, to an ideology, or to her constituents. Coverage of women like Belinda Stronach and former Prime Minister Kim Campbell are foremost illustrations. Political parties may think especially hard about choosing women for party leadership posts given the exaggeration of their attack-style behaviours in the news media, unless perhaps the political climate and party ideology favour a "tough" approach. At times, women can make the iron maiden frame work for them, as Margaret Thatcher and other women have in the past, although some women may judge the costs to be too steep.

For those concerned about fairness and equality in political representation, the patterns examined in this book have worrying parallels for other marginalized groups whose under-representation is well documented. Similar processes result in racialized coverage of visible minority candidates and politicians, who are framed in stereotypical ways. Like female candidates, news reports often question minority candidates' electoral viability – either explicitly or subtly, their issue priorities and positions are framed in stereotypical ways, and their markers of difference tend to be highlighted in news coverage (e.g., Fleras and Kunz 2001; Gershon 2012; Henry and Tator 2002; Saunders 1991; Terkildsen and Damore 1999; Tolley 2012; Zilber and Niven 2000a, 2000b). Granted, the candidate, the medium, and the campaign can all contribute to variance in media coverage – a central point in this book – and this is no less important for coverage of visible minority candidates. Like women, minority candidates may seize on the opportunities presented by their backgrounds and characteristics. They may strategically emphasize their ethnic backgrounds or stress issues of particular salience to minority voters, provision-related patterns that are logical responses to the fact that minority candidates often run in districts with high concentrations of minority voters, as well as the fact that visibility in the news can be gained when one stands out. That said, the media undoubtedly play their part in racializing minority candidates, subtly presenting them as awkward fits in a political realm that takes whiteness as its norm.

Prospects for Change

The last question to be addressed is simple: what can be done? What strategies can be adopted to eliminate barriers to women's representation in politics? The menu for reform is extensive: from formal government-mandated policy prescriptions – such as quotas – that could alter political party nomination procedures to less formal changes in societal attitudes. In the case of press coverage of politicians, policy-mandated reform is tricky terrain, because media regulation is a contentious issue in any democracy, whether Canada or elsewhere. Most newspapers, television news outlets, the Canadian Broadcast Standards Council and the Canadian Association of Broadcasters have already adopted guidelines on sex-role portrayal to encourage gender-neutral reporting. These may miss the mark, for on the surface, gender neutrality is often accomplished by covering women the same as covering men, using masculine frames and imagery that have the effect of highlighting the incongruence between feminine stereotypes and archetypical political leadership. For many, gender neutrality in reporting may simply require the avoidance of blatantly sexist language and themes. News stories sometimes violate even this relatively low bar, to say nothing of coverage that is much more nuanced in its gendering of political women.

Beyond these voluntary measures, it is not clear what policy solution to force the media to report on female politicians differently is feasible or desirable. Surely, we cannot regulate the media to the point where journalists are prohibited from using game frames and phrases such as "hammers home" and "slam dunk" to report on women, and certainly, there can be no ban on covering political women's private lives and appearances. Few citizens would desire such restrictions on the news. Likewise, we cannot force the media to overhaul their occupational culture and organizational structures. None of these policy-based prescriptions are consonant with the idea of a free and independent media, which is an integral component of democratic life.

Another oft-proposed remedy for gendered mediation is to increase the number of female journalists. If the journalistic profession was more gender equitable in its staffing, the argument goes, we would see more gender equitable coverage of male and female politicians. Some female journalists are vigilantly progressive in their coverage of female politicians, and, thus, a concerted effort to hire and promote more female journalists would undoubtedly produce the desired results in certain times and places. The experiences of some of my interviewees speak to this potential. In the main, however, skepticism is warranted about this prescription. Rank-and-file journalists have relatively little control over their topic assignments, and in television news, reporters rarely write their own copy. In other words, the average journalist has little control over what and how she (or he) reports. For women to have substantial influence on coverage, they need to occupy decision-making positions in the profession. Unfortunately, "the higher, the fewer rule" (Bashevkin 1993) tends to hold in news organizations as it does in political organizations. Female journalists are disproportionately clustered at the lower levels of the news profession. Although 55 percent of reporters for Canadian dailies were women in 1995, only 8 percent of "star" reporters, 4 percent of desk heads, and 2 percent of editors-in-chief were women (Robinson 2005, 43). The distribution of women in decision-making positions in television news was very similar in Robinson's study (57), and in my analyses of women's standings in both print and television news in 2011, as discussed in Chapter 3.

Moreover, the extent to which individual female journalists are willing to identify and combat gendered mediation will depend largely on whether they are feminist or they possess a gender consciousness. This leads very powerfully to the ultimate point: even when willing, female journalists are seldom *able* to act on their feminist sensibilities in order to produce gender-neutral reportage. The masculine narrative that pervades news coverage of politics functions at a systemic level. Two meta-level factors, in particular, govern how the news is produced: the sociology of newswork and the political economy of the news business, both of which are dominated by men. The organization and practice of newswork likely reduces – or perhaps eradicates altogether – the influence of journalists' gender on news coverage. Enhancing women's presence and status in journalism would be symbolically important in its own right; there are, however, fundamental limitations on the potential for such a change to eradicate gendered mediation of female politicians.

All this said, media coverage *has* been consistently identified as a force inhibiting women's political representation, and change is required. The United Nations Fourth World Conference on Women, held in Beijing in 1995, identified media as one of twelve sites requiring strategic action and noted, as well, that gendered production and programming are global patterns.[1] One of the core themes connecting research on women in politics is a focus on collectively held, deeply ingrained gender-role stereotypes. This dimension of the problem should be the real target for reform. Stereotypes establish expectations about individuals, based on their group membership, and stereotypes also have a prescriptive element, because they tell people what types of behaviour are *appropriate* for a particular group. Stereotypes help explain why news content tends to be gendered. Indeed, counter-stereotypical behaviours – such as a female leader attacking a political rival – is newsworthy because it is unexpected and dramatic, and this is why women's aggressive behaviours tend to be exaggerated in the news. Female politicians themselves often see culturally constituted stereotypes as straightjackets, particularly since they occupy positions that were historically for men only.

The bad news is that stereotypes are notoriously resistant to change at both the aggregate and individual levels. At the aggregate level, stereotypes are part of our collective culture. At the individual level, as Festinger (1957) noted more than five decades ago, people tend to resist new information that contradicts their existing knowledge and beliefs. Until our collectively held beliefs are more accepting of the notion that women belong in the political world, and that their private and public lives are not necessarily more in tension than those of men, female politicians' gendered experience of the media and of politics will persist.

This is a bleak prognosis. My conclusion does not, however, mean prescriptions are impossible. Put simply, female politicians are not powerless, and they have not seen themselves as powerless. One of the advantages of the provision-presentation distinction put forth in this book is its recognition that women have some control over how they are covered in the media. Moreover, initiatives like campaign schools that provide specific training on media relations seem to help female politicians. Successful self-presentation to the media does not seem to be intuitive but, instead, requires expertise. We have to consider the possibility that women's socialization experiences and occupational backgrounds tend to provide them with less confidence and skill for successful media presentation. Resources for female candidates and office holders to produce their own communication materials, particularly in the form of candidate-sponsored advertisements, could also help. Part of the problem with political self-presentation is that candidates and legislators rarely present themselves directly to voters. Self-presentation is done through media intermediaries, who provide unpredictable and sometimes negative coverage. If women had better access to candidate-controlled, versus media-controlled, communications, they might be able to represent themselves to the public on their own terms. Whatever strategy is chosen, it is clear that some responsibility rests with political parties for ensuring that the women they nominate and who sit in their caucuses have access to the resources, financial and otherwise, required for making the most of their public personas.

Media organizations and their employees constitute important political actors that are difficult to regulate and impossible to ignore. Unfortunately, change in the collectively held assumptions of journalists about who is and is not suited for political office moves at a snail's pace, a direct result of the fact that culturally defined beliefs are incredibly enduring. In the meantime, female politicians, their male allies, and their political parties need to share knowledge collaboratively about how to navigate the media terrain. At the same time, they would be advised to take every opportunity to challenge prevailing (masculine) norms about the traits and behaviours of the archetypical politician, for this is likely the only viable route to dismantling the powerful cultural forces that lie at the heart of gendered news and its negative effects.

Appendix 1
Issue Coding

For each data set, issues were coded. From these issue codings, I constructed several broader groupings of issues (which are not mutually exclusive). These are listed below.

Health Care Issues *(CBC 2000, Party Press Releases 2000)*
Health care – general
Health care – funding
Health care – privatization
Health care – user fees
Health care – two-tier system

Health Care Issues *(OMPP 2006)*
Healthcare (e.g., waiting times, privatization, two-tier system, user fees)

Public Finance Issues *(CBC 2000, Party Press Releases 2000)*
Public finances (general)
Spending
Deficit
Debt
Surplus (use of)
Taxes

Economy and Public Finance Issues *(OMPP 2006)*
Deficit/Government spending/Fiscal responsibility (e.g., budget, surplus, debt, deficit)
Economy (general)
Energy/Hydro/Gas prices
Inflation/Cost of living
Taxes
Unemployment/Jobs
Value of Canadian dollar
Income trusts

Law and Order Issues[*] *(CBC 2000, Party Press Releases 2000)*
Crime (general)
Tougher sentencing
Death penalty
Rehabilitation
Anti-gang biker law
Gun control

Law and Order Issues *(OMPP 2006)*
Crime (e.g., gun control)

Social Issues *(CBC 2000, Party Press Releases 2000)*
Social issues (general)
Social programs
Day care
Unemployment insurance
Poverty
Education
Environment
Aboriginals
Immigration
Lifestyle issues
Abortion
Youth crime
Moral/Personal beliefs of politicians

[*] Youth crime was classified as a social issue, not a law and order issue.

Social Issues *(OMPP 2006)*
Aboriginal issues
Decline of community/morals
Education
Environment
Health care (e.g., waiting times, privatization, two-tier system, user fees)
Housing
Immigration
Public transportation
Racism/Discrimination
Same-sex marriage
Senior citizens' issues
Welfare/Poverty/Homelessness
Social programs (e.g., day care, abortion)

Government, Leadership, and Governance Issues *(OMPP 2006)*
Government/Leadership (e.g., accountability corruption, ethics, patronage, rules)
Minority government/Coalition
Constitution – general (e.g., use of notwithstanding clause, change)
Democratic reform/Turnout (e.g., elected Senate)
Intergovernmental relations
Gomery Inquiry/Sponsorship Scandal

"Hard" Issues[*] *(CBC 2000, Party Press Releases 2000)*
Economic (general)
Job creation/unemployment
International trade
Public finances (general)
Spending
Deficit
Debt
Surplus (use of)
Taxes
Crime (general)
Tougher sentencing

[*] Not all issues are classifiable as either "hard" issues or "soft" issues. Issues such as national unity and referenda are examples of issues not classified into either category.

Death penalty
Rehabilitation
Anti-gang biker law
Gun control
Election process (general)
Election dates
Referenda
Electoral system
Constitution (general)
National unity
Division of powers
Quebec
Defence

"Hard" Issues[*] *(OMPP 2006)*
Constitution – general (e.g., use of notwithstanding clause, change)
Crime (e.g., gun control)
Deficit/Government spending/Fiscal responsibility (e.g., budget, surplus, debt, deficit)
Democratic reform/Turnout (e.g., elected Senate)
Economy (general)
Energy/Hydro/Gas prices
Inflation/Cost of living
Intergovernmental relations
International affairs/Defence
Minority government/Coalition
National unity/Separatism
Taxes
Trade and industry
Unemployment/Jobs
Value of Canadian dollar
Income trusts

"Soft" Issues[*] *(CBC 2000, Party Press Releases 2000)*
Health care – general
Health care – funding

[*] Not all issues are classifiable as either "hard" issues or "soft" issues. Issues such as national unity and referenda are examples of issues not classified into either category.

Health care – privatization
Health care – user fees
Health care – two-tier system
Abortion – general
Referendum on abortion
Ethics – general
Patronage/Corruption
Grand-Mère affair
Rules and guidelines
Social issues – general
Social programs
Day care
Youth crime
Unemployment insurance
Poverty
Education
Environment
Immigration
Lifestyle issues
Moral/Personal beliefs of politicians

"Soft" Issues[*] *(OMPP 2006)*
Aboriginal issues
Decline of community/morals
Education
Environment
Health care (e.g., waiting times, privatization, two-tier system, user fees)
Housing
Immigration
Public transportation
Racism/Discrimination
Same-sex marriage
Senior citizens' issues
Welfare/Poverty/Homelessness
Social issues/programs (e.g., day care, abortion)

---

[*] Not all issues are classifiable as either "hard" issues or "soft" issues. Issues such as national unity and referenda are examples of issues not classified into either category.

Appendix 2
Coding for CES and Media Reception Study

Dependent Variable

News Ratings

For each story, participants rated whether the story was "very good," "quite good," "neither good nor bad," "quite bad," or "very bad" for the party that was the main focus of the story.

- 1 = very bad
- 2 = bad
- 3 = neither good nor bad
- 4 = good
- 5 = very good

Independent Variables

Participants' Sex

- 1 = female
- 0 = male

Participants' Party Identification

Coded 1 if the news story is about a party (or leader of party) that respondent identifies with; coded 0 if party identification is not the same as the party/leader that the news story is about (includes other party identifiers, no party identifiers, "don't knows," and refusals). Party identification variables are from the post-election wave of the 2000 CES.

For example, respondents who identify with the Liberal party are assigned scores of 1 for all stories about Jean Chrétien/the Liberals, and all other respondents are assigned a score of 0 for all Chrétien/Liberal stories. Thus, those who receive a score of 0 for Chrétien/Liberal stories are those who identify with some party other than the Liberals, including no party affiliation, as well as those who provided "don't know" responses or refused to respond to the CES party identification questions.

Likewise, for stories about Alexa McDonough/the NDP, respondents who identify with the NDP are assigned a score of 1, and all other respondents (including the respondent in the previous example who was assigned a 1 for all the Liberal stories) are given a score of 0.

Leader Feeling Thermometers
The original question from CES asked respondents to rate each leader on a scale of 0 to 100, from "strong dislike" to "strong like" of the leader.

This variable was rescaled 0 to 1, and "don't know" responses were assigned scores of 0.5.

For each story, models only include ratings of the leader that the story was mainly about. For stories about Stockwell Day/the Alliance, it is how participants feel about Day that is included in the model. For stories about Jean Chrétien/the Liberals, it is the Chrétien feeling thermometer that is included in the model.

Leader Aggressivity
This variable is from the content analysis of CBC news of the 2000 federal election campaign, and it indicates the extent to which a leader engaged in verbal and/or non-verbal aggressive behaviour in a news story. Leader aggressivity in each news story was coded in the following way:

0 = no verbal attack of a party/leader and no aggressive body language in the story
0.5 = either verbal attack or aggressive body language
1 = both verbal attack of a party/leader and aggressive body language

In other words, the 0 to 1 coding represents a movement from no aggressive or conflictive behaviour to combined verbal and non-verbal conflictive behaviour.

Body language coded as aggressive: finger pointing, fist clenching, and hand chopping.

Notes

INTRODUCTION

1 Supply-side explanations for women's political under-representation focus on the attributes of candidates themselves, such as viability, quality, and experience, as well as the very important trait, willingness to run. Supply-side explanations ask questions about whether women in the candidate eligibility pool, which has grown dramatically, are willing to run for and are capable of winning elected office. Demand-side explanations focus not on the candidates, but on the outside forces – typically institutional or structural – that raise barriers to women's political aspirations. Together, these explanations highlight how factors such as the electoral system, campaign fundraising and spending rules, party elites, and voters hinder women's attempts to gain office, typically at the nomination and general election stages. In focusing on both the content of the news and on the effects of the news, this book hopes to make an important contribution to our understanding of the forces that structure the supply of and demand for female political candidates and legislators.
2 Adjusted for gender differences in the total number of hours worked per year, because men tend to work more hours than women do. Without factoring in the number of hours worked, the gender wage gap is 70.5 cents for every dollar earned by men.
3 Canada is tied for fourth place with England, after Korea, Japan, and Germany. See OECD, *Gender Brief* (March 2010). http://www.oecd.org/dataoecd/23/31/44720649.pdf.
4 Statistics Canada, CANSIM, "Table 282-0009: Labour Force Survey Estimates (LFS), by National Occupational Classification for Statistics (NOC-S) and Sex" (2008). http://cansim2.statcan.ca/cgi-win/cnsmcgi.exe?Lang=E&RootDir=CII/&ResultTemplate=CII/CII___&Array_Pick=1&ArrayId=2820009.

5 Michael Ornstein, "Racialization and Gender of Lawyers in Ontario," Report for the Law Society of Upper Canada (2010). http://www.lsuc.on.ca/latest-news/a/racialization-and-gender-of-lawyers-in-ontario/.
6 Television news data are derived from the Canadian Election Study's two content analysis studies of the 2000 campaign. The first one analyzes news coverage across the four networks already mentioned. The second is a richer, more detailed coding of coverage featured on CBC's *The National*. This book uses both data sets.
7 Stuart N. Soroka, Antonia Maioni, and Blake Andrew, *Federal Election Newspaper Content Analysis* (Observatory on Media and Public Policy, McGill University, 2006). www.ompp.mcgill.ca.
8 Data from the 2000 CES were provided by the Institute for Social Research, York University. The survey was funded by the Social Sciences and Humanities Research Council of Canada (SSHRC), and was completed for the 2000 CES investigators: André Blais (Université de Montréal), Elisabeth Gidengil (McGill University), Richard Nadeau (Université de Montréal), and Neil Nevitte (University of Toronto). Neither the Institute for Social Research, the SSHRC, nor the CES investigators is responsible for the analyses and interpretations presented in this book.

CHAPTER 1: VISIBILITY IN THE NEWS

1 E.g., *Gender Guidelines* (Ottawa: CBC, 1998).
2 E.g., *CBC Annual Report to HRSD for 2008: Employment Equity* (Ottawa: CBC, 2008). http://www.cbc.radio-canada.ca/docs/equity/pdf/ee-exec2008e.pdf.
3 The NDP later lost two of its 21 MPs due to defections; so when Parliament was dissolved for the 2000 federal election, the NDP caucus had 19 members.
4 This is an example of a news program's headlines from the 2000 campaign from the opening credits of the 22 November broadcast of *The National*: "Tonight. Exonerated ... The ethics counsellor says Jean Chrétien did nothing wrong by helping a constituent get a controversial loan. Punishing pace ... Stockwell Day pulls out all the stops in his drive to break through in Ontario. And mercy mission. Police and social workers round up some of those gasoline-sniffing children in Sheshatshui, Labrador."
5 Sound bites are not completely unmediated, because newsmakers choose when a sound bite starts and ends, as well as which sound bites to use in a news story. Therefore, a sound bite is not a form of completely unmediated news coverage, even though it "poses" as relatively unmediated to viewers.
6 In the context of the 2000 federal election campaign, high-profile candidates were people like Sheila Copps (Liberal cabinet member), Paul Martin (Liberal cabinet member), Deborah Grey (long-serving and highly vocal Alliance member; first Reform Party member elected to the House), and Bill Blaikie (NDP member and one of the longest-serving members of the House at that point).
7 Although leaders are candidates in their respective ridings, results presented for candidates exclude data on party leaders.
8 Also referred to as "AdScam" or "Sponsorgate." The federal government set up a fund, following the 1995 referendum on Quebec sovereignty, to help promote federalism and Canadian sentiment in Quebec. The program ran from 1996 to 2004. The fund was badly managed and misused. In the early spring of 2002, Chrétien asked Auditor General Sheila Fraser to launch a full investigation. Fraser released her

report on 10 February 2004, which outlined that $100 million of the $250 million sponsorship program was awarded to Liberal-friendly advertising firms and Crown corporations for little or no work. Not long after Chrétien's departure from the Liberal leadership post, in December 2003, Prime Minister Paul Martin asked Justice John H. Gomery to head up a public inquiry into how the Sponsorship Program was handled. Martin promised to resign if there was evidence that he knew about fraud in the program. Testimony in the inquiry started in September 2004. Justice Gomery released his first report on 1 November 2005, and his final report on 1 February 2006. The final report consisted mostly of recommendations for changes to the civil service and its relationship to government.
9 An announcement was officially made by Goodale in the evening on 23 November 2005, after trading had closed for the day in financial markets, that he would not impose a tax on income trusts, as had been feared. In an attempt to "level the playing field" between corporations and trusts, Goodale lowered the tax on dividends paid by corporations as well. Allegations were made shortly afterwards that some Bay Street actors knew details early because of an advance leak of the information and spent the hours before the announcement making money by trading on information that most investors didn't have – essentially an insider trading scandal. The RCMP launched a criminal investigation, in late December 2005, during the election campaign, into whether information was leaked from the finance minister's office. Despite calls for his resignation, Goodale would not step down while the RCMP investigated, but he did maintain a lower profile during the second part of the campaign (hence, being unavailable for comment in news stories, particularly stories about the income trusts probe). The RCMP's investigation cleared Goodale of any wrongdoing, but did charge an official in Goodale's department with a breach of trust as a result of the leak.
10 Canadian Newspaper Association. *Circulation Data Report 2009* (April 2010). http://www.cna-acj.ca/en/system/files/2009CirculationDataReport_1.pdf.

CHAPTER 2: QUALITY OF NEWS COVERAGE
1 Linda Trimble, "Memo to Belinda Stronach: You're Being Framed," *Globe and Mail*, 21 Jan. 2004.
2 *Winnipeg Sun*, 8 May 2005.
3 Jean Lapierre, Liberal MP for Shefford, Quebec, left the Liberal caucus in 1990 to sit as a member of the Bloc Québécois. Lapierre later returned to the Liberals, and took his seat as a Liberal MP after the 2004 federal election. Scott Brison left the Progressive Conservatives (PCs) in 2004 to join the Liberals. Brison's decision to switch parties was a result of the PC Party's merger with the Canadian Alliance to form the Conservative Party of Canada in 2004. Keith Martin left the Canadian Alliance in 2004 to join the Liberals upon the former's merger into the CPC.
4 CBC Newsworld, 18 May 2005.
5 CBC's *The National*, 19 Nov. 2000.
6 Personal interview with Alexa McDonough, 25 Feb. 2005.
7 "These Women Not Two of a Kind," *Globe and Mail*, 6 April 1993, A6.
8 I use various indicators of aggressive behaviour. First, the data indicate whether a politician was shown in a story to be attacking another party or leader verbally.

"Attack" was not equated simply with criticism or negative evaluation. A story that showed Alliance leader Stockwell Day criticizing the Liberal government for its failure to increase defence spending is not necessarily an attack. This may, in fact, be a valid critique of government spending priorities, and valid critique is part of the opposition's mandate. As Mutz and Reeves (2005) emphasize, conflict is what politics is about, a fact that citizens know and accept. "On the attack" refers, rather, to instances where untrue or unsubstantiated allegations were made; where the tone is unduly harsh, rude, or confrontational; and particularly where name calling and mud slinging that go beyond mere criticism were depicted. In addition to verbal attacks, politicians' body language was also coded according to its level of aggressivity. From the content analysis of the CBC news, three types of body language were coded as aggressive: finger pointing, fist clenching, and hand chopping. This classification is in line with psychology, communications, and linguistics research on how these three types of gestures are typically interpreted (ibid.). For example, Henley and Freeman (1995) describe finger pointing as "a subtle, nonverbal threat." For an application of this body language typology to research on gender, media, and politics, see Gidengil and Everitt (2000, 2003a). In the training period, coders were given detailed instructions in order to distinguish between what may be viewed as normal political conflict and what is better labelled "political attack." However, there is certainly an element of subjectivity involved, and coders were instructed on this. Measuring such variables is much less straightforward than measuring structural features of media content such as story length. Coders completed approximately fifteen hours of coder training, the objectives of which were to explain what the coding instrument's categories meant, communicate expectations about coding, provide "rules of thumb" for variables where subjective judgment inevitably was involved (such as the coding of attack behaviour), and instruct coders how to record the coding. As part of the training, the coders practised using the coding instrument by analyzing the content of select portions of CBC television news coverage of the 1997 federal election. Practice coding sessions permitted concrete discussion of application of the coding instrument as well as an assessment, or "pre-test," of the validity of the coding instrument.

9 Cohen's kappa = 0.867 for the verbal attack variable, a level of intercoder reliability that essentially meets conventionally acceptable standards. As Riffe et al. note (1998, 145), "coefficients of .90 or greater would be acceptable to all, .80 or greater would be acceptable in most situations, and below that there exists great disagreement." In a meta-analysis of two hundred articles indexed in *Communication Abstracts* that used the term *content analysis* and were published from 1994 to 1998, Lombard, Snyder-Duch, and Bracken (2002, 599) report that "the mean minimum accepted reliability level was .75."

10 Intercoder reliability for the three types of body language: finger pointing kappa = 0.856, fist clenching kappa = 0.942, hand chopping kappa = 0.913.

11 Also called "soft" news (vs. hard news) and the "tabloidization" of news, "infotainment"-style news refers to the use of entertainment-genre production formulas geared towards making information presented in the news more entertaining and dramatic.

12 I would like to thank Emmanuelle Hébert for suggesting this categorization of objects.

13 CBC's *The National*, 24 Oct. 2000.
14 Ibid.
15 E.g., *The National*, 10 Oct. and 10 Nov. 2000.
16 *The National*, 23 Nov. 2000.
17 *The National*, 26 Nov. 2000.
18 See Appendix 1 for the full list of issue categories coded for CBC election stories. Not all stories were coded as having a "main" or "primary" issue: 46 of the 163 stories (28% of the 163 stories) had no single dominant issue. Stories coded as having no primary or main issue tended to mention issues, but did not have a single, main issue focus. Appendix 1 also provides detailed information on the coding of "hard" and "soft" issues.
19 Lead-ins, voice-overs, and wrap-ups were coded as descriptive, analytical, or evaluative (e.g., Robinson and Shehan 1983; Gidengil and Everitt 2000). *Descriptive* means that the segment contains statements that merely report events and facts without judgment, explanation, in-depth discussion, commentary, interpretation, or inference. *Analytical* means that the segment contains explanation, interpretation, synthesis, or inference of some intangible entity, such as a leader's or candidate's emotions, thoughts, or motivations. Analytical statements tell viewers not only what happened but also how the event should be interpreted, regarded, or explained. For example, a voice-over telling viewers that Stockwell Day held up a "No 2-Tier Health Care" sign during the English-language leaders' debate is coded as descriptive, for it does not elaborate or speculate on Day's motivations for using the sign or how the sign affected perceptions of his performance in the debate. Conversely, a voice-over that says Day held up the sign because of his association with the Klein government, which had arguably made moves towards a two-tier system in the years prior to the election, is classified as analytical. In this instance, the story attempts to attribute motives to Day's use of the sign. *Evaluative* means the segment contains some normative component including but not limited to judgment, ranking of the parties or leaders, criticism, praise, and so on. I combine the analytical and evaluative categories, treating them as a single, larger category that I call *interpretive*, which is then compared with levels of purely descriptive coverage.
20 Clark's first sound bite in the story was this: "The Reform Alliance has no understanding of what life is like in Atlantic Canada, and no understanding of the history and society of Quebec. And now their plan to betray the health care system has become clear. But even before Reform, the Liberal party of Jean Chrétien broke its trust with Atlantic Canada." Joe Clark. *The National*, 1 Nov. 2000.
21 *The National*, 1 Nov. 2000.
22 Evidence would include reference to polls, the party policy booklet, past election performance, comments from experts, statements from the party campaign headquarters, and so forth. Essentially, *evidence* refers to a source of information external to the news organization that corroborates what the anchor or reporter says about the leader. Evidence does not have to be convincing or even accurate; coders were simply told to indicate whether any evidence was offered or mentioned.
23 *The National*, 17 Nov. 2000.
24 *The National*, 12 Nov. 2000.

25 This would be any explicit mention of external appearances, including hair, weight, clothes, shoes, and/or facial expression, and it would also include general descriptors of appearance, such as "beautiful," "glamorous," or "trim." The following were not considered explicit mentions of appearance: reference to race/ethnicity or age, although an argument could certainly be made that these are implicit mentions of appearance.
26 This would include explicit reference to the fact that a candidate is married, divorced, widowed, single, or the like, as well as explicit reference to a partner, using phrases such as "wife of," "husband of," and "partner of."
27 This would include explicit reference to the presence or absence of children, or naming or giving the ages of children with a clear mention that the candidate is the mother or father. Calling a candidate a "mother" or "father" in the story would also constitute explicit reference to the candidate's parental status.
28 Vaughn Palmer, "Conservative Discipline Forces Humour-Seekers to Look Elsewhere," *Vancouver Sun*, 21 Jan. 2006, A3.
29 Linda Diebel, "'We Did It,' Exclaims Triumphant Stronach," *Toronto Star*, 24 Jan. 2006, A3.
30 John Ivison, "Stronach's Switch Still Stings for Some," *National Post*, 8 Dec. 2005, A1.
31 Martin Cash, "TV Star Brings Glamour Factor to Churchill: Tina Keeper," *National Post*, 28 Dec. 2005, A6.
32 Julie Smyth, "Alberta MP Puts New Face on Tory Child-Care Stance," *National Post*, 7 Dec. 2005, A6.
33 Patrick Evans, "The Doctor, the Anchor and the Economist," *Toronto Star*, 4 Dec. 2005, A6.
34 Ibid.
35 Gary Mason, "Fur Likely to Fly as Robinson, Fry Square Off," *Globe and Mail*, 3 Dec. 2005, A11.
36 Roy MacGregor, "Why Nystrom Thinks a Second Comeback May Be Possible," *Globe and Mail*, 2 Dec. 2005, A2.
37 Surya Bhattacharya, "Candidates Show New Face of Politics in Diverse Riding," *Toronto Star*, 22 Dec. 2005, B2.
38 Andrew Mills, "Schreyer's Bid for Seat Makes Political History," *Toronto Star*, 16 Dec. 2005, A8.
39 This would include explicit reference to a degree, diploma, or other qualification; to having studied at some specific institution; to having studied some particular topic in college, university, or other educational institution; and the like.
40 This would include explicit reference to a former and/or current job and/or profession (e.g., doctor, lawyer, professor, city councillor, business person, business owner).
41 This would include explicit reference to incumbency, the holding of a cabinet or critic post, the holding of elected office in the past or at some other level, and a past run at a seat, whether successful or not.
42 Allan Kellogg, "Ambrose a Rising Star Who'll Likely Have a Seat at the Cabinet Table," *Edmonton Journal*, 6 Jan. 2006, A2.
43 Smyth, "Alberta MP Puts New Face on Tory Child-Care Stance."
44 Carol Goar, "Tory Women Step to the Fore," *Toronto Star*, 25 Jan. 2006, A22.

45 Irwin Black, "Tight Race Has Frulla Energized," *Montreal Gazette*, 20 Jan. 2006, A13.
46 John Ivison, "Campaign Ambitions in a Nutshell: Parties Woo the Commuter Belt around Toronto," *National Post*, 21 Dec. 2005, A8.
47 E.g., Lisa Diebel, "More than the Boss's Daughter," *Toronto Star*, 17 Dec. 2005, A6.
48 Janet Bagnall, "The Stronach Factor," *Montreal Gazette*, 13 Jan. 2006, A21.
49 Stan Josey, "Hargrove, Stronach Cozy Up," *Toronto Star*, 18 Jan. 2006, B2.
50 Diebel, "More than the Boss's Daughter."
51 Sarah Sacheli and Anne Jarvis, "Whelan's Strategy Questioned: Ex-MP Not the Incumbent," *Windsor Star*, 5 Dec. 2005, A1.
52 E.g., Juliet Strauss, "Contest in Icy Manitoba Riding Heats Up," *Globe and Mail*, 26 Dec. 2005, A4.
53 Ibid.
54 Cash, "TV Star Brings Glamour Factor to Churchill."
55 Kellogg, "Ambrose a Rising Star."
56 The scheme used by the Observatory codes two types of tone, story tone and tone of people discussed in stories. I use the second measure, obviously, since it is directly linkable to candidates.
57 Soroka et al., *2006 Federal Election Newspaper Content Analysis Codebook*.

CHAPTER 3: WHO IS RESPONSIBLE?

1 I would like to thank Stuart Soroka for first suggesting the specific term *provision-presentation distinction*, as well as for prompting further analysis of the relationship between the two.
2 See, e.g., "1972: Nixon's Last Campaign," *Manchester Union-Leader*, 1 Nov. 2004. Ironically, this is the newspaper that provoked the crying incident with its comments about Muskie's wife, Jane. See also, "Media Frenzies in Our Time," *Washington Post*, 27 March 1998; "FBI Finds Nixon Aides Sabotaged Democrats," *Washington Post*, 10 Oct. 1972; "One Man's Primary – and How He Lost," *New York Times*, 21 May 1972.
3 Note that there is some debate about whether or not empathy, warmth, and trustworthiness are becoming more important as political character attributes, particularly given the series of public governance scandals that have happened in the United States (e.g., Enron) and Canada (e.g., Sponsorship Scandal, Human Resources Development Canada) in recent years. Indeed, several authors have pointed out that we may see men and women both starting to emphasize traditionally "feminine" traits in their self-presentations to citizens and the media.
4 The following discussion of the structure and operation of a news organization is based on Schultz's text, unless otherwise noted.
5 http://www.cbc.ca/news/live/newscentre.html.
6 Ibid.
7 The issue codes for the press release data set are identical to those for the Canadian Election Study's 2000 media content analyses, meaning that the same issues are grouped into hard, soft, and uncodeable categories as in Chapter 2. See Appendix 1 for further details on how issues were coded.
8 E.g., Laurie Monsebraaten, "Child Care Splits Parties, Parents," *Toronto Star*, 16 Jan. 2006, A8; Andrew Duffy, "Family Becomes a Serious Wedge Issue," *Ottawa Citizen*,

19 Dec. 2005, A5; Smyth, "Alberta MP Puts New Face on Tory Child-Care Stance"; Gloria Galloway, "Provinces Worry Plans for Child Care Will Suffer," *Globe and Mail*, 7 Dec. 2005, A4.

CHAPTER 4: BACKLASH OR BOOST?

1 In the last possibility, the observation of no difference in voters' responses to male and female attacks could occur because (1) the effects of attack-style behaviour are not conditional upon the sex of the aggressor, an outcome that has been reported in the literature (e.g., Brooks 2011), or (2) both backlash and boost effects occur, cancelling each other out and resulting in no net gain or loss for women politicians relative to their male counterparts. I simply list the different explanations for a no-effects finding here. This chapter does not explore these in greater detail, and focuses instead on the backlash and boost outcomes.
2 The literature has focused primarily on the former, as do the analyses in this chapter.
3 In this stacked data set, each participant-news story pairing is a separate case. Each participant provided ratings of each news story. There are 56 participants, and 163 news stories. Therefore, each participant appears in the data set 163 times. This results in 9,046 news ratings (or "cases"). The media reception study is a classic example of clustering, because each of the 56 participants underwent repeated measurement in terms of recording ratings for each of the 163 news stories. Thus, there are 56 clusters in the data, one for each of the participants. In these data, therefore, because observations are clustered, heteroskedasticity and serial correlation are potential worries (Fox 1991). The problem is addressed by including the *cluster* option, a standard feature of *Stata*'s regression commands, which produces robust standard errors that, in effect, correct for non-independence of repeated observations.
4 The original variable formed a 5-point scale from "very bad" (score of 1) to "very good" (score of 5), with a neutral option for "neither bad nor good," as well as more moderate options for "somewhat bad" and "somewhat good." In the recoded version of the dependent variable reported in this chapter, the extreme ("very") and moderate ("somewhat") categories on both the good and bad ends of the scale are collapsed. The neutral option was coded as missing in order to provide an unambiguous test of the two possible effects of aggressive depictions for the female leader compared with the male leaders: boost (good ratings) or backlash (bad ratings).
5 I considered alternative codings of the leader aggressivity variable (e.g., 0 = no aggressivity, 1 = either or both forms). Arguably, the combination of the two forms is more powerful or perceived as more aggressive than one or the other occurring on its own, so in the end, I chose a coding strategy that reflected this intuitive notion, and that distinguished a single form of aggressive behaviour (verbal or non-verbal) from the combination of the two.
6 This indicator is similar to those used by other scholars (e.g., Gidengil 1995; Greenstein 2000) and my own work in other contexts (Goodyear-Grant and Croskill 2011) to measure gender ideology, although a better operationalization would be to use an index of questions that could measure the different dimensions of the concept (gender arrangements in the public sphere, etc.). The 2000 CES offers limited options on this front. There are other questions that could have been used, but most of these were in the mail-back wave of the survey, which had a low response rate.

7 All predicted probabilities were generated using the Clarify application (King, Tomz, and Wittenberg 2000; Tomz, Wittenberg, and King 2001). The values generated indicate the predicted probability of positive news ratings at different values of the leader aggressivity variables while holding the values of all non-manipulated variables at their means.
8 This value comes from a 0 to 1 scale, where a predicted probability of 1 would indicate that all respondents are predicted to assign a positive rating to McDonough's news stories, and a score of 0 suggests that none of the respondents are predicted to assign a positive rating to McDonough's news stories.
9 I have no way to test this proposition with these data, but speculatively, it seems natural that a sitting executive would be seen in a positive light when he behaves in a masculine or authoritative manner, a reaction that may be conditional, however, on party or favorability ratings. Indeed, part of the argument about why women seldom occupy executive political positions is that the traits associated with the highest levels of office are decidedly masculine, even more so than those associated with office holding generally.

CHAPTER 5: MEDIA EFFECTS ON POLITICIANS' EXPERIENCES OF THEIR POLITICAL CAREERS

A version of this chapter also appears in Elizabeth Goodyear-Grant, "Crafting a Public Image: Women MPs and the Dynamics of Media Coverage," in *Are Doors Opening Wider? Studies of Women's Political Engagement in Canada*, ed. Sylvia Bashevkin, 147-65 (Vancouver: UBC Press, 2009).

1 Telephone interview with Kim Campbell, 22 Sept. 2005.
2 Personal interview with Rahim Jaffer, 21 Feb. 2005.
3 When he was first elected to Parliament in 1997, Jaffer was "at the tender age of 25," as his online biography noted at the time
4 As a brief aside, Jaffer did not mention radio media at all, perhaps because of a short-lived scandal in 2001 whereby one of his parliamentary assistants impersonated him on the radio. The story in the media following the incident was that Jaffer had been double-booked; thus, his assistant, Matthew Johnston, stepped in to take Jaffer's place on a call-in show at a Vancouver radio station. Unfortunately, Jaffer initially lied and said that he had done the interview himself, but then later admitted that his assistant had done the interview. See "The Great Rahim Jaffer Phone-in Hoax," *National Post*, 21 March 2001.
5 Edward Greenspon and Jeff Sallot, "How Campbell Self-Destructed," *Globe and Mail*, 27 Oct. 1993, A1.
6 "They're Off!" *Montreal Gazette*, 9 Sept. 1993, A1.
7 Greenspon and Sallot, "How Campbell Self-Destructed."
8 "Staying the Course with Campbell," *Globe and Mail*, 14 Sept. 1993, A1.
9 "Liberal Leader Has Had It Easy," *Globe and Mail*, 30 Sept. 1993, A1.
10 "Quote of the Day," *Globe and Mail*, 8 Oct. 1993, A1.
11 The Fraser Institute. 1993. "Election '93: What Role Did Television Play in the Outcome?" *On Balance* 6(9), 3.
12 "Liberals Go After 'Protest' Vote," *Globe and Mail*, 9 Oct. 1993, A6.
13 "A Gaffe Is When You Tell the Truth," *Globe and Mail*, 14 Sept. 1993, A16.
14 Personal interview with Alexa McDonough, 25 Feb. 2005.

15 *Ottawa Citizen*, 3 Oct. 1998, B4.
16 Although McDonough believed the piece was a news story, it was a political gossip column called "What the Gargoyle Heard."
17 McDonough makes this point again in *Why Women Run* (1999), a National Film Board documentary on her 1997 effort to win the federal constituency of Halifax against two-time Liberal incumbent Mary Clancy.
18 E.g., "Clark's Daughter Big Part of Campaign," *Toronto Star*, 26 Oct. 2000, 1; "The Catherine Factor," *Kitchener-Waterloo Record*, 26 Oct. 2000, A8; "Helping Dad Means Picking Out His Tie," *Toronto Star*, 30 Oct. 2000, 1.
19 Personal interview with Gurmant Grewal, 24 Feb. 2005.
20 Each party has a lounge with direct access to the House of Commons. These lounges have telephones and computers as well as food and beverage services. Stockwell Day explained to me that many of the MPs come in and out of their party's lounge through the course of a typical day in the House. They also use the lounges to meet with people, and have messengers who take notes in and out of the party lounges, since access is restricted to caucus members.
21 The "Rat Pack" was the nickname given to a group of highly visible Liberal opposition MPs during the 1980s. The Rat Pack included Don Boudria, Brian Tobin, Sheila Copps, and John Nunziata, and the group was known for its sharp and relentless critique of Mulroney and the PC governments both in the House of Commons and to the media.
22 The Copps family dominated Hamilton-area politics for some time. Both her father and mother held public office – her father Victor Copps was an influential mayor of Hamilton (1962-1976), and her mother Geraldine Copps was a Hamilton city councillor (1985-2000). Copps Coliseum, Hamilton's primary sports and entertainment centre, is named after Victor Copps.
23 Personal interview with Stockwell Day, 24 Feb. 2005. Day was a Conservative MLA in the Alberta legislature from 1986 to 2000, and became Alberta's treasurer, the equivalent of finance minister, in 1997.
24 *The Fundamental Day* aired on 14 Nov. 2000, about midway through the campaign. It questioned the links between Day's religious and political beliefs, particularly how his alleged belief in creationism would affect policy. The documentary described Day's time in Bentley, Alberta, "the heart of Alberta's Bible belt," and claimed that Bentley is the place where Day "first mixed religion and politics." The documentary also mentioned Jim Keegstra, a teacher who taught anti-Semitic beliefs in high school classrooms, and pointed out that Keegstra lived just thirty minutes down the road from Day. The documentary also claimed that Day once called homosexuality "a mental disorder," said women who were victims of incest or rape "should not get government-funded abortions unless their pregnancy is life-threatening," and supported banning *Of Mice and Men*, "calling the language ... blasphemous."

CONCLUSION

1 United Nations, *Report of the Fourth World Conference on Women*, A/CONF.177/20, chap. 4(j), 1995.

Works Cited

Abu-Laban, Yasmeen, and Linda Trimble. 2006. "Print Media Coverage of Muslim Canadians during Recent Federal Elections." *Electoral Insight* 8, 2: 35-41.

Aday, Sean, and James Devitt. 2001. "Style over Substance: Newspaper Coverage of Elizabeth Dole's Presidential Bid." *Harvard International Journal of Press/Politics* 6, 2: 52-73.

Alexander, D., and K. Anderson. 1993. "Gender as a Factor in the Attribution of Leadership Traits." *Political Research Quarterly* 46, 3: 527-45.

Alexander-Floyd, Nikol G. 2008. "Framing Condi(licious): Condoleezza Rice and the Storyline of 'Closeness' in US National Community Formation." *Politics and Gender* 4, 3: 427-49.

Altschull, J. Herbert. 1997. "Boundaries of Journalistic Autonomy." In *Social Meanings of News: A Text-Reader*, ed. D. Berkowitz, 259-68. Thousand Oaks, CA: Sage.

Ansalobehere, Stephen, Roy Behr, and Shanto Iyengar. 1993. *The Media Game.* New York: Macmillan.

Ansolabehere, Stephen, and Shanto Iyengar. 1991. "Why Candidates Attack: Effects of Television Advertising in the 1990 California Gubernatorial Campaign." Paper presented at the annual meeting of the Western Political Science Association.

–. 1994. "Riding the Wave and Claiming Ownership Over Issues: The Joint Effects of Advertising and News Coverage in Campaigns." *The Public Opinion Quarterly* 58, 3: 335-57.

–. 1995. *Going Negative: How Political Advertisements Shrink and Polarize the Electorate.* New York: Free Press.

Ansalobehere, Stephen, Shanto Iyengar, Adam Simon, and Nicholas Valentino. 1994. "Does Attack Advertising Demobilize the Electorate?" *American Political Science Review* 88, 4: 829-38.

Argyle, Michael, F. Alkema, and R. Gilmour. 1971. "The Communication of Friendly and Hostile Attitudes by Verbal and Nonverbal Signals." *European Journal of Social Psychology* 1, 3: 385-402.

Argyle, Michael, Veronica Salter, Hilary Nicholson, Marilyn Williams, and Philip Burgess. 1970. "The Communication of Inferior and Superior Attitudes by Verbal and Non-verbal Signals." *British Journal of Social and Clinical Psychology* 9, 3: 222-31.

Banwart, M.C., and M.S. McKinney. 2005. "A Gendered Influence in Campaign Debates? Analysis of Mixed-Gender United States Senate and Gubernatorial Debates." *Communication Studies* 56, 4: 353-73.

Bartels, Larry M. 1988. *Presidential Primaries and the Dynamics of Public Choice*. Princeton, NJ: Princeton University Press.

–. 2002. "The Impact of Candidate Traits in American Presidential Elections." In *Leaders' Personalities and the Outcomes of Democratic Elections*, ed. Anthony King, 44-69. New York: Oxford University Press.

Bashevkin, Sylvia B. 1993. *Toeing the Lines: Women and Party Politics in English Canada*, 2nd ed. Toronto: Oxford University Press.

–. 2009. *Women, Power, Politics: The Hidden Story of Canada's Unfinished Democracy*. Don Mills: Oxford University Press.

Basil, Michael, Caroline Schooler, and Byron Reeves. 1991. "Positive and Negative Political Advertising: Effectiveness of Advertisements and Perceptions of Candidates." In *Television and Political Advertising*, 1, *Psychological Processes*, ed. F. Biocca, 245-62. Hillsdale, NJ: Erlbaum.

Bathla, Sonia. 1998. *Women, Democracy and the Media: Cultural and Political Representation in the Indian Press*. New Delhi: Sage.

–. 2000. "Covering Women in the Indian Press: A Brahmanical Cultural Paradigm." In *Gender, Politics and Communication*, ed. A. Sreberny and L. van Zoonen, 183-204. Cresskill, NJ: Hampton Press.

Bean, Clive, and Anthony Mughan. 1989. "Leadership Effects in Parliamentary Elections in Australia and Britain." *American Political Science Review* 83, 4: 1165-79.

Bélanger, Éric. 2003. "Issue Ownership by Canadian Political Parties 1953-2001." *Canadian Journal of Political Science* 36, 3: 539-58.

Bennett, W. Lance. 2003. *News: The Politics of Illusion*, 5th ed. New York: Addison Wesley Longman.

Benson, Rodney. 2004. "Bringing the Sociology of Media Back In." *Political Communication* 21: 275-92.

Best, Deborah L., and John E. Willams. 1990. *Measuring Sex Stereotypes: A Thirty-Nation Study*. Beverly Hills, CA: Sage.

Bittner, Amanda. 2011. *Platform or Personality? The Role of Party Leaders in Elections*. Oxford: Oxford University Press.

Bittner, Amanda, and Elizabeth Goodyear-Grant. 2013. "A Laggard No More? Women in Newfoundland and Labrador Politics." In *Stalled: The Representation of Women in Canadian Legislatures*, ed. L. Trimble, J. Arscott, and M. Tremblay, 115-34. Vancouver: UBC Press.

Black, Jerome, and Lynda Erickson. 2003. "Women Candidates and Voter Bias: Do Women Politicians Need to Be Better?" *Electoral Studies* 22, 1: 81-100.

Blais, André, Elisabeth Gidengil, Richard Nadeau, and Neil Nevitte. 2002a. *Anatomy of a Liberal Victory: Making Sense of the Vote in the 2000 Canadian Election*. Peterborough, ON: Broadview.

–. 2002b. "Do Party Supporters Differ?" In *Citizen Politics: Research and Theory in Canadian Political Behaviour*, ed. J. Everitt and B. O'Neill, 184-201. Don Mills, ON: Oxford University Press.

–. 2003. "Campaign Dynamics in the 2000 Canadian Election: How the Leader Debates Salvaged the Conservative Party." *PS: Political Science and Politics* 36, 1: 45-50.

Blais, André, Neil Nevitte, Elisabeth Gidengil, and Richard Nadeau. 2000. "Do People Have Feelings toward Leaders about Whom They Say They Know Nothing?" *Public Opinion Quarterly* 64, 4: 452-63.

Blumler, Jay G., and Michael Gurevitch. 1988. "The Political Effects of Mass Communication." In *Culture, Society and the Media*, ed. M. Gurevitch, T. Bennett, J. Curran, and J. Woolacott, 236-67. London: Routledge.

Blumler, Jay G., and D. Kavanagh. 1999. "The Third Age of Political Communication: Influences and Features." *Political Communication* 16, 3: 209-30.

Bode, Leticia, and Valerie M. Hennings. 2012. "Mixed Signals? Gender and the Media's Coverage of the 2008 Vice Presidential Candidates." *Politics and Policy* 40, 2: 221-57.

Bonde, Hans. 2009. "The Great Male Cycle: Sport, Politics and European Masculinity Today." *The International Journal of the History of Sport* 26, 10: 1540-54.

Bratton, Kathleen A. 2005. "Critical Mass Theory Revisited: The Behavior and Success of Token Women in State Legislatures." *Politics and Gender* 1, 1: 97-125.

Brians, Craig Leonard. 2005. "Women for Women? Gender and Party Bias in Voting for Female Candidates." *American Politics Research* 33: 357-75.

Brooks, Deborah Jordan. 2010. "A Negativity Gap? Voter Gender, Attack Politics, and Participation in American Elections." *Politics and Gender* 6, 3: 319-41.

–. 2011. "Testing the Double Standard for Candidate Emotionality: Voter Reactions to the Tears and Anger of Male and Female Politicians." *Journal of Politics* 73, 2: 597–615.

Broverman, J.K., S.R. Vogel, D.M. Broverman, F.E. Clarkson, and P.S. Rosenkrantz. 1972. "Sex-Role Stereotypes: A Current Appraisal." *Journal of Social Issues* 28, 2: 59-78.

Brown, Mary Ellen, and Darlaine C. Gardetto. 2000. "Representing Hillary Rodham Clinton: Gender, Meaning, and News Media." In *Gender, Politics and Communication*, ed. A. Sreberny and L. van Zoonen, 21-52. Cresskill, NJ: Hampton Press.

Brown, Rosemary. 1989. *Being Brown: A Very Public Life*. Toronto: Random House.

Brown, Steven, Ronald Lambert, Barry Kay, and James Curtis. 1988. "In the Eye of the Beholder: Leader Images in Canada." *Canadian Journal of Political Science* 21, 4: 729-55.

Burrell, Barbara C. 1994. *A Woman's Place Is in the House: Campaigning for Congress in the Feminist Era*. Ann Arbor: University of Michigan Press.

Bussey, Kay, and Albert Bandura. 1999. "Social Cognitive Theory of Gender Development and Differentiation." *Psychological Review* 106, 4: 676-713.

Butler, Doré, and Florence L. Geis. 1990. "Nonverbal Affect Responses to Male and Female Leaders: Implications for Leadership Evaluations." *Journal of Personality and Social Psychology* 58, 1: 48-59.

Bystrom, Dianne G. 2006. "Advertising, Web Sites, and Media Coverage: Gender and Communication along the Campaign Trail." In *Gender and Elections*, ed. S.J. Carroll and R.L. Fox, 239-62. New York: Cambridge University Press.

Bystrom, Dianne G., Mary Christine Banwart, Lynda Lee Kaid, and Terry A. Robertson. 2004. *Gender and Candidate Communication*. New York: Routledge.

Bystrom, Dianne, and Linda L. Kaid. 2002. "Are Women Candidates Transforming Campaign Communication? A Comparison of Advertising Videostyles in the 1990s." In *Women Transforming Congress*, ed. C. S. Rosenthal, 146-69. Norman: University of Oklahoma Press.

Bystrom, Dianne, and J.L. Miller. 1999. "Gendered Communication Styles and Strategies in Campaign 1996: The Videostyles of Women and Men Candidates." In *The Electronic Election: Perspectives on the 1996 Campaign Communication*, ed. L.L. Kaid, and D.G. Bystrom, 293-302. Mahwah, NJ: Erlbaum.

Bystrom, Dianne, T. Robertson, and M.C. Banwart. 2001. "Framing the Fight: An Analysis of Media Coverage of Female and Male Candidates in Primary Races for Governor and US Senate in 2000." *American Behavioral Scientist* 44, 12: 1999-2013.

Campbell, A., P.E. Converse, W.E. Miller, and D.E. Stokes. 1960. *The American Voter*. New York: Wiley.

Campbell, Kim. 1996. *Time and Chance: The Political Memoirs of Canada's First Woman Prime Minister*. Toronto: Doubleday.

Cantrell, Tania H., and Ingrid Bachmann. 2008. "Who is the Lady in the Window? A Comparison of International and National Press Coverage of First Female Government Heads." *Journalism Studies* 9, 3: 429-46.

Carbert, Louise. 2009. "Are Cities More Congenial? Tracking the Rural Deficit in the House of Commons." In *Opening Doors Wider: Women's Political Engagement in Canada*, ed. Sylvia Bashevkin, 70-92. Vancouver: UBC Press.

Carli, L.L. 1990. "Gender, Language, and Influence." *Journal of Personality and Social Psychology* 59, 5: 941-51.

Carli, L.L., S. LaFleur, and C.C. Loeber. 1995. "Nonverbal Behavior, Gender, and Influence." *Journal of Personality and Social Psychology* 68, 6: 1030–41.

Carlin, Diana B., and Kelly L. Winfrey. 2009. "Have You Come a Long Way, Baby? Hillary Clinton, Sarah Palin, and Sexism in 2008 Campaign Coverage." *Communication Studies* 60, 4: 326-43.

Carlson, Tom. 2001. "Gender and Political Advertising across Cultures: A Comparison of Male and Female Political Advertising in Finland and the US." *European Journal of Communication* 16, 2: 131-54.

Carroll, Susan J. 2009. "Reflections on Gender and Hillary Clinton's Presidential Campaign: The Good, the Bad, and the Misogynic." *Politics and Gender* 5, 1: 1-20.

Carroll, Susan J., and Ronnee Schreiber. 1997. "Media Coverage of Women in the 103rd Congress." In *Women, Media, and Politics*, ed. P. Norris, 131-49. New York: Oxford University Press.

Carter, C., G. Branston, and S. Allen, ed. 1998. *News, Gender and Power*. London: Routledge.

Chambers, Deborah, Linda Steiner, and Carole Fleming. 2004. *Women and Journalism*. London and New York: Routledge.

Chang, Chingching, and Jacqueline Hitchon. 1997. "Mass Media Impact on Voter Response to Women Candidates: Theoretical Development." *Communication Theory* 7, 1: 29-52.

Childs, Sarah. 2008. *Women and British Party Politics: Descriptive, Substantive and Symbolic Representation*. London: Routledge.

Clark, Cal, and Janel Clark. 1993. "The Gender Gap 1988: Compassion, Pacifism and Indirect Feminism." In *Women and Politics: Outsiders or Insiders?* ed. Lois Lovelace Duke, 32-45. Englewood Cliffs, NJ: Prentice Hall.

Coe, Kevin, David Domke, Meredith M. Bagley, Sheryl Cunningham, and Nancy Van Leuven. 2007. "Masculinity as Political Strategy: George W. Bush, the 'War on Terrorism,' and an Echoing Press." *Journal of Women, Politics and Policy* 29, 1: 31-55.

Cohen, B. 1963. *The Press and Foreign Policy*. Princeton, NJ: Princeton University Press.

Copps, Sheila. 1986. *Nobody's Baby: A Survival Guide to Politics*. Toronto: Deneau.

–. 2004. *Worth Fighting For*. Toronto: McClelland and Stewart.

Covert, Catherine L. 1981. "Journalism History and Women's Experience: A Problem in Conceptual Change." *Journalism History* 8, 1: 2-6.

Craft, Stephanie, and Wayne Wanta. 2004. "Women in the Newsroom: Influence of Female Editors and Reporters on the News Agenda." *Journalism and Mass Communication Quarterly* 81, 1: 124-38.

Dabbousa, Yasmine, and Amy Ladleya. 2010. "A Spine of Steel and a Heart of Gold: Newspaper Coverage of the First Female Speaker of the House." *Journal of Gender Studies* 19, 2: 181-94.

Dalton, Russell J., and Martin P. Wattenberg, ed. 2000. *Parties without Partisans: Political Change in Advanced Industrial Democracies*. New York: Oxford University Press.

Davis, J. 1982. "Sexist Bias in Eight Newspapers." *Journalism Quarterly* 59, 3: 456-60.

Davis, Rebecca Howard. 1997. *Women and Power in Parliamentary Democracies: Cabinet Appointments in Western Europe, 1968-1992*. Lincoln, NB: University of Nebraska Press.

Davis, Shannon N., and Theodore N. Greenstein. 2009. "Gender Ideology: Components, Predictors, and Consequences." *Annual Review of Sociology* 35: 87-105.

Derks, Belle, Naomi Ellemers, Colette van Laar, and Kim de Groot. 2011. "Do Sexist Organizational Cultures Create the Queen Bee?" *British Journal of Social Psychology* 50, 3: 519-35.

Deutchman, Iva E., and Anne Ellison. 2004. "When Feminists Don't Fit: The Case of Pauline Hanson." *International Feminist Journal of Politics* 6, 1: 29-52.

DeVaus, David, and Ian McAllister. 1989. "The Changing Politics of Women: Gender and Political Alignments in 11 Nations." *European Journal of Political Research* 17, 3: 241-62.

Devitt, James. 2002. "Framing Gender on the Campaign Trail: Female Gubernatorial Candidates and the Press." *Journalism and Mass Communication Quarterly* 79, 2: 445-63.

Dolan, Kathleen. 1998. "Voting for Women in the 'Year of the Woman.'" *American Journal of Political Science* 42, 1: 272-93.

–. 2002. "Electoral Context, Issues, and Voting for Women in the 1990s." *Women and Politics* 23, 1/2: 21-36.

–. 2004. *Voting for Women: How Voters Evaluate Women Candidates*. Boulder, CO: Westview Press.

–. 2005. "Do Women Candidates Play to Gender Stereotypes? Do Men Candidates Play to Women? Candidate Sex and Issues Priorities on Campaign Websites." *Political Research Quarterly* 58, 1: 31–44.

Dornan, Christopher, and Jon H. Pammett, eds. 2001. *The Canadian General Election of 2000*. Ottawa: Dundurn Press.

Dougherty, Kevin, John Geddes, and Alan Toulin. 1993. "Tories Set to Unveil Social Policy." *Financial Post*, 25 September: 5.

Druckman, James N. 2005. "Media Matter: How Newspapers and Television News Cover Campaigns and Influence Voters." *Political Communication* 22, 4: 463-81.

Eagly, Alice H. 2007. "Female Leadership Advantage and Disadvantage: Resolving the Contradictions." *Psychology of Women Quarterly* 31, 1: 1-12.

Eagly, Alice H., and Maureen Crowley. 1986. "Gender and Helping Behavior: A Meta-Analytic Review of the Social Psychological Literature." *Psychological Bulletin* 100: 283-306.

Eagly, A.H., and B.T. Johnson. 1990. "Gender and Leadership Style: a Meta-Analysis." *Psychological Bulletin* 108: 233-56.

Eagly, Alice H., and Steven J. Karau. 2002. "Role Congruity Theory of Prejudice toward Female Leaders." *Psychological Review* 109, 3: 573-98.

Eagly, Alice H., Steven J. Karau, and M.G. Makhijani. 1995. "Gender and the Effectiveness of Leaders: A Meta-Analysis." *Psychological Bulletin* 117: 125-45.

Eagly, Alice H., Mona G. Makhijani, and Bruce G. Klonsky. 1992. "Gender and the Evaluation of Leaders: A Meta-Analysis." *Psychological Bulletin* 111, 1: 3-22.

Eagly, Alice H., and Valerie J. Steffen. 1984. "Gender Stereotypes Stem from the Distribution of Women and Men into Social Roles." *Journal of Personality and Social Psychology* 46: 735-54.

Eichenberg, Richard C. 2003. "Gender Differences in Public Attitudes toward the Use of Force by the United States, 1990-2003." *International Security* 28, 1: 110-41.

–. 2005. "Victory Has Many Friends: U.S. Public Opinion and the Use of Military Force, 1981-2005." *International Security* 30, 1: 140-77.

Entman, Robert M. 1993. "Framing: Towards Clarification of a Fractured Paradigm." *Journal of Communication* 43, 4: 51-8.

Ericson, Richard, Patricia Baranek, and Janet Chan. 1987. *Visualizing Deviance: A Study of News Organization*. Toronto: University of Toronto Press.

–. 1992. "Representing Order." In *Seeing Ourselves: Media Power and Policy in Canada*, 1st ed., ed. H. Holmes and D. Taras, 232-49. Toronto: Harcourt Brace Jovanovich.

Erie, S. P., and M. Rein. 1988. "Women and the Welfare State." In *The Politics of the Gender Gap*, ed. C.M. Mueller, 173-91. Newbury Park, CA: Sage.

Escobar-Lemmon, Maria, and Michelle M. Taylor-Robinson. 2005. "Women Ministers in Latin American Government: When, Where, and Why?" *American Journal of Political Science* 49, 4: 829-44.

Eveland Jr., William P., Mihye Seo, and Krisztina Marton. 2002. "Learning from the News in Campaign 2000: An Experimental Comparison of TV News, Newspapers, and Online News." *Media Psychology* 4, 4: 353-78.

Everitt, Joanna. 1998. "The Gender Gap in Canada: Now You See it, Now You Don't." *Canadian Review of Sociology and Anthropology* 35, 2: 1-29.

–. 2002. "Gender Gaps on Social Welfare Issues: Why Do Women Care?" In *Citizen Politics: Research and Theory in Canadian Political Behaviour*, ed. J. Everitt and B. O'Neill, 110-25. Toronto: Oxford University Press.

–. 2003. "Media in the Maritimes: Do Female Candidates Face a Bias?" *Atlantis* 27, 2: 90-8.

–. 2005. "Gender, Media, and Politics: A Critical Review Essay." *Political Communication* 22: 387-416.

Everitt, Joanna, and Michael Camp. 2009a. "One Is Not Like the Others: Allison Brewer's Leadership of the New Brunswick NDP." In *Opening Doors Wider: Women's Political Engagement in Canada*, ed. Sylvia Bashevkin, 127-46. Vancouver: UBC Press.

–. 2009b. "Changing the Game Changes the Frame: The Media's Use of Lesbian Stereotypes in Leadership versus Election Campaigns." *Canadian Political Science Review* 3, 3: 24-39.

Festinger, Leon. 1957. *A Theory of Cognitive Dissonance*. Stanford: Stanford University Press.

Fiske, S. T. 1984. "Schema-based versus Piecemeal Politics: A Patchwork Quilt, but Not a Blanket, of Evidence." In *Political Cognition: The 19th Carnegie Symposium on Cognition*, ed. R. R. Lau and D.O. Sears, 141-58. Hillsdale, NJ: Erlbaum.

Fleras, Augie, and Jean Kunz. 2001. *Media and Minorities: Diversity in Multicultural Canada*. Toronto: Thomson.

Fountaine, Susan, and Judy McGregor. 2002. "Reconstructing Gender for the 21st Century: News Media Framing of Political Women in New Zealand." Refereed paper presented at the annual conference of the *Australian and New Zealand*

Communications Association. Brisbane. http://webenrol.massey.ac.nz/massey/fms/Colleges/College%20of%20Business/NZCWL/pdfs/JMcGregorSFountainePaper.pdf.

Fowler, Linda, and Jennifer L. Lawless. 2009. "Looking for Sex in All the Wrong Places: Press Coverage and the Electoral Fortunes of Gubernatorial Candidates." *Perspectives on Politics* 7, 3: 519-36.

Fox, Richard Logan. 1997. *Gender Dynamics in Congressional Elections.* Thousand Oaks, CA: Sage.

Funk, Carolyn L. 1997. "Implications of Political Expertise in Candidate Trait Evaluations." *Political Research Quarterly* 50, 3: 675-97.

Gamson, William. 1988. "Political Discourse and Collective Action." *International Social Movement Research* 1: 219-44.

Garcia, Mario R., and Pegie Stark. 1991. *Eyes on the News.* St. Petersburg, Florida: The Poynter Institute.

Geer, John G. 2006. *In Defense of Negativity: Attack Ads in Presidential Campaigns.* Chicago: University of Chicago Press.

Gershon, Sarah. 2012. "When Race, Gender, and the Media Intersect: Campaign News Coverage of Minority Congresswomen." *Journal of Women, Politics and Policy* 33, 2: 105-25.

Ghanem, Salma. 1997. "Filling in the Tapestry: The Second Level of Agenda-Setting." In *Communication and Democracy: Exploring the Intellectual Frontiers in Agenda-Setting Theory*, ed. M E. McCombs, D.L. Shaw, and D. Weaver, 3-14. Mahwah, NJ: Laurence Erlbaum Associates.

Gidengil, Elisabeth. 1995. "Economic Man – Social Woman? The Case of the Gender Gap in Support for the Canada-US Free Trade Agreement." *Comparative Political Studies* 28, 3: 384-408.

Gidengil, Elisabeth, André Blais, Joanna Everitt, Patrick Fournier, and Neil Nevitte. 2006. "Back to the Future? Making Sense of the 2004 Canadian Election outside Quebec." *Canadian Journal of Political Science* 39, 1: 1-25.

Gidengil, Elisabeth, André Blais, Richard Nadeau, and Neil Nevitte. 2003. "Women to the Left? Gender Differences in Political Beliefs and Policy Preferences." In *Gender and Electoral Representation in Canada*, ed. Manon Tremblay and Linda Trimble, 140-59. Don Mills, ON: Oxford University Press.

–. 2004. *Citizens.* Vancouver: UBC Press.

Gidengil, Elisabeth, and Joanna Everitt. 1999. "Metaphors and Misrepresentation: Gendered Mediation in News Coverage of the 1993 Canadian Leaders' Debates." *Harvard International Journal of Press/Politics* 4, 1: 48-65.

–. 2000. "Filtering the Female: Television News Coverage of the 1993 Canadian Leaders' Debates." *Women and Politics* 21, 4: 105-31.

–. 2002. "Damned If You Do, Damned If You Don't: Television News Coverage of Female Party Leaders in the 1993 Federal Election." In *Political Parties, Representation and Electoral Democracy in Canada*, ed. William Cross, 223-37. Don Mills, ON: Oxford University Press.

–. 2003a. "Conventional Coverage/Unconventional Politicians: Gender and Media Coverage of Canadian Leaders' Debates, 1993, 1997, 2000." *Canadian Journal of Political Science* 36, 3: 559-77.

–. 2003b. "Talking Tough: Gender and Reported Speech in Campaign News Coverage." *Political Communication* 20, 3: 209-32.

Gilens, Martin. 1988. "Gender and Support for Reagan: A Comprehensive Model of Presidential Support." *American Journal of Political Science* 32, 1: 19-49.

Gilligan, Carol. 1982. *In a Different Voice: Psychological Theory and Women's Development*. Cambridge, MA: Harvard University Press.

Gingras, Anne-Marie. 1997. "Les métaphores dans la langue politique." *Politiques et Sociétés* 30: 159-71.

Gingras, François-Pierre. 1995. "Daily Male Delivery: Women and Politics in the Daily Newspapers." In *Gender and Politics in Contemporary Canada*, ed. F.-P. Gingras, 191-208. Toronto: Oxford University Press.

Goffman, Erving. 1959. *The Presentation of Self in Everyday Life*. Garden City, NY: Doubleday.

Gold, Howard J. 2005. "Explaining Third-Party Success in Gubernatorial Elections: The Cases of Alaska, Connecticut, Maine and Minnesota." *Social Science Journal* 42, 4: 523-40.

Golebiowska, Ewa. 2002. "Political Implications of Group Stereotypes: Campaign Experiences of Openly Gay Political Candidates." *Journal of Applied Social Psychology* 32, 3: 590-607.

Goodyear-Grant, Elizabeth. 2009. "Crafting a Public Image: Women MPs and the Dynamics of Media Coverage." In *Opening Doors Wider: Women's Political Engagement in Canada*, ed. Sylvia Bashevkin, 147-65. Vancouver: UBC Press.

–. 2013. "Women Voters, Candidates, and Legislators: A Gender Perspective on Recent Party and Electoral Politics." In *Parties, Elections, and the Future of Canadian Politics*, ed. A. Bittner and R. Koop, 119-39. Vancouver: UBC Press.

Goodyear-Grant, Elizabeth, and Julie Croskill. 2011. "Gender Affinity Effects in Vote Choice in Westminster Systems: Assessing 'Flexible' Voters in Canada." *Politics and Gender* 7, 2: 223-50.

Gordon, Ann, David M. Shafie, and Ann N. Crigler. 2003. "Is Negative Advertising Effective for Female Candidates: An Experiment in Voters' Uses of Gender Stereotypes." *Harvard International Journal of Press/Politics* 8, 3: 35-53.

Greenstein, Theodore N. 2000. "Economic Dependence, Gender, and the Division of Labor in the Home: A Replication and Extension." *Journal of Marriage and Family* 62, 2: 322-35.

Gulati, Girish J. 2004. "Members of Congress and Presentation of Self on the World Wide Web." *Harvard International Journal of Press/Politics* 9, 1: 22-40.

Hall, Judith. 1984. *Nonverbal Sex Differences: Communication Accuracy and Expressive Style*. Baltimore: Johns Hopkins University Press.

Halpern, Diane F. 1988. "Sex Difference in Cognitive Abilities." *American Journal of Psychology* 101: 452-54.

Hayes, Danny. 2011. "When Gender and Party Collide: Stereotyping in Candidate Trait Attribution." *Politics and Gender* 7, 2: 133-65.

Heath, Roseanna Michelle, Leslie A. Schwindt-Bayer, and Michelle M. Taylor-Robinson. 2005. "Women on the Sidelines: Women's Representation on

Committees in Latin American Legislatures." *American Journal of Political Science* 49, 2: 420-36.
Heilman, Madeline E. 2001. "Description and Prescription: How Gender Stereotypes Prevent Women's Ascent up the Organizational Ladder." *Journal of Social Issues* 57, 4: 657-74.
Heldman, Caroline, Sue Carroll, and Stephanie Olson. 2005. "She Brought Only a Skirt: Print Media Coverage of Elizabeth Dole's Bid for the Presidential Nomination." *Political Communication* 22, 3: 315-35.
Henderson, Ailsa. 2004. "Regional Political Cultures in Canada." *Canadian Journal of Political Science* 37, 3: 595-615.
Henley, Nancy, and Jo Freeman. 1995. "The Sexual Politics of Interpersonal Behaviour." In *Women: A Feminist Perspective*, 5th ed., ed. J. Freeman, 79-91. Mountain View, CA: Mayfield.
Henningham, J.P., and A. Delano. 1998. "British Journalists." In *The Global Journalist: News People around the World*, ed. D. Weaver, 143-60. Cresskill, NJ: Hampton Press.
Henry, Frances, and Carol Tator. 2002. *Discourses of Domination: Racial Bias in the Canadian English-Language Press*. Toronto: University of Toronto Press.
Herrnson, Paul S., J. Celeste Lay, and Atiya Kai Stokes. 2003. "Women Running 'as Women': Candidate Gender, Campaign Issues, and Voter-Targeting Strategies." *Journal of Politics* 65, 1: 244-55.
Hitchon, Jacqueline C., and Chingching Chang. 1995. "Effects of Gender Schematic Processing on the Reception of Political Commercials for Men and Women Candidates." *Communication Research* 22, 4: 430-58.
Hitchon, Jacqueline, Chingching Chang, and Rhonda Harris. 1997. "Should Women Emote? Perceptual Bias and Opinion Change in Response to Political Ads for Candidates of Different Genders." *Political Communication* 14, 1: 49-69.
Holian, David B. 2004. "He's Stealing My Issues! Clinton's Crime Rhetoric and the Dynamics of Issue Ownership." *Political Behavior* 26, 2: 95-124.
Hoskins, Colin, Stuart McFadyen, and Adam Finn. 2001. "Refocusing the CBC." *Canadian Journal of Communication* 26, 1: 17-30.
Huddy, Leonie. 1994. "The Political Significance of Gender Stereotypes." In *Research in Micropolitics: New Directions in Political Psychology*, ed., Michael X. Delli Carpini, Leonie Huddy, and Robert Y. Shapiro, 169-93. Greenwich, CT: JAI Press.
Huddy, Leonie, and Teresa Capelos. 2002. "Gender Stereotyping and Candidate Evaluation: Good News and Bad News for Women Politicians." In *The Social Psychology of Politics*, ed. V.C. Ottati, R.S. Tindale, J. Edwards, F.B. Bryant, L. Heath, D.C. O'Connell, Y. Suarez-Balcazar, and E. Posavac, 29-53. New York: Kluwer Academic Press.
Huddy, Leonie, and Nayda Terkildsen. 1993a. "The Consequences of Gender Stereotypes for Women Candidates at Different Levels and Types of Office." *Political Research Quarterly* 46, 3: 503-25.
–. 1993b. "Gender Stereotypes and the Perception of Male and Female Candidates." *American Journal of Political Science* 37, 1: 119-47.

Inglehart, Ronald, and Pippa Norris. 2003. *Rising Tide: Gender Equality and Cultural Change around the World*. New York: Cambridge University Press.

Iyengar, Shanto, 1990. "The Accessibility Bias in Politics: Television News and Public Opinion." *International Journal of Public Opinion Research* 2, 1: 1-15.

–. 1991. *Is Anyone Responsible? How Television Frames Political Issues*. Chicago: University of Chicago Press.

Iyengar, Shanto, and Donald Kinder. 1987. *News that Matters: Television and American Opinion*. Chicago: University of Chicago Press.

Iyengar, Shanto, Nicholas Valentino, Stephen Ansolabehere, and Adam Simon. 1997. "Running as a Woman: Gender Stereotyping in Women's Campaigns." In *Women, Media, and Politics*, ed. Pippa Norris, 77-98. New York: Oxford University Press.

Jacobson, Gary C. 1992. *The Politics of Congressional Elections*, 3rd ed. New York: HarperCollins.

James, Curtis. 2000. "Low-income, Low Priority." *Marketing* 26 October: 36-38.

Jamieson, Kathleen Hall. 1995. *Beyond the Double Bind: Women and Leadership*. New York: Oxford University Press.

Janoff-Bulman, R. and M.B. Wade. 1996. "The Dilemma of Self-Advocacy for Women: Another Case of Blaming the Victim?" *Journal of Social and Clinical Psychology* 15, 2: 143-52.

Johnston, Richard. 2002. "Prime Ministerial Contenders in Canada." In *Leaders' Personalities and the Outcomes of Democratic Elections*, ed. Anthony King, 158-83. New York: Oxford University Press.

Johnston, Richard, André Blais, Henry E. Brady, and Jean Crête. 1992. *Letting the People Decide: Dynamics of a Canadian Election*. Montreal: McGill-Queen's University Press.

Kahn, Kim Fridkin. 1992. "Does Being Male Help? An Investigation of the Effects of Candidate Gender and Campaign Coverage on Evaluations of US Senate Candidates." *Journal of Politics* 54, 2: 497-517.

–. 1993. "Gender Differences in Campaign Messages: The Political Advertisements of Men and Women Candidates for U.S. Senate." *Political Research Quarterly* 46, 3: 481-502.

–. 1994. "The Distorted Mirror: Press Coverage of Women Candidates for Statewide Office." *Journal of Politics* 56, 1 (1994): 154-74.

–. 1996. *The Political Consequences of Being a Woman*. New York: Columbia University Press.

Kahn, Kim Fridkin, and Edie N. Goldenberg. 1991. "Women Candidates in the News: An Examination of Gender Differences in US Senate Campaign Coverage." *Public Opinion Quarterly* 55, 2: 180-99.

Kahn, Kim Fridkin, and Patrick J. Kenney. 1999. "Do Negative Campaigns Suppress or Mobilize Turnout? Clarifying the Relationship between Negativity and Participation." *American Political Science Review* 93, 4: 877-89.

Kanter, Rosabeth Moss. 1977a. "Some Effects of Proportions on Group Life: Skewed Sex Ratios and Responses to Token Women." *American Journal of Sociology* 82, 5: 965-90.

–. 1977b. *Men and Women of the Corporation*. New York: Basic Books.
Kathlene, Lyn. 1994. "Power and Influence in State Legislative Policymaking: The Interaction of Gender and Position in Committee Hearing Debates." *American Political Science Review* 88, 3: 560-76.
Kaufmann, Karen M. 2004. "Disaggregating and Reexamining Issue Ownership and Voter Choice." *Polity* 36, 2: 283-99.
Kendall, Kathleen E. 2000. *Communication in the Presidential Primaries: Candidates and the Media, 1912-2000*. Westport, CT: Praeger.
Kinder, Donald, Mark Peters, Robert Abelson, and Susan Fiske. 1980. "Presidential Prototypes." *Political Behavior* 2, 4: 315-37.
King, Gary, Robert O. Keohane and Sidney Verba. 1994. *Designing Social Inquiry: Scientific Inference in Qualitative Research*. Princeton, NJ: Princeton University Press.
King, Gary, Michael Tomz, and Jason Wittenberg. 2000. "Making the Most of Statistical Analyses: Improving Interpretation and Presentation." *American Journal of Political Science* 44, 2: 341-55.
Kittilson, Miki Caul, and Kim Fridkin. 2008. "Gender, Candidate Portrayals and Election Campaigns: A Comparative Perspective." *Politics and Gender* 4, 3: 371-92.
Krook, Mona Lena, and Diana Z. O'Brien. 2010. "All the President's Men? Numbers and Portfolio Allocations of Female Cabinet Ministers." Paper presented at the Midwest Political Science Association National Conference, Chicago, IL, 22-25 April.
Law, Ian. 2002. *Race in the News*. New York: Palgrave.
Lawless, Jennifer. 2005. "Women, War, and Winning Elections: Gender Stereotyping in the Post-September 11th Era." *Political Research Quarterly* 57, 3: 479-90.
Lawless, Jennifer L., and Richard Logan Fox. 2005. *It Takes a Candidate: Why Women Don't Run for Office*. New York: Cambridge University Press.
–. 2010. *It Still Takes a Candidate: Why Women Don't Run for Office*. New York: Cambridge University Press.
Lawrence, Regina G., and Melody Rose. 2009. *Hillary Clinton's Race for the White House: Gender Politics and the Media on the Campaign Trail*. Boulder, CO: Lynne Rienner.
Lawson, Erica. 2002. "Images in Black: Black Women, Media and the Mythology of an Orderly Society. In *Back to the Drawing Board: African-Canadian Feminisms*, ed. Njoki Nathani Wane, Katerina Deliovsky, and Erica Lawson, 199-223. Toronto: Sumach.
Leeper, Mark Stephen. 1991. "The Impact of Prejudice on Female Candidates: An Experimental Look at Voter Inference." *American Politics Quarterly* 19, 2: 248-61.
Lemish, D., and C.E. Tidhar. 1999. "Still Marginal: Women in Israel's 1996 Television Election Campaign." *Sex Roles* 41, 5/6: 389-412.
Lenart, S. 1997. "Naming Names in a Midwestern Town: The Salience of Democratic Presidential Hopefuls in Early 1992." *Political Behavior* 19, 4: 365-82.
Liebler, Carol M., and Susan J. Smith. 1997. "Tracking Gender Differences: A Comparative Analysis of Network Correspondents and their Sources." *Journal of Broadcasting and Electronic Media* 41, 1: 58-68.

Lippmann, Walter. 1922. *Public Opinion*. New York: Harcourt Brace.
Lombard, Matthew, Jennifer Snyder-Duch, and Cheryl Campanella Bracken. 2002. "Content Analysis in Mass Communication: Assessment and Reporting of Intercoder Reliability." *Human Communication Research* 28, 4: 587-604.
Lundell, Åsa Kroon and Mats Ekström. 2008. "The Complex Visual Gendering of Political Women in the Press." *Journalism Studies* 9, 6: 891-910.
Mandel, Ruth. 1981. *In the Running: The New Woman Candidate*. New York: Ticknor and Fields.
Manheim, Jarol B. 1986. "A Model of Agenda Dynamics." In *Communication Yearbook 10*, ed. M.L. McLaughlin, 499-516. Newbury Park, CA: Sage.
Matland, Richard E. 1994. "Putting Scandinavian Equality to the Test: An Experimental Evaluation of Gender Stereotyping of Political Candidates in a Sample of Norwegian Voters." *British Journal of Political Science* 24, 2: 273-92.
Matland, Richard and David King. 2002. "Women as Candidates in Congressional Elections." In *Women Transforming Congress*, ed. Cindy Simon Rosenthal, 119-45. Norman: University of Oklahoma Press.
Matland, Richard, and K. Montgomery. 2003. "Recruiting Women to National Legislatures: A General Framework with Applications to Post-Communist Democracies." In *Women's Access to Political Power in Post-Communist Europe*, ed. R. Matland and K. Montgomery, 19-43. Oxford: Oxford University Press.
McCombs, M.E., and D.L. Shaw. 1972. "The Agenda-Setting Function of Mass Media." *Public Opinion Quarterly* 36: 176-87.
McDermott, Monika L. 1997. "Voting Cues in Low-Information Elections: Candidate Gender as a Social Information Variable in Contemporary United States Elections." *American Journal of Political Science* 41, 1: 270-83.
—. 1998. "Race and Gender Cues in Low-Information Elections." *Political Research Quarterly* 51, 4: 895-918.
McKee, John P., and Alex C. Sheriffs. 1957. "The Differential Evaluation of Males and Females." *Journal of Personality* 25: 356-71.
McKenzie, Judith. 2000. "Political Biography and Autobiography and the Study of Women in Politics in Canada: The Case of Political Ambition." *Journal of Legislative Studies* 6, 4: 91-114.
McLaughlin, Audrey. 1992. *A Woman's Place: My Life and Politics*. Toronto: Macfarlane Walter and Ross.
Mendelsohn, Matthew. 1996. "Television News Frames in the 1993 Canadian Election." In *Seeing Ourselves: Media Power and Policy in Canada*, 2nd ed., ed. H. Holmes and D. Taras, 8-22. Toronto: Harcourt Brace.
Mendelson, Andrew. 2003. "The Impact of Role-Congruency and Photo Presence on the Processing of News Stories about Hillary Clinton." *Atlantic Journal of Communication* 11, 2: 135-48.
Mills, Kay. 1997. "What Difference Do Women Journalists Make?" In *Women, Media, and Politics*, ed. P. Norris, 41-55. New York: Oxford University Press.
Mondak, Jeffrey J. 1995. "Competence, Integrity, and the Electoral Success of Congressional Incumbents." *Journal of Politics* 57, 4: 1043-69.
Monière, Denis, and Julie Fortier. 2000. *Radioscopie de l'information télévisée au Canada*. Montreal: Les Presses de l'Université de Montréal.

Moon, Jeremy, and Imogen Fountain. 1997. "Keeping the Gates? Women and Ministers in Australia, 1970-1996." *Australian Journal of Political Science* 32, 3: 455-66.
Mueller, Carol M. 1986. "Nurturance and Mastery: Competing Qualifications for Women's Access to High Public Office?" In *Women and Politics: Activism, Attitudes, and Office-holding*, ed. Gwen Moore and Glenna D. Spitze, 211-32. Greenwich, CT: JAI Press.
Mueller, Melinda A. 2008. "Gender Differences in the 2006 House Elections: The Effect of Gender on Campaign Messages about the Iraq War." *Thomas Jefferson Law Review* 31, 1: 53-88.
Muir, Kathie. 2005. "Political Cares: Gendered Reporting of Work and Family Issues in Relation to Australian Politicians." *Australian Feminist Studies* 20, 46: 77-90.
Mullen, B., and L. Hu. 1989. "Perceptions of Ingroup and Outgroup Variability: A Meta-Analytic Integration." *Basic and Applied Social Psychology* 10, 3: 233-52.
Mutz, Diana. 1997. "Mechanisms of Momentum: Does Thinking Make It So?" *Journal of Politics* 59, 1: 104-25.
Mutz, Diana C., and Byron Reeves. 2005. "The New Videomalaise: Effects of Televised Incivility on Political Trust." *American Political Science Review* 99, 1: 1-16.
Nadeau, Richard, and André Blais. 1990. "Do Canadians Distinguish between Parties? Perceptions of Party Competence." *Canadian Journal of Political Science* 23, 2: 317-33.
National Film Board of Canada. 1991. *Sisters in the Struggle*. Montreal: National Film Board of Canada.
Newman, Brian. 2002. "Bill Clinton's Approval Ratings: The More Things Change, The More They Stay the Same." *Political Research Quarterly* 55, 4: 781-804.
Niven, David and Jeremy Zilber. 2001a. "Do Women and Men in Congress Cultivate Different Images? Evidence from Congressional Websites." *Political Communication* 18, 4: 395-405.
–. 2001b. "How Does She Have Time for Kids and Congress? Views on Gender and Media Coverage from House Offices." *Women and Politics* 23, 1/2: 147-65.
Noddings, Nel. 1984. *Caring: A Feminine Approach to Ethics and Moral Education*. Berkeley: University of California Press.
Norris, Pippa. 1988. "The Gender Gap: A Cross-National Trend?" In *The Politics of the Gender Gap*, ed. C.M. Mueller, 217-34. Newbury Park, CA: Sage.
–. 1997. "Women Leaders Worldwide: A Splash of Color in the Photo Op." In *Women, Media, and Politics*, ed. P. Norris, 149-65. New York: Oxford University Press.
Okimoto, Tyler G., and Victoria L. Brescoll. 2010. "The Price of Power: Power Seeking and Backlash against Female Politicians." *Personality and Social Psychology Bulletin* 36, 7: 923-36.
O'Neill, Brenda. 2002. "Sugar and Spice? Political Culture and the Political Behaviour of Canadian Women." In *Citizen Politics: Research and Theory in Canadian Political Behaviour*, ed. J. Everitt and B. O'Neill, 40-55. Don Mills, ON: Oxford University Press.

Ornstein, Michael. 2010. "Racialization and Gender of Lawyers in Ontario." Report for the Law Society of Upper Canada.

Paolino, Phillip. 1995. "Group-Salient Issues and Group Representation: Support for Women Candidates in the 1992 Senate Elections." *American Journal of Political Science* 39, 2: 294-313.

Petrocik, John R. 1996. "Issue Ownership in Presidential Elections, with a 1980 Case Study." *American Journal of Political Science* 40, 3: 825-50.

Petrocik, John R., William L. Benoit, and Glenn J. Hansen. 2003. "Issue Ownership and Presidential Campaigning, 1952-2000." *Political Science Quarterly* 118, 4: 599-626.

Phelan, Julie E., and Laurie A. Rudman. 2010. "Prejudice toward Female Leaders: Backlash Effects and Women's Impression Management Dilemma." *Social and Personality Psychology Compass* 4, 10: 807-20.

Poggione, Sarah. 2004. "Exploring Gender Differences in State Legislators' Policy Preferences." *Political Research Quarterly* 57, 2: 305-14.

Popkin, Samuel L. 1991. *The Reasoning Voter: Communication and Persuasion in Presidential Campaigns*. Chicago: University of Chicago Press.

Powers, T.A., and D.C. Zuroff. 1988. "Interpersonal Consequences of Overt Self-Criticism: A Comparison with Neutral and Self-enhancing Presentations of Self." *Journal of Personality and Social Psychology* 54, 6: 1054-62.

Prentice, Deborah A., and Erica Carranza. 2002. "What Women and Men Should Be, Shouldn't Be, Are Allowed to Be, and Don't Have to Be: The Contents of Prescriptive Gender Stereotypes." *Psychology of Women Quarterly* 26, 4: 269-81.

Rahn, Wendy M. 1993. "The Role of Partisan Stereotypes in Information Processing about Political Candidates." *American Journal of Political Science* 37, 2: 472-96.

Rakow, Lana F., and Kimberlie Kranich. 1991. "Women as Sign in Television News." *Journal of Communication* 41, 1: 8-23.

Reese, Stephen D., and Jane Ballinger. 2001. "The Roots of a Sociology of News: Remembering Mr. Gates and Social Control in the Newsroom." *Journalism and Mass Communication Quarterly* 78, 4: 641-58.

Reynolds, Andrew. 1999. "Women in the Legislatures and Executives of the World: Knocking at the Highest Glass Ceiling." *World Politics* 51, 4: 547–72.

Robertson, T., A. Conley, K. Scymcznska, and A. Thompson. 2002. "Gender and the Media: An Investigation of Gender, Media and Politics in the 2000 Election." *New Jersey Journal of Communication* 10, 1: 104-17.

Robinson, Gertrude. 1978. "Women, Media Access and Social Control." In *Women and the News*, ed. L.K. Epstein, 87-108. New York: Hastings House.

–. 2005. *Gender, Journalism, and Equity: Canadian, US, and European Perspectives*. Cesskill, NJ: Hampton Press.

Robinson, Gertrude, and Armande Saint-Jean (with Christine Rioux). 1991. "Women Politicians and Their Media Coverage: A Generational Analysis." In *Women in Canadian Politics: Toward Equity in Representation*, ed. K. Megyery, 127-69. Ottawa and Toronto: Royal Commission on Electoral Reform and Party Financing and Dundurn Press.

Robinson, Gertrude, and Armande Saint-Jean. 1995. "The Portrayal of Women Politicians in the Media." In *Gender and Politics in Contemporary Canada*, ed. F.-P. Gingras, 176-90. Toronto: Oxford University Press.

–. 1996. "From Flora to Kim: Thirty Years of Representation of Canadian Women Politicians." In *Seeing Ourselves: Media Power and Policy in Canada*, 2nd ed., ed. H. Holmes and D. Taras, 23-56. Toronto: Harcourt Brace.

Robinson, Michael J., and Margaret A. Shehan. 1983. *Over the Wire and on TV*. New York: Russell Sage Foundation.

Rodgers, Shelly, and Esther Thorson. 2003. "A Socialization Perspective on Male and Female Reporting." *Journal of Communication* 53, 4: 658-75.

Rosenthal, Robert, Judith A. Hall, M. Robin DiMatteo, Peter L. Rogers, and Dane Archer. 1979. *Sensitivity to Nonverbal Communication: The PONS Test*. Baltimore: Johns Hopkins University Press.

Rosenwasser, Shirley, and Norma Dean. 1989. "Gender Role and Political Office: Effects of Perceived Masculinity/Femininity of Candidate and Political Office." *Psychology of Women Quarterly* 13, 1: 77-85.

Rosenwasser, Shirley and Jana Seale. 1988. "Attitudes Toward a Hypothetical Male or Female Presidential Candidate – A Research Note." *Political Psychology* 9, 4: 591-98.

Ross, Karen. 2002. *Women, Politics, Media: Uneasy Relations in Comparative Perspective*. Cresskill, NJ: Hampton Press.

Ross, Karen, and Annabelle Sreberny. 2000. "Women in the House: Media Representations of British Politicians." In *Gender, Politics and Communication*, ed. A. Sreberny and L. van Zoonen, 79-100. Cresskill, NJ: Hampton Press.

Rossiter, Clinton. 1960. *The American Presidency*, 2nd ed. New York: Harcourt, Brace and World.

Rossmann, Liliana Castañeda. 2010. "Tears, Unity, Moose Burgers, and Fashion: A Tale of Two Candidates." *American Behavioral Scientist* 54, 3: 239-64.

Rubin, Irene S., and Herbert J. Rubin. 2004. *Qualitative Interviewing: The Art of Hearing Data*, 2nd ed. Thousand Oaks, CA: Sage.

Rudman, Laurie A. 1998. "Self-Promotion as a Risk Factor for Women: The Costs and Benefits of Counterstereotypical Impression Management." *Journal of Personality and Social Psychology* 74, 3: 629-45.

Rudman, Laurie A., and Kimberly Fairchild. 2004. "Reactions to Counterstereotypic Behavior: The Role of Backlash in Cultural Stereotype Maintenance." *Journal of Personality and Social Psychology* 87, 2: 157-76.

Rudman, Laurie A., and Peter Glick. 1999. "Feminized Management and Backlash toward Agentic Women: The Hidden Cost to Women of a Kinder, Gentler Image of Middle Managers." *Journal of Personality and Social Psychology* 77, 5: 1004-10.

–. 2001. "Prescriptive Gender Stereotypes and Backlash toward Agentic Women." *Journal of Social Issues* 57, 4: 745-62.

Rudman, Laurie A., and Stephanie Goodwin. 2004. "Gender Differences in Automatic In-Group Bias: Why Do Women Like Women More than Men Like Men?" *Journal of Personality and Social Psychology* 87, 4: 494-509.

Rudman, Laurie A., and J.E. Phelan. 2008. "Backlash Effects for Disconfirming Gender Stereotypes in Organizations." In *Research in Organizational Behavior*, ed., A.P. Brief and B.M. Staw, 61-79. New York: Elsevier.
Safire, W. 2005. "The Way We Live Now: On Language." *New York Times*. 12 February.
Sampert, Shannon, and Linda Trimble. 2003. "'Wham, Bam, No Thank You Ma'am': Gender and the Game Frame in National Newspaper Coverage of Election 2000." In *Women and Electoral Politics in Canada*, ed. M. Tremblay and L. Trimble, 211-27. Don Mills, ON: Oxford University Press.
Sanbonmatsu, Kira. 2002. "Gender Stereotypes and Vote Choice." *American Journal of Political Science* 46, 1: 20-34.
–. 2004. "Political Knowledge and Gender Stereotypes." *American Politics Research* 31, 6: 575-94.
Sanbonmatsu, Kira, and Kathleen Dolan. 2009. "Do Gender Stereotypes Transcend Party?" *Political Research Quarterly* 62, 3: 485-94.
Sapiro, Virginia. 1982. "If US Senator Baker Were a Woman: An Experimental Study of Candidate Image." *Political Psychology* 3, 1/2: 61-83.
–. 1983. *The Political Integration of Women: Roles, Socialization, and Politics*. Urbana: University of Illinois Press.
Sapiro, Virginia, and Pamela Johnston Conover. 1993. "Gender, Feminist Consciousness, and War." *American Journal of Political Science* 37, 4: 1079-99.
Sapiro, Virginia, Katherine Cramer Walsh, Patricia Strach, and Valerie Hennings. 2011. "Gender, Context, and Television Advertising: A Comprehensive Analysis of 2000 and 2002 House Races." *Political Research Quarterly* 64, 1: 107-19.
Saunders, Eileen. 1991. "Mass Media and the Reproduction of Marginalization." In *Reporting the Campaign: Electoral Coverage in Canada*, ed. Frederick J. Fletcher, 273-321. Volume 22 of the Research Studies for the Royal Commission on Electoral Reform and Party Financing. Toronto: Dundurn Press.
Scarrow, Howard, A. 1965. "Distinguishing between Political Parties – The Case of Canada." *Midwest Journal of Political Science* 9, 1: 61-76.
Schaffner, Brian F. 2005. "Priming Gender: Campaigning on Women's Issues in U.S. Senate Elections." *American Journal of Political Science* 49, 4: 803-17.
Schokkenbroek, C. 1999. "News Stories – Structure, Time and Evaluation." *Time and Society* 8, 1: 59-98.
Schudson, Michael. 1989. "The Sociology of News Production." *Media, Culture and Society* 11, 3: 263-82.
Schultz, Brad. 2005. *Broadcast News Producing*. Thousand Oaks, CA: Sage.
Schultz, Cindy, and S. Mark Pancer. 1997. "Character Attacks and Their Effects on Perceptions of Male and Female Political Candidates." *Political Psychology* 18, 1: 93-102.
Schwindt-Bayer, Leslie A. 2006. "Still Supermadres? Gender and the Policy Priorities of Latin American Legislators." *American Journal of Political Science* 50, 3: 570-85.
Serini, Shirley A., Angela A. Powers, and Susan Johnson. 1998. "Of Horse Race and Policy Issues: A Study of Gender in Coverage of a Gubernatorial Election by Two Major Metropolitan Newspapers." *Journalism and Mass Communication Quarterly* 75, 1: 194-204.

Shames, Shauna. 2003. "The 'Un-Candidates': Gender and Outsider Signals in Women's Political Advertisements." *Women and Politics* 25, 1/2: 115-47.

Shanks, J. Merrill, and Warren E. Miller. 1991. "Policy Direction and Performance Evaluation: Complementary Explanations of the Reagan Elections." *British Journal of Political Science* 20, 2: 143-235.

Shapiro, Robert, and Harpreet Mahajan. 1986. "Gender Differences in Policy Preferences: A Summary of Trends from the 1960s to the 1980s." *Public Opinion Quarterly* 50: 42-61.

Sharpe, Sydney. 1994. *The Gilded Ghetto: Women and Political Power in Canada*. Toronto: HarperCollins.

Shen, Fei. 2008. "Staying Alive: The Impact of Media Momentum on Candidacy Attrition in the 1980-2004 Primaries." *Harvard International Journal of Press/Politics* 13, 4: 429-50.

Sigelman, Lee, and Emmett H. Buell Jr. 2003. "You Take the High Road and I'll Take the Low Road? The Interplay of Attack Strategies and Tactics in Presidential Campaigns." *Journal of Politics* 65, 2: 518-31.

Simeon, Richard, and David Elkins. 1974. "Regional Political Cultures in Canada." *Canadian Journal of Political Science* 7, 3: 397-437.

Smith, Kevin B. 1997. "When All's Fair: Signs of Parity in Media Coverage of Female Candidates." *Political Communication* 14, 1: 71-82.

Smith, K.C., S.E. Ulch, J.E. Cameron, J.A. Cumberland, M.A. Musgrave, and N. Tremblay. 1989. "Gender-Related Effects in the Perception of Anger Expression." *Sex Roles* 20, 9/10: 487-99.

Soroka, Stuart, and Blake Andrew. 2009. "Media Coverage of Canadian Elections: Horserace Coverage and Negativity in Election Campaigns." In *Mediating Canadian Politics*, ed. Shannon Sampert and Linda Trimble, 213-28. Toronto ON: Pearson.

Sreberny-Mohammadi, Annabelle, and Karen Ross. 1996. "Women MPs and the Media: Representing the Body Politic." *Parliamentary Affairs* 49: 103-15.

Stalsburg, Brittany L. 2010. "Voting For Mom: The Political Consequences of Being a Parent for Male and Female Candidates." *Politics and Gender* 6, 3: 373-404.

Stephens, Mitchell. 1996. "On Shrinking Soundbites." *Columbia Journalism Review*. 35, 3: 22.

Studlar, Donley T., and Gary F. Moncrief. 1999. "Women's Work? The Distribution and Prestige of Portfolios in the Canadian Provinces." *Governance: An International Journal of Policy and Administration* 12, 4: 379-95.

Terkildsen, Nayda and David F. Damore. 1999. "The Dynamics of Racialized Media Coverage in Congressional Elections." *Journal of Politics* 61, 3: 680-99.

Thomas, Gwynn, and Melinda Adams. 2010. "Breaking the Final Glass Ceiling: The Influence of Gender in the Elections of Ellen Johnson-Sirleaf and Michelle Bachelet." *Journal of Women, Politics and Policy* 31, 2: 105-31.

Thomas, Sue. 1991. "The Impact of Women on State Legislative Policies." *The Journal of Politics* 53, 4: 958-76.

–. 1994. *How Women Legislate*. Oxford: Oxford University Press.

Thomas, Sue, and Susan Welch. 1991. "The Impact of Gender on Activities and Priorities of State Legislators." *Western Political Quarterly* 44, 2: 445-56.
Tolleson-Rinehart, Sue. 1992. *Gender Consciousness and Politics*. New York: Routledge.
Tolley, Erin. 2012. "Black and White or Shades of Grey? Racial Mediation in Canadian Politics." Paper presented at the Annual Meeting of the Canadian Political Science Association. Edmonton, Alberta, 13 June.
Tomz, Michael, Jason Wittenberg, and Gary King. 2003. CLARIFY: Software for Interpreting and Presenting Statistical Results, version 2.1. Stanford University, University of Wisconsin, and Harvard University. http://gking.harvard.edu/.
Tremblay, Manon, et Nathalie Bélanger. 1997. "Femmes chefs de partis politiques et caricatures éditorials: l'élection fédérale canadienne de 1993." *Recherches féministes* 10, 1: 35-75.
Trimble, Linda. 2005. "Who Framed Belinda Stronach? National Newspaper Coverage of the Conservative Party of Canada's 2004 Leadership Race." Paper presented at the annual meeting of the *Canadian Political Science Association*. London, ON, 4 June.
–. 2007. "Gender, Political Leadership and Media Visibility: Globe and Mail Coverage of Conservative Party of Canada Leadership Contests." *Canadian Journal of Political Science* 40, 4: 969-93.
Trimble, Linda, and Jane Arscott. 2003. *Still Counting: Women in Politics across Canada*. Peterborough, ON: Broadview.
Trimble, Linda, and Joanna Everitt. 2010. "Belinda Stronach and the Gender Politics of Celebrity." In *Mediating Canadian Politics*, ed. S. Sampert and L. Trimble, 50-74. Toronto: Pearson.
Trimble, Linda, and Shannon Sampert. 2004. "Who's in the Game? The Framing of the Canadian Election 2000 by the *Globe and Mail* and the *National Post*." *Canadian Journal of Political Science* 37, 1: 51-72.
Trimble, Linda and Natasja Treiberg. 2010. "'Either Way, There's Going to Be a Man in Charge': Media Representations of New Zealand Prime Minister Helen Clark." In *Cracking the Highest Glass Ceiling: A Global Comparison of Women's Campaigns for Executive Office*, ed. Rainbow Murray, 116-36. Santa Barbara: Praeger.
Trimble, Linda, Natasja Treiberg, and Sue Girard. 2010. "'Kim-Speak': l'effet du genre dans la médiatisation de Kim Campbell durant la campagne pour l'élection nationale canadienne de 1993." ("'Kim-Speak': Gendered Mediation of Kim Campbell during the 1993 Canadian National Election"). *Recherches féministes* 23, 1: 29-52.
Tuchman, Gaye. 1978. *Making News: A Study in the Construction of Reality*. New York: Free Press.
Tversky A., and D. Kahneman. 1974. "Judgment under Uncertainty: Heuristics and Biases." *Science* 185: 1124-31.
van Zoonen, Liesbet. 1994. *Feminist Media Studies*. London and Thousand Oaks, CA: Sage.

–. 1998. "'Finally I Have My Mother Back': Politicians and Their Families in Popular Culture." *Harvard International Journal of Press/Politics* 3, 1: 48-64.
–. 2000a. "Broken Hearts, Broken Dreams? Politicians and Their Families in Popular Culture." In *Gender, Politics and Communication*, ed. A. Sreberny and L. van Zoonen, 101-20. Cresskill, NJ: Hampton Press.
–. 2000b. "The Personalization of Politics: Opportunities for Women." *International Journal for Politics and Psychology* 9, 3/4: 19-35.
–. 2005. *Entertaining the Citizen: When Politics and Popular Culture Converge.* Oxford: Rowman and Littlefield.
–. 2006. "The Personal, the Political and the Popular: A Woman's Guide to Celebrity Politics." *European Journal of Cultural Studies* 9, 3: 287-301.
Warren, Carol A.B. 2001. "Qualitative Interviewing." In *Handbook of Interview Research: Content and Method*, ed. Jaber F. Gubrium, and James A. Holstein, 83-102. Thousand Oaks, CA: Sage.
Wattenberg, Martin P. 1995. *The Rise of Candidate-Centered Politics.* Cambridge, MA: Harvard University Press.
Weaver, David, and G. Cleveland Wilhoit. 1996. *The American Journalist in the 1990s: U.S. News People at the End of an Era.* Mahwah, NJ: Erlbaum.
Weikart, Lynne, Greg Chen, Daniel W. Williams, and Haris Hromic. 2006. "The Democratic Sex: Gender Differences and the Exercise of Power." *Journal of Women, Politics and Policy* 28, 1: 119-40.
White, Theodore Harold. 1973. *The Making of the President, 1972.* New York: Atheneum.
Wilcox, Clyde, Lara Hewitt, and Dee Allsop. 1996. "The Gender Gap in Attitudes toward the Gulf War: A Cross National Perspective." *Journal of Peace Research* 33, 1: 67-82.
Wiley, M.G, and A. Eskilson. 1985. "Speech Style, Gender Stereotypes, and Corporate Success: What If Women Talk More Like Men?" *Sex Roles* 12, 9/10: 993-1007.
Wolf, Naomi. 1997. *The Beauty Myth.* Toronto: Vintage.
Wood, Elizabeth A. 2011. "Performing Memory: Vladimir Putin and the Celebration of World War II in Russia." *The Soviet and Post-Soviet Review* 38, 2: 172-200.
Yoder, J.D. 1991. "Rethinking Tokenism: Looking Beyond Numbers." *Gender and Society* 5, 2: 178-92.
Young, Lisa. 2002. "Representation of Women in the New Canadian Party System." In *Political Parties, Representation, and Electoral Democracy in Canada*, ed. William Cross, 181-200. Don Mills, ON: Oxford University Press.
–. 2005. "Campaign Finance and Women's Representation in Canada and the United States. In *The Delicate Balance between Political Equity and Freedom of Expression: Political Party and Campaign Financing in Canada and the United States*, ed. Steven Griner and Daniel Zovatto, 47-59. Stockholm: International IDEA.
Young, Lisa, and William Cross. 2003. "Women's Involvement in Canadian Political Parties." In *Women and Electoral Politics in Canada*, ed. M. Tremblay and L. Trimble, 91-108. Don Mills, ON: Oxford University Press.

Zaller, John. 1996. "The Myth of Massive Media Impact Revived: New Support for a Discredited Idea." In *Political Persuasion and Attitude Change*, ed. D.C. Mutz, P.M. Sniderman, and R.A. Brody, 17-78. Ann Arbor: University of Michigan Press.
–. 1998. "Monica Lewinsky's Contribution to Political Science." *PS: Political Science and Politics* 31, 2: 182-89.
Zilber, Jeremy, and David Niven. 2000a. "Congress and the News Media: Stereotypes in the News Media Coverage of African-Americans in Congress." *Harvard International Journal of Press/Politics* 5, 1: 32-49.
–. 2000b. *Racialized Coverage of Congress: The News in Black and White*. Westport: Praeger.

Index

Ablonczy, Diane, 96-97, 128
agenda-setting by news media, 10, 25
Ahluwalia, Raj, 87
Ambrose, Rona: association with soft issues in 2006 campaign, 133; cabinet appointment in 2006, 128; coverage of education and experience in 2005-06 campaign, 96-97; "horserace" coverage in 2005-06 campaign, 99; media coverage of personal life in 2005-06 campaign, 92-93, 170; mentions of childlessness, 93, 170
Ashton, Niki, 98
attack-style politics and media coverage: aggression closely associated with politics, 143, 146, 159; analysis data, methods, and limitations, 148-51, 157-58; attack-style press releases in 2000 campaign, 133-35; "backlash effect" on women leaders, 20-21, 29, 43, 69, 142-45, 159-60, 163, 188; body language studied, 69, 150, 203-4n8; oncounter-stereotypical female behaviour, 143; coverage of party leaders in 2000 campaign, 69-71, 72-74, 133-35, 139-40, 159-60, 188; effect on leaders in 2000 campaign, 151-55, 156t, 159-60; electoral advantage of, 140; exaggeration of female aggressivity (gendered mediation), 71-76, 105, 129, 133-34, 139-40, 142, 159-60, 188; gender, and voter response to attack-style behaviour, 147-48, 155; indicators (verbal attack, aggressive body language), 69, 205n8; level of tolerance for aggression, 153, 155; political climate and reaction to female aggression, 159; political party (right- or left-wing) and evaluation of aggressive behaviour, 157-58; successful aggressive women in politics, 158-59, 189; verbal attacks, definition, 149-50; "viability boost" for women leaders/politicians, 145-47, 155; women's self-presentation to media (to avoid iron-maiden frame), 72

Index

Bachelet, Michelle, 125
Bains, Navdeep Singh, 95
Bashevkin, Sylvia B., 1, 23, 114, 131
The Beauty Myth (Wolf), 60
Bennett, Carolyn, 46, 94, 97
Bennett, W. Lance, 39
Benson, R., 6
Bhutto, Benazir, 158
Biden, Joe, 28
Black, Jerome, 72
Blais, André, 83, 84
Bloc Québécois and 2000 election campaign: attack-style press releases, 134t; challengers and incumbents, by gender, 132t, 133t; distribution of news stories, 34-35; length of news stories, by political party, 35-36; overview of campaign, 31-34, 83, 84; percentage of female candidates and MPs, by year (2004-08), 127f; seats in House of Commons (pre- and post-election), 31, 32t, 34; "soft" vs. "hard" issues, 83, 131t. *See also* broadcast news coverage of 2000 federal election campaign; Duceppe, Gilles
Blumler, Jay G., 9
Braaten, Bev, 78
Brescoll, Victoria L., 143
Brewer, Allison, 58
Brison, Scott, 59, 95, 203n3
British Columbia, women candidates in 2005-06 election campaign, 51
Broadbent, Ed: media coverage according to party connections, 174; personal interview with author, 17; preference for print media, 166; on Question Period in House of Commons, 176, 177
broadcast news coverage of 2000 federal election campaign: coverage of issues in stories about party leaders, 83-84, 101; data from CES, 15, 29, 199-200; distribution of coverage, by political party, 34-35; evidence for media interpretation, 87-89, 105, 205n22; features of 2000 campaign (parties, leaders, platforms), 31-34; focus of news stories about party leaders, 80-81; leader-focused news coverage, 30-31, 34-36; length of news stories, by political party, 35-36; nature of lead-ins in stories about party leaders, 86-87; polling data pre-election, 33-34; prominence of stories (placement and headline), 36-38; salience cues to voters, 10, 25; seats in House of Commons (pre- and post-election), 31, 32t, 34, 38; "soft" vs. "hard" issue coverage, 83-84, 101, 104, 130-31; "spin" and framing in news stories' wrap-up, 39; viability coverage (polls, debates, strategy, electoral battles), female vs. male party leaders, 79-80, 81-82. *See also* CBC coverage of 2000 federal election campaign
Brooks, Deborah Jordan, 144, 147
Brown, Rosemary, 173
Bush, George W., 140

Calgary Herald, 50-51, 115t
Camp, Michael, 95
Campbell, Kim: attack-style behaviour exaggerated in 2000 debates, 134; comments taken out of context by media, 165-68; descriptive vs. interpretative coverage in 1993 campaign, 85-86; gendered behaviour on her part, 20, 108; gendered double standard regarding private life, 29, 172; leader of PC Party in 1993 federal election, 2; on masculine nature of journalism, 182; media assumptions about female politicians, 175-76; media attention to appearance and personal life, 66, 166-67, 170; media coverage of ad mocking Chrétien in 1993 election campaign, 52; media

visibility vs. that of male contenders for party leader, 28; personal interview with author, 17, 165; preferences for certain media formats, 165-68; "psychological price" of appearing neutered or masculine, 183; *Time and Chance* (autobiography), 165-66; tough or aggressive stances viewed unfavourably, 29, 178-79

Canadian Alliance party and 2000 election campaign: attack-style press releases, 134-35; distribution of news stories, 34, 35f; Grand-Mère affair, 88-89; length of news stories, by political party, 35-36; overview of 2000 federal campaign, 31-34, 83, 84, 148; recruitment of women candidates, 3; seats in House of Commons (pre- and post-election), 31, 32t, 34; "soft" vs. "hard" issues, 83-84, 130, 131t. *See also* broadcast news coverage of 2000 federal election campaign; Day, Stockwell

Canadian Association of Broadcasters, 190

Canadian Broadcast Standards Council, 190

Canadian Broadcasting Corporation. *See* CBC coverage of 2000 federal election campaign

Canadian Election Study 2000 (CES), 15, 29, 199-200. *See also* broadcast news coverage of 2000 federal election campaign

Carlin, Diana B., 57

Carranza, Erica, 143

CBC coverage of 2000 federal election campaign: attack-style behaviour of party leaders, 69-71, 70f, 72-74; clips and sound bites of leaders with family members, 66-68; clips (video footage), by party leader, on *The National*, 40-42; coverage of Clark's viability, 82-83; coverage of party-switching by male MPs, 59; descriptive lead-ins for news stories on *The National*, 87-89; evidence for media interpretation in news stories, 87-89, 105, 205n22; exaggeration of female aggressivity, 71, 74-76, 159-60; *Fundamental Day* (on Day's religious beliefs), 181, 210n24; guidelines for sex-role portrayal, 30; lead-ins for news stories on *The National*, 38-39; mentions of female vs. male leaders' background and experience, 77-78; negative coverage of McDonough's viability on *The National*, 81-83; sound bites, by party leader, on *The National*, 39-41, 85; sound bites, by sex, on CBC news, 42-43, 85; sound bites, ratio to clips, by party leader, on *The National*, 41-42; symbols of power in sound bites and clips of party leaders, 76-77, 105; wrap-up for news stories on *The National*, 39

Chow, Olivia, 46, 90, 170

Chrétien, Jean, and 1993 election campaign: descriptive vs. interpretative coverage, 85-86; media coverage of ad mocking his facial expression, 52

Chrétien, Jean, and 2000 election campaign: attack-style behaviour, media stories, 69-70, 72-74; attack-style politics, effect on voters, 151-55, 156t, 188; attack-style press releases, 134-35; campaign gaffes, media reporting of, 165, 168; clips and sound bites with family, 66-67; coverage of issues (soft, hard) in media, 83-84; distribution of news stories, 34, 35f; evidence for media interpretation in news stories, 88; experience leading up to campaign, 31-34; family members visible in campaigns, 171; focus of news stories, 81t; length of news stories, by political party, 35-36; media coverage of appearance, 60; mention of political experience in media, 77; nature of lead-ins in news stories, 86-87; prominence of stories (placement and headline), 36-38; sound bites, ratio to clips, by party leader, on CBC's *The National*, 41-42; sound bites on CBC's *The National*, 40-41; symbols of power in sound bites and clips, 76-77; viability coverage, 79-80. *See also* Liberal Party of Canada

Clark, Catherine, 62, 171

Clark, Christy, 2

Clark, Helen, 66, 68-69

Clark, Joe, and 2000 federal election campaign: attack-style behaviour and media stories, 69-70, 72-74; attack-style politics, effect on voters, 151-55, 156t; clips and sound bites with family, 66-67; coverage compared with that of McDonough, 37-38; coverage of issues (soft, hard) in media, 83-84; daughter campaigning with him, 62, 171; evidence for media interpretation in news stories, 87-88; focus of news stories about him, 80-81; nature of lead-ins in news stories, 86-87, 205n20; news stories' distribution in, 34-35; news stories' length, by political party, 35-36; party leader, 31-34; prominence of stories (placement and headline), 36-38; sound bites, ratio to clips, by party leader, on CBC's *The National*, 41-42; sound bites on CBC's *The National* in 2000 federal election, 40-41; symbols of power in sound bites and clips, 76-77; viability coverage, 79-80, 82-83. *See also* Progressive Conservative (PC) Party

Clinton, Bill, 62

Clinton, Hillary: benefits of using stereotypical traits, 21; emphasis on candidature, not gender, 135; media focus on appearance and personal life, 59; portrayal as "iron maiden," 64, 189; public approval of "soft" feminine attribute (crying), 110; reticence about opening up private life to media, 170

clips (video) in 2000 election campaign: of leaders with family members, 66-68; by party leader, on *The National*, 40-42; ratio to sound bites, by party leader, on *The National*, 41-42; symbols of power in clips of party leaders, 76-77

Conservative Party of Canada (CPC): challengers and incumbents, by gender, in 2006 campaign, 131-33; overview of 2005-06 federal election, 44-45; percentage of female candidates and MPs, by year (2004-08), 127-28. *See also* Harper, Stephen

Copps, Sheila: assertiveness portrayed negatively in media, 64, 129; comfort level with adversarial Question Period, 177; member of the Rat Pack, 177, 210n21; speculation re. sexual orientation, 171

Craft, Stephanie, 118

culture. *See* gendered culture

Davies, Libby, 46, 51

Day, Stockwell, and 2000 election campaign: attack-style behaviour, media stories, 69-70, 72-74; attack-style politics, effect on voters, 151-55, 156t; clips and sound bites with family, 66-67; coverage of issues (soft, hard) in media, 83-84; distribution of news stories, 34,

35f; electoral advantage gained from aggressive and masculine portrayal, 140; evidence for media interpretation in news stories, 88-89; experience leading up to campaign, 32-34; focus of news stories, 81t; on *Fundamental Day* (CBC documentary), 181, 183, 210*n*24; length of news stories, by political party, 35-36; media coverage of Question Period, 176; mention in media of background and political experience, 77; nature of lead-ins in news stories, 86-87; personal interview with author, 17; prominence of stories (placement and headline), 36-38; relationships with journalists, 180-81; Sea-Doo press conference, 140, 161-62; sound bites, ratio to clips, by party leader, on CBC's *The National*, 41-42; sound bites on CBC's *The National*, 40-41; symbols of power in sound bites and clips, 76-77; viability coverage, 79-80. *See also* Canadian Alliance party

Devitt, James, 63
Dole, Elizabeth, 59, 86
Dosanjh, Ujjal, 47
Duceppe, Gilles, and 2000 election campaign: coverage of issues (soft, hard) in media, 83-84; distribution of news stories, 34, 35f; focus of news stories, 81t; length of news stories, by political party, 35-36; prominence of stories (placement and headline), 36-38; viability coverage, 79-80. *See also* Bloc Québécois
Dunderdale, Kathy, 2

Ekström, Mats, 55
Entman, Robert M., 13
Erickson, Lynda, 72

Everitt, Joanna: on backlash effect against aggressive female politicians, 144; on limitations of celebrity politics for women, 66; on married male politicians' media coverage, 62; on media concentration of female leaders' aggressiveness in debates, 71, 120, 134-35; on use of gay stereotypes in media coverage, 95

Fairclough, Ellen, 11
federal election campaign (2000). *See* broadcast news coverage of 2000 federal election campaign
federal election campaign (2005-06). *See* print news coverage of 2005-06 federal election campaign
Festinger, Leon, 192
Finley, Diane, 128
Fountaine, Susan, 66
framing: contribution to prominence in media, 26; "iron maiden" frame for political women, 14, 56-57, 64-65, 71, 139, 186; media structuring of a news item, 10; "mother" frame for political women, 14, 61-64, 65-66, 186; "pet" frame for political women, 14, 64, 186; photos of candidates (framing mechanism), by sex, 48-49, 51; "sex object" frame for political women, 14, 56, 58-61, 65-66, 186; "spin" and framing in wrap-up to news story, 39; woman-to-woman conflict as "catfight," 178-79; of women politicians using masculine language/imagery, 13, 190-91. *See also entries beginning with* representations
Fridkin, Kim, 27
Frulla, Liza, 46, 93, 97
Fry, Hedy, 46, 51, 93, 94-95
Fundamental Day (CBC documentary), 181, 210*n*24

Index

Gamson, William, 6
Gandhi, Indira, 158
gender ideology: assessing in attack-style politics analysis, 150; voter responses to attack-style behaviour, 147-48, 155
gender schema theory: description, 6; female politicians and "schema incompatibility," 13, 29, 75, 110-11; gender stereotypes (*see under* gendered culture)
gendered coverage by media: assumptions about how female politicians get ahead, 175-76; benefits for women of feminine stereotypes, 44, 55, 69, 72, 74, 187-88; data used in analysis, 15-17; data used in analysis, issue coding, 15-17, 194-98; exaggeration of female aggressivity, 71, 74-76, 129, 133-35; female journalists' conforming to masculine norms, 116-18, 182; female journalists' remedial effects very limited, 17, 115-16, 191-92; gendered mediation approach to women candidates, 65, 71-76; guidelines on sex-role portrayal, 190; international gendered coverage, 169, 170-71; lessening with time, 161-62, 187; male model of politician viewed as the norm, 5, 55, 56, 110-11; news biases at systemic level, 118; "outgroup homogeneity bias" toward women in politics, 175; parallels with coverage of non-traditional (gay, lesbian, minority) politicians, 8, 55-56; regulation undesirable, 191; willingness of women to run and, 7, 22-23, 55, 189; women politicians as novel, alien, and different, 5, 7, 14-15, 23, 28, 54-55, 74-75, 125-26, 179-80; women politicians as outsiders, 72, 175, 179-80; women politicians covered because of their novelty, 46-47, 179-80. *See also* broadcast news coverage of 2000 federal election campaign; print news coverage of 2005-06 federal election campaign; quality of media coverage of female politicians; visibility of female politicians in news
gendered culture: aggressive stances by female politicians viewed unfavourably, 20-21, 29, 43, 129, 178-79; exaggeration of female aggressivity, 71, 74-76, 129, 133-35, 139-40, 142, 159-60, 188; frames (*see* framing); "gentlemanly" norms and attacks on female politicians, 178; male politicians viewed as the norm, 5, 55, 56, 110-11; media coverage of women politicians and, 5-6, 23, 74, 107, 109-11, 187-88; men stereotyped as competent, assertive, and independent, 74, 142-43; politics viewed as masculine domain, 111; women stereotyped as altruistic, trustworthy, and ethical, 21, 44, 55, 72; women stereotyped as warm, compassionate and cooperative, 21, 69, 74. *See also entries beginning with* representations
gendered mediation thesis: categories for analyzing gendered news coverage, 13-14; counter-stereotypical female behaviour magnified by media, 43, 65, 74-75, 111, 129, 142-43; descriptive vs. interpretive coverage of female vs. male politicians, 15, 18-19, 57, 84-89, 205n19; female politicians' behaviour evaluated more than male, 14; female politicians shown less often with symbols of power, 76-77; framework for analyzing gendered news coverage, 12-14; news media reflection of gendered

culture, 5-6, 23, 74, 107, 109-11, 187-88; premise of male-dominated media and masculine nature of news, 109; seemingly gender-neutral coverage, 5, 12-13; substance and style/format of the news, 13-14; women framed using masculine language and imagery, 13, 190-91. *See also* gendered coverage by media; news media's masculine nature
Gershon, Sarah, 173
Gidengil, Elisabeth: on backlash effect against aggressive female politicians, 144; on gender differences re. issues and priorities, 121-22; on media concentration of female leaders' aggressiveness in debates, 71, 120, 134-35
Gilligan, Carol, 122
Globe and Mail: coverage of Belinda Stronach as "sex object," 58; coverage of contenders for Conservative party leader, by sex, 28; coverage of male vs. female candidates in 2005-06 campaign, by sex, 49-51; male domination of news production, 114-15
Goodale, Ralph, 49, 102, 203*n*9
Gordon, Ann, 145
government, federal: 2000 federal election (*see* broadcast news coverage of 2000 federal election campaign); 2005-06 federal election (*see* print news coverage of 2005-06 federal election campaign); House of Commons party standings in 2000 (pre- and post-election), 31, 32t, 34, 38; percentage of women MPs in House of Commons, 1-2, 185; Question Period in House of Commons, 176-79
government, provincial: number of women premiers, 2; percentage of female MPs, 2; print coverage of provincial elections (1999, 2000), 43
Graham, Laurie, 89
Grewal, Gurmant, 90, 172, 173-74
Grewal, Nina, 90, 172
Grey, Deborah, 171
Guergis, Helena, 128
Gurevitch, Michael, 9

Halonen, Tarja, 170
Halpern, Diane F., 6
Halsema, Femke, 170
Hanson, Pauline, 59
Harper, Stephen, 44, 60, 128, 171. *See also* Conservative Party of Canada
Hayes, Danny, 158
Hitchon, Jacqueline C., 145
House of Commons: party standings in 2000 (pre- and post-election), 31, 32t, 34, 38; percentage of women MPs, 1-2, 185; Question Period, 176-79
Huddy, Leonie, 110-11, 145

Jaffer, Rahim: ethnic minority status, 174; format preferences for media, 166; "Phone-in Hoax" (2001), 209*n*4; on Question Period in House of Commons, 177-78; re. relationships with journalists, 181
Johnson-Sirleaf, Ellen, 125, 158
journalists: female journalists' conforming to masculine norms, 116-18, 182; female journalists' remedial effects very limited, 17, 115-16, 191-92; female journalists' support for female politicians, 182; gender stereotyping of issues of new/inexperienced politicians, 103-4, 105, 109; journalism norms masculine in nature, 112; politicians' relationships with, 180-82; provincial vs. Ottawa journalists, 181. *See also* framing

Kahn, Kim Fridkin, 178
Kanter, Rosabeth Moss: on effect of token status on female politicians, 145; "iron maiden" frame to portray professional women, 56-57, 64-65, 186; "mother" frame to portray female politicians, 56-57, 61-64, 186; "pet" frame to portray female politicians, 56-57, 64, 186; "sex object" frame to portray female politicians, 56-57, 58-61, 186
Keeper, Tina, 92, 98-99
Kelly, Jackie, 64
Kittilson, Miki Caul, 27
Kranich, Kimberlie, 85

La Presse, 49-51
Lapierre, Jean, 47, 59, 203*n*3
Lawless, Jennifer L., 141
Lawrence, Carmen, 170
Layton, Jack, 44, 60
Le Devoir, 50-51
Leeper, Mark Stephen, 145-46
Liberal Party of Canada: attack-style press releases in 2000 campaign, 134-35; challengers and incumbents, by gender, in 2006 campaign, 132t, 133t; distribution of news stories in 2000 federal election, 34, 35f; Grand-Mère affair in 2000 campaign, 88-89; length of news stories in 2000 federal campaign, by political party, 35-36; overview of 2000 federal campaign, 31-34, 83, 84, 148; overview of 2005-06 federal campaign, 44-45; percentage of female candidates and MPs, by year (2004-08), 127f; seats in House of Commons in 2000 (pre- and post-election), 31, 32t, 34; "soft" vs. "hard" issues in 2000 election, 83-84, 130, 131t; Sponsorship Scandal, 44, 202*n*8. *See also* broadcast news coverage of 2000 federal election campaign; Chrétien, Jean; print news coverage of 2005-06 federal election campaign
Loubier, Yvan, 42
Lubbers, Ruud, 62
Lundell, Åsa Kroon, 55

MacDonald, Flora, 12, 28, 66
MacKay, Peter, 68
Mancini, Peter, 78
Mandel, Ruth, 142
Manheim, Jarol B., 25-26
Manning, Preston, 59
Mansbridge, Peter, 87. *See also* CBC coverage of 2000 federal election campaign
Marois, Pauline, 2
Martin, Keith, 59, 203*n*3
Martin, Paul, 44, 171
McDonough, Alexa, and 2000 election campaign: accomplishments for NDP party, 32-33; attack-style behaviour, media stories, 69-71, 72-74, 74t, 105, 134, 139-40; attack-style politics, effect on voters, 29, 151-55, 156t, 188; behaviour in leaders' debates, 71, 134; broadcast news coverage compared with that for Clark, 37-38, 52; clips and sound bites with family, 66-67; conflicts between women in politics viewed as "catfights," 179; evidence for media interpretation in news stories, 87-89, 105; focus of news stories, 80-81; gendered mediation approach of media, 71-76; leader of NDP party, 2, 30, 31-34; media confusion between her and McLaughlin, 175; media focus on physical appearance, 168-69; mentions of background and experience in media coverage, 77; nature of lead-ins in news stories, 86-87; news stories' distribution,

34t, 35, 38; news stories' length, by political party, 35-36, 38; personal interview with author, 17, 165; print new stories (placement and headline), 36-38; on relations with journalists, 181, 182; self-censorship of personal life for media consumption, 66-68, 170; "soft" vs. "hard" issue coverage, 83-84, 101, 104, 130-31; sound bites, ratio to clips, by party leader, on CBC's *The National*, 41-42; sound bites on CBC's *The National*, 40-41; symbols of power in sound bites and clips, 76-77, 105; viability coverage, 79-80, 105. *See also* New Democratic Party

McGill Media Observatory, 15-16, 199-200

McGregor, Judy, 66

McLaughlin, Audrey: confusion in media between her and McDonough, 175; leader of NDP party in 1993 federal election, 2; marital status and the media, 68; media story about her outfit, 169; "psychological price" of appearing neutered or masculine, 183-84; speculation re. sexual orientation, 171; tough or aggressive stances viewed unfavourably, 29

McLellan, Anne, 20, 42, 46, 93

Meir, Golda, 158

Merkel, Angela, 170

military action, attitudes toward, by gender, 122

Minna, Maria, 46

Mulroney, Brian, 60, 171

Muskie, Edmund, 110

Mutz, Diana, 70

National Post, 49-51, 114-15

NDP. *See* New Democratic Party

New Brunswick, and coverage of female politicians, 58

New Democratic Party (NDP): attack-style press releases in 2000 campaign, 134-35; challengers and incumbents, by gender, in 2006 campaign, 103, 130-32, 133t; coverage in 2000 federal campaign compared with that for PC Party, 37-38; main issues in 2000 campaign, 83, 84, 148; news stories' distribution in 2000 federal election, 34t, 35, 38; news stories' length in 2000 federal campaign, by political party, 35-36, 38; overview of 2000 federal campaign, 31-34; percentage of female candidates and MPs, by year (2004-08), 127-28; prominence of stories (placement and headline) in 2000 federal election, 37-38; recruitment policies for women candidates, 3; seats in House of Commons (pre- and post-election), 31, 32t, 34, 38; "soft" vs. "hard" issues in 2000 election, 83-84, 104, 130-31. *See also* broadcast news coverage, 2000 federal election campaign; McDonough, Alexa; McLaughlin, Audrey

news media: agenda-setting by, 10, 25; assumptions about how female politicians get ahead, 175-76; celebritization of politics, 65-66, 140; condensed and selective take on the real world, 8; effects on politics (1920s to present), 9-11; framing (*see* framing); marginalized groups' coverage, 8, 55-56; politicians' attitude to "no such thing as bad press," 180; priming, 11; replacement for direct experience with politicians, 8, 193; role in shaping voters' perceptions of candidates, 4, 11, 163, 186; salience cues to voters, 10, 25, 47. *See also* gendered coverage by media; news media's masculine nature

news media's masculine nature: male-dominated industry, 6-7, 113-15; masculine character of news, 6, 19, 74, 109; masculine norms, with female journalists conforming, 112, 116-18, 182; news biases at systemic level, 118; political economic structure slanted toward male preferences, 112-13; remedial effects of having female journalists very limited, 17, 115-16, 191-92; status of men and women in TV and print news, 113-15. *See also* gendered mediation thesis

Niven, David, 103-4

Nystrom, Lorne, 95

Oda, Bev, 97, 128

Okimoto, Tyler G., 143

Ottawa Citizen, story about McDonough, 168-69

Palin, Sarah, 28, 59, 108, 135

Pelosi, Nancy, 59

Pettigrew, Pierre, 47

political parties: gatekeeping role in selecting candidates, 2-3, 185, 189, 201*n*1; left-wing parties more supportive of women candidates, 3; members of left-wing parties, 131; partisan loyalties weaker since 1940s, 9; percentage of female candidates and MPs, by year and party (2004-08), 127-28; recruitment policies aimed at women candidates, 3, 185, 189; type of parties with women leaders, 131. *See also* Bloc Québécois; Canadian Alliance party; Conservative Party of Canada; Liberal Party of Canada; New Democratic Party

politics: aggression closely associated with politics, 143, 146, 159; candidate's self-selection to run, 2, 143, 185, 189, 201*n*1; changes in political landscape since 1940s, 9-10; counter-stereotypical behaviour by female politicians, reaction, 143, 159-60, 188; male model of politician viewed as the norm, 5, 55, 56, 110-11; political parties' selection of candidates, 2-3, 185, 189, 201*n*1; viewed as masculine domain, 111; women under-represented in politics, 1-2, 185, 201*n*1

Prentice, Deborah A., 143

Primarolo, Dawn, 169

priming by news media, 11

print news, male domination of news production, 114-15

print news coverage of 2005-06 federal election campaign: of appearance and personal lives of female vs. male politicians, 89-96, 105; comparison of coverage of male vs. female candidates, 49-51; data obtained from McGill Media Observatory, 15-16, 199-200; direct quotes of candidates, by sex, 49-50, 85; features of 2005-06 campaign (parties, issues), 44-45; of female candidates' education and experience, 96-99; first mentions, placement in print news, 47-48, 50-51; first mentions of candidates, by sex and candidate type (incumbent, challenger), 45-47, 50; coverage of female candidates because of their novelty, 46-47; focus of analysis on candidates' media coverage, 30-31; gender stereotyping of new/inexperienced politicians by journalists, 103-4, 105, 109; gendered coverage of aggressive behaviour by female politicians, 94-95, 105-6, 133-35; "horserace" vs. issue coverage of candidates, by sex, 99-100, 101, 105, 117t, 186; number of women candidates vs. male candidates, 45; photos of candidates (framing mechanism), by sex, 48-49, 51; references to powerful men in coverage of female politicians, 98-99, 105; salience cues to voters, 10, 47; "soft" vs. "hard" news coverage of female challengers vs. incumbents, 102-3, 131-32, 136, 186-87; Sponsorship Scandal, 44, 202n8; tone of stories on candidates, 99-101, 105

Progressive Conservative (PC) Party, and 2000 election campaign: attack-style press releases, 134-35; coverage compared with that of NDP, 37-38; distribution of news stories, 34-35; length of news stories, by political party, 35-36; main issues, 31-34, 83, 84, 148; seats in House of Commons (pre- and post-election), 31, 32t, 34, 38; "soft" vs. "hard" issues, 83-84, 131t. *See also* broadcast news coverage of 2000 federal election campaign; Clark, Joe; Conservative Party of Canada

provision-presentation, by and of women: candidacies and cabinet appointments, by gender, 120, 126-30; challengers and incumbents, by gender, in 2006 campaign, 130-33; description of "provision," 119-20; gender differences in issue positions and priorities, 121-24, 129-31, 136, 188; gender differences in moral reasoning, 122-23; gendered coverage result of provision, presentation, or both, 108, 119-20, 124-26, 136, 187; McDonough's self-censorship of personal life, 66-68, 170; news a combination of provision and presentation, 119-20; "provision" of news in Question Period, 177-79; self-censoring to avoid gendered coverage, 22, 67-68, 71-72, 123, 129, 136-37, 162, 170-72; self-presentation training, 176, 193; "soft" vs. "hard" news coverage of female challengers vs. incumbents in 2006 election, 102-3, 131-32, 136, 186-87; strategic use of being perceived as an outsider, 72, 125; strategic use of being seen as less prone to corruption, 44, 55, 125; strategic use of campaigning as a woman, 123, 124-25, 136, 187-88; type of political parties with women leaders, 131; value of provision-presentation distinction, 136-37; women in left-wing parties, 131; women more visible because of their difference, 5, 7, 14-15, 23, 28, 54-55, 74-75, 125-26; women politicians' need to navigate gendered news media, 7; women's gendered behaviour, as legislators, 123; women's tendency to undervalue their credentials, 78-79. *See also* attack-style politics and media coverage; *entries beginning with* representations

public perception and gendered coverage: aggressive behaviour by right- or left-wing candidates, 157-58; gendered coverage of female candidates and, 20, 55, 183; lack of bias against women candidates, 4; media's role in shaping perceptions of female politicians, 4; political climate and reaction to aggressive female politicians, 159; politics associated more with masculine traits, 140; public's level of tolerance for aggression, 153, 155; "viability boost" for aggressive stances by women, 145-47, 155; voters' responses to attack-style behaviour, by gender, 147-48, 155; women politicians as novel, alien, and different, 5, 7, 14-15, 23, 28, 54-55, 179-80

Putin, Vladimir, 140

quality of media coverage of female politicians: attack-style behaviour's negative effect on women leaders, 20-21, 29, 43, 69, 159-60, 163, 188; descriptive vs. interpretative coverage, 15, 18-19, 57, 84-89, 205*n*19; disproportionate focus on appearance and personal lives, 5, 13-14, 48-49, 54, 58-61, 89-96, 105, 168-72, 186; evidence in news stories for media interpretation, 87-89, 105, 205*n*22; female candidates speaking agentically, or paraphrased, 15, 41-42, 57, 85-86; frames used to report on female politicians, 13-14, 56-57, 61-65, 186; framing by journalists when paraphrasing candidates' words, 57, 85-86; "iron maiden" frame of political women, 14, 56-57, 64-65, 71, 139, 186; issues (*see* representations of issues and positions); male model of politician viewed as the norm, 5, 55, 56; "mother" frame of political women, 14, 61-64, 65-66, 186; personal attributes (*see* representations of the personal); "pet" frame of political women, 14, 64, 186; professional qualifications (*see* representations of the professional); "sex object" frame of political women, 14, 56, 58-61, 65-66, 186; viability as candidate (*see* representations of viability); women framed using masculine language and imagery, 13, 190-91; women politicians perceived as "alien" and "different," 5, 7, 14-15, 23, 28, 54-55, 74-75, 125-26; women's self-presentations to media (to avoid iron maiden frame), 72

quantity of media coverage of female politicians. *See* visibility of female politicians in news

racial minorities: media focus on appearance and ethnicity, 172-73; portrayal in media as novel and "the other," 8, 55-56, 173-74; potential of media to depict unfavourably, 8

Rakow, Lana F., 85

Rebick, Judy, 179

Reeves, Byron, 70

Reform Party, 3

Reno, Janet, 68-69, 171

representations of issues and positions: benefits for women of feminine stereotypes, 55, 72, 187; description, 14; emphasis by media on "soft" or "women's" issues, 54, 63, 109; framing of issues (soft, hard) of party leaders in 2000 campaign, 83-84, 101, 117t, 130-31; gender stereotyping of new/inexperienced politicians by journalists, 103-4, 105, 109; "horserace" vs. issue coverage, 99-100, 101, 117t, 186; issue coverage of candidates, by sex, 2005-06 campaign, 101-2, 105, 186; issue coverage of incumbents vs. challengers, by sex, 2005-06 campaign, 102-4, 105; women's self-presentations to media (to avoid iron maiden frame), 72

representations of the personal: attack-style behaviour, coverage of party leaders in 2000, 69-71, 72-74, 133-35, 139-40, 159-60, 188; attack-style behaviour's negative effect on women leaders, 20-21, 29, 43, 69, 159-60, 163, 188; autonomous speaking by female politicians vs.

paraphrasing, 65; benefits for women of feminine stereotypes, 44, 55, 69, 72, 187-88; celebritization of politics, 65-66, 140; clips and sound bites of leaders in 2000 campaign, 66-68, 85; comments re. sexual orientation, 68-69, 94-95, 171; description, 13-14; divorced or single women, 67-69; double bind of women politicians' being too hard or soft, 64-65, 142; double bind of women politicians' marital status, 68; focus on appearance and personal lives of female vs. male politicians, 5, 13-14, 48-49, 54, 58-61, 89-96, 105, 168-72, 186; focus on childlessness or number of children, 61-62, 65-67, 93, 96, 170; framing of female politicians in 2000 campaign, 65-76; framing of female politicians in 2005-06 campaign, 89-95; gendered double standards re. private lives, 28-29, 59-61; "iron maiden" frame of political women, 14, 56-57, 64-65, 71, 139, 186; McDonough as "confrontational" in media coverage in 2000, 69-71, 72-74; media's exaggeration of female aggressivity (gendered mediation), 71-76, 105, 129, 133-34, 139-40, 142, 159-60, 188; mediated coverage of female politicians, 65, 71-76; "mother" frame and role conflict of political women, 14, 61-64, 65-66, 186; "pet" frame of political women, 14, 64, 186; political competence questioned with emphasis on appearance, 61; "sex object" frame of political women, 14, 56, 58-61, 65-66, 186

representations of the professional: coverage of female candidates' education and experience in 2005-06 campaign, 96-99, 104-5; coverage of female vs. male leaders' background and experience in 2000 campaign, 54, 76-79; description, 14; framing of female politicians in 2000 campaign, 76-79; references to powerful men in coverage of female politicians, 98-99, 105; symbols of power in sound bites and clips in 2000 campaign, 76-77, 105; women's tendency to undervalue their credentials, 78-79. *See also* representations of viability

representations of viability: description, 14; doubts raised re. women's viability as candidates and officials, 14, 54, 186; focus of coverage about party leaders in 2000 campaign, 80-81; framing of female politicians in 2000 campaign, 79-83; "horserace" vs. issue coverage of candidates, 10, 13-14, 79, 99-100, 101, 117t, 186; tone of stories on candidates, by sex, in 2005-06 campaign, 99-101, 105; "viability boost" with aggressive behaviour by women leaders/politicians, 145-47, 155; viability coverage (polls, debates, strategy, electoral battles), female vs. male party leaders, 79-80, 81-82, 145-47, 155; visibility in the news and, 24-25. *See also* representations of the professional

Rice, Condoleezza, 59
Robinson, Gertrude, 57, 190
Robinson, Svend, 94-95
Rock, Allan, 42, 78
Ross, Karen, 5, 136, 166, 169
Rossiter, Clinton, 111
Rudman, Laurie A., 147

Saint-Jean, Armande, 57
salience transfer, by citizens from media, 10, 25

Schreyer, Ed, 95-96
Schwarzenegger, Arnold, 140
Sgro, Judy, 178
Shames, Shauna, 72
Shipley, Jenny, 66
Sisters in the Struggle (National Film Board), 173
Skelton, Carol, 128
Smith, Allison, 67
Société Radio-Canada's *Le Téléjournal*, 30. *See also* broadcast news coverage of 2000 federal election campaign
Sorensen, Eric, 89
sound bites, in media in 2000 campaign: definition, 39; of leaders with family members, 66-68; mediation by newsmakers, 72-74, 202*n*5; by party leader, on *The National*, 39-41, 85; ratio to clips, by party leader, on *The National*, 41-42; by sex, on CBC news, 42-43, 85; symbols of power in sound bites of party leaders, 76-77
Sponsorship Scandal (in 2000 federal election campaign), 44, 202*n*8
Sreberny-Mohammadi, Annabelle, 5, 166, 169
Stronach, Belinda: coverage of education and experience in 2005-06 campaign, 97-98; coverage of relationship status in 2000 campaign, 68; first mentions in print news, 2005-06 election campaign, 45-47; framed by media as "sex object," 58-59, 66, 90-92, 189; gendered behaviour toward her by McLellan, 20; gendered double standard regarding private life, 29; media visibility vs. that of male contenders for party leader, 28; personal (appearance, relationships, parental status) media coverage in 2005-06 campaign, 90-92, 170, 171-72

Terkildsen, Nayda, 110-11, 145
Thatcher, Margaret ("Iron Lady"), 64, 158, 189
Time and Chance (Campbell), 165-66
Toronto Star, 49-51, 90-92, 115t
Torsney, Paddy, 97
Trimble, Linda, 47, 66, 68
Trudeau, Pierre Elliott, 60, 62
Tuchman, Gaye, 11-12, 25
2000 federal election campaign. *See* broadcast news coverage of 2000 federal election campaign
2005-06 federal election campaign. *See* print news coverage of 2005-06 federal election campaign

United Nations Fourth World Conference of Women (1995), 192
United States: elections of females in 1992 "Year of the Woman" election, 27-28, 55, 121, 125; media coverage of female office holders, 27-28

Van Dusen, Julie, 182
van Zoonen, Lisbet, 66, 126
Vancouver Sun, 50-51, 115t
Verner, Josée, 96, 128
video clips. *See* clips (video)
visibility of female politicians in news: aggressive stances by female politicians viewed unfavourably, 20-21, 29, 43, 129, 178-79; attack-style behaviour's negative effect on women leaders, 20-21, 29, 43, 69, 159-60, 163, 188; candidates perceived as novel, alien, and different, 5, 7, 14-15, 23, 28, 54-55, 74-75, 125-26; coverage because of their novelty, 46-47, 179-80; coverage compared with male candidates, 18, 26-28, 52, 186; gendered double standards regarding private lives, 28-29; invisible often in media (symbolic annihilation), 11-12, 25; print

coverage of provincial elections (1999, 2000), 43; in Question Period in House of Commons, 176-79; role of party connections, 174-75; seriousness with which media view women politicians, 175-76. *See also* broadcast news coverage of 2000 federal election campaign; print news coverage of 2005-06 federal election campaign; quality of media coverage of female politicians

visibility of politicians in news: importance for candidates and party leaders, 24-26; in Question Period in House of Commons, 176-79

Wanta, Wayne, 118
Wayne, Elsie, 42
Weir, Elizabeth, 58
Whalen, Susan, 98
Winfrey, Kelly L., 57
Wolf, Naomi, 60
women politicians: candidates' gender gap with respect to income, 3, 201n2; capitalizing on gender stereotypes, 44, 55, 72, 123, 124-25, 136, 187-88; fundraising ability, 3-4; gendered experiences lessening with time, 161-62, 187; gendered media and willingness of women to run, 7, 22-23, 55, 189; growth in supply pool of candidates, 4; interview methodology, 163-65; male and female expectations re. media coverage, 162; media assumptions about how female politicians get ahead, 175-76; media focus on appearance and personal lives, 5, 13-14, 48-49, 54, 58-61, 89-96, 105, 168-72, 186; media interest in personal lives, 169-72, 186; preferences for certain media formats, 165-68; underrepresentation in politics, 1-2, 185, 201n1

Wynne, Kathleen, 2

Zaller, John, 8
Zilber, Jeremy, 103-4